Another Opening, Another Show

Another Opening, Another Show

A Lively Introduction to the Theatre

Tom Markus   **Linda Sarver**

University of Utah and Pioneer Theatre Company

Illustrations by Linda Sarver

Mayfield Publishing Company

Mountain View, California

London · Toronto

Library of Congress Cataloging-in-Publication Data

Markus, Tom.
    Another Opening, Another Show / Tom Markus and Linda Sarver; illustrations by Linda Sarver.
       p. cm.
    Includes bibliographical references and index.
    ISBN 0-7674-1616-3
       1. Theater.   I. Sarver, Linda, 1953- II. Title.

PN2037.M327 2000
792—dc21

00-028055

Manufactured in the United States of America
10   9   8   7   6   5   4   3

Mayfield Publishing Company
1280 Villa Street
Mountain View, California 94041

Sponsoring editor, Janet M. Beatty; *production editor,* Carla White Kirschenbaum; *manuscript editor,* Karen Dorman; *text and cover designer,* Susan Breitbard; *art editor,* Robin Mouat; *illustrators:* Linda Sarver, Joan Carol, and Judy and John Waller; *manufacturing manager,* Randy Hurst; *photo researcher,* Brian Pecko. The text was set in 9.5/12 Palatino by Black Dot Group and printed on 45# Somerset Matte by R. R. Donnelley & Sons Company.

Cover image: © Joan Markus. Broadway production of Kiss Me Kate. Starring Brian Stokes Mitchell and Marin Mazzle. Scenic designer: Robin Wagner. Costume designer: Martin Pakledinaz. Chorus (from left to right): Jerome Vivona, JoAnn M. Hunter, Robert Ousley, John Horton, Nancy Lemenager, Darren Lee

Contents

PART IV   CURTAIN'S UP

Preface

We listened to our students before we wrote this book. We met with a group who volunteered to discuss the standard textbooks assigned in introductory theatre appreciation courses. They identified the pros and cons of each, and then we asked them what *they* wanted in a textbook. After listening to the traits they described, we distilled their "wish list" down to six:

- They described themselves as audiences, and they want a book that's geared to *their* learning experience. Whether they are nonmajors encountering theatre for the first time or young actors hoping for a career, they want to learn how to understand and enjoy theatre when they go to it.

- They want a book that's fun to read, instead of one that's impersonal, dry, and academic. They want a book that's not too long, and they'd like a book with a sense of humor.

- They want to learn how theatre is made, instead of learning how to read and analyze a play at home. Dramatic literature and theatre history are for advanced classes, they tell us.

- They want an insider's look at the theatre, not an academician's critique of it. They don't want gossip, but they want to know how theatre *really* works.

- They want a book with pictures that illustrate the ideas in the text, instead of merely decorating it.

- They want a book that doesn't cost a lot; they'd rather spend money *going* to the theatre instead of reading about it.

With this list in mind, we undertook the writing of an entertaining and accessible guide that describes what theatre is, why so many people value it, and how to enjoy the theatrical experience. It is also a survey of the theatre landscape, touching on the kinds of plays that students might attend, the kinds of work that people in the theatre do, what theatre is like as a business, and the place of theatre in our culture.

We've enlivened the chapters with behind-the-scenes stories from our careers in the profession. Our students have responded enthusiastically to this book, and we believe yours will too.

HOW WE ORGANIZED THE BOOK

The text's major innovation is that it's organized according to the sequence of experiences students have when they go to the theatre. It begins with short chapters that define theatre and describe its origins and value, and then, like a travel guide book, it helps students find out where and when plays are performed, how to buy tickets, what kind of behavior and customs theatregoers have, and what they will experience when they go to the theatre—from the kinds of plays they'll encounter, to what they'll see when the curtain rises, to how the actors do their work, to how they can judge a performance and tell their friends what they have experienced.

FEATURES

- The text introduces all the standard topics covered in theatre appreciation texts, and it assumes no prior knowledge on the students' part.
- The practical information in Part II, "Planning Your Trip to the Theatre," offers apt advice on finding what's on, getting tickets, and learning what is expected of an audience. It also provides some looks behind the scenes of "show biz."
- The unique middle section of the book, "Let's Look at Theatre," helps students understand how the visual arts of theatre communicate, so they will appreciate how the scenery, costume, and lighting designs affect their experience. The photographs, drawings, and discussions of a single play demonstrate how design influences the audience's experience and how the same script can be interpreted in many different ways.
- Musical theatre is celebrated in a chapter that explains why it is an especially American art form.
- The exercises at the ends of chapters relate theatre to the students' own lives, from noticing ads for theatrical productions in their community to analyzing characters in performances they have attended.
- The photos and drawings are carefully selected to illustrate the ideas in the text, and the special section of color photos includes up-to-date Broadway musicals.
- The book highlights different categories of information, so students find it easy to understand. Boxes set off important ideas, and there are lists leading to the topics discussed in the following paragraphs. Checklists actively engage students after they have read about a topic, and we've included anecdotes and illustrations to flesh out the ideas in an entertaining and stimulating way.
- Unfamiliar words are printed in bold and defined in the glossary.
- At the back of the book is an extensive, annotated list of plays, books, and videotapes that will help students explore the subject of theatre further.

SUPPLEMENTARY MATERIAL

We've shared our teaching experience in an *Instructor's Manual* that includes sample syllabi; a chapter-by-chapter list of new terms, suggestions for classroom activities ranging from field trips to Internet searches, and video resources that will augment and illustrate the text; a tool to help students with written assignments called "What Is an Essay?"; and a test bank of multiple-choice, true/false, and essay questions.

ACKNOWLEDGMENTS

We are deeply indebted to Robert Potter, University of California, Santa Barbara, Frank Kuhn, University of Southern Mississippi, and Diane Hostetler, North Seattle Community College, for their detailed and extensive suggestions; to Jack Axelrod and the late John Harrop for their comments on the chapter "Actors and Characters," and to Gage Williams for his responses to the entire section "Let's Look at Theatre." We thank Roger Benington and Barbara Smith, and the hundreds of students who read and offered suggestions on early drafts of the book. We're grateful to the following instructors for their helpful reviews of the manuscript: Mark Adams, College of the Mainland; Michael Corriston, Southeast Community College; Virginia Ludders, Glendale Community College; Joyce Porter, Moraine Valley Community College; Michelle Rebollo, St. Louis Community College at Meramec; Michael Sevareid, Elizabethtown College; and Larry Waters, University of Nevada, Reno. The book's successes owe much to these kind colleagues; the errors and failures are entirely our own.

We thank the editorial and production staff at Mayfield, particularly Jan Beatty who saw the potential in our approach and guided us throughout with a firm hand, wry smile, and a quick e-mail response to cries for help; Carla Kirschenbaum who shepherded the manuscript through to publication; Karen Dorman who has a sense of humor as well as a fine copyeditor's eye; and the many other folks who helped along the way, including Star MacKenzie, Robin Mouat, Brian Pecko, Marty Granahan, and Irina Raicu.

1

Flying Fish and Dying Villains

If you're new to theatre, it may seem like you've come to a foreign land. Theatre is a world with its own vocabulary and its own history, and it's as different from biology as biology is from accounting. This text is written as a guidebook that will help you make sense of unfamiliar territory and at the same time enjoy what you discover. Yes, we said "enjoy." After all, theatre aims to be entertaining, and a text introducing you to theatre ought to be entertaining as well.

We have written this text in the first person instead of in that vague and indefinite voice that you find in most textbooks. We'll make it clear that you're reading our personal observations about theatre. The pages are filled with facts and with conventional academic wisdom, but they also contain opinions, observations, and behind-the-scenes stories. You may wonder whose opinions you're reading and why in the world you should pay attention to them. A fair question—let us introduce ourselves.

Age before beauty: I'm Tom Markus. I'm not a famous actor or a household name. But I am someone who has been a professional theatre artist for more than forty years and a professional educator for even longer. As a director and actor, I have been in films, on TV, and on stage with some of the major actors of our time—and I was once in a Broadway show. It flopped, and I never acted in another, but being in a Broadway show is, for an actor, like cutting a major label CD is for a musician or making an NBA team is for a basketball player. You may not be the top-o'-the-heap, but not very many have done what you've done. Maybe your CD didn't sell as many copies as one of Madonna's, or maybe you only got into a couple of games during your one season and never even played against Michael Jordan, but at least you were there. I've been there—as an actor, as a director, and as a professor who earned a Ph.D. nearly four decades ago and who has taught at Yale, at the University of California, and as far away as Flinders University in Australia.

And my learning and my experience combine to qualify me to share what I know and believe—they qualify me to "profess" the subject of Theatre.

I'm Linda Sarver, and I'll add many of my theatre experiences to Tom's. Sometimes you'll hear my voice as you read, and sometimes Tom's; we take turns and talk about the subjects we know best. I'm a professional costume designer and an educator who has been working in this field for twenty years. I've designed in Canada and Hong Kong and for many professional theatres and Shakespeare festivals across America. I've also worked on some feature films, and I was part of a team that won an Emmy for costuming the TV miniseries *North and South*. I have a Master of Fine Arts degree, and I've taught at Florida State University, Marquette University, and the University of Utah. I've spent many exciting, pleasurable, and rewarding years in this profession.

So why have we happily spent so much of our lives in theatre? What makes theatre so special? There are probably a million stories that explain what theatre is all about. Here are two of our favorites.

The first anecdote really happened. I was hired by the Oregon Shakespeare Festival to direct a production of Shakespeare's rollicking comedy *The Merry Wives of Windsor* (this is Tom speaking). The central character is Sir John Falstaff, a fat and foolish middle-aged knight who attempts to woo two very respectable women in the city of Windsor. He deludes himself that these married women will adore him. The two women find Falstaff ludicrous, and they decide to play a sequence of tricks upon him to humiliate him. Mrs. Ford invites him to her home, but as soon as he arrives she tells him that her insanely jealous husband is coming back unexpectedly and that he'd better sneak out of the house before her husband finds him there. The two women hide Falstaff in a wicker basket of dirty laundry so that their servants can carry him out of the house. Later, the audience learns that Falstaff was thrown into the river along with the dirty laundry in the basket. The actors and I decided to bring Falstaff on stage for his next entrance dripping wet from his filthy dunking. We hoped the audience would laugh. In rehearsals, I suggested that the actor carry his boots, as though he had taken them off because they were wet. Then he could turn one of them upside down and pour out the water that had filled it. We expected a second laugh from the audience. Then someone suggested that Falstaff reach into the other boot and pull out a fish! We found some frozen rainbow trout at the grocery store, and when we thawed them out they flopped about in the actor's hand as though they were just pulled out of the river. We anticipated a third laugh from the sight of the fish. The actor came up with the idea that Falstaff had caught a cold from being tossed into the river, so he could give a big "Ah-choo" on one or more occasions and hopefully prompt yet more laughter. At one rehearsal I said, "Why don't you hold the fish by the tail, turn away from the audience, give a big sneeze, and toss the fish over your head and out into the audience?" "Are you serious?" the actor asked. "Nobody's going to want to get hit by a fish!" "Trust me," I replied. "For the one person who might not like it, the other 999 people in the audience will howl with laughter. Everybody loves to see some-one else in trouble." We debated the idea, we rehearsed it, and on opening night the actor threw the fish (Figure 1.1).

As I had anticipated, the audience howled. But things didn't go exactly as planned. The actor turned, sneezed, and tossed the fish. The audience laughed. But while the actor waited for the laughter to subside, somebody tossed the fish back onto the stage. When the actor turned around, he saw the fish, mistakenly assumed he had failed to reach the audience with it, turned his back again, sneezed again, tossed the fish again, and turned back toward the audience. The fish came flying back onto the stage. The audience was in paroxysms of laughter. The actor picked the fish up and carried it offstage when he exited. But he saved it for the curtain call, and when he took his bow, he tossed the fish back into the audience one final time. The comic business was a triumph. The production continued delighting large audiences for sev-eral performances, until one night a surprise occurred. Apparently word had gotten around the community about the flying fish, for that night, when Fal-staff turned his back, sneezed, and tossed the fish over his head, out of the audience came twenty fish flying up onto the stage! It took a while to clear the stage before the performance could continue.

The second anecdote is often told in theatrical circles. We don't know if it happened or not, but it's a funny story. Johnny Weismuller was a movie star who played the role of Tarzan in many films and was celebrated in the days of black-and-white movies for his muscles, his innocent charm, and his monosyl-labic dialogue that prompted parodies like "Me Tarzan, you Jane." The story goes that early in his career he did some stage roles. Usually he was cast in tongue-in-cheek melodramas as the honorable jungle boy so he could stride around in his loincloth and save the virgin from the villain. One of the perfor-mances required him to shoot the bad guy late in the third act. Weismuller wrestled the pistol from the villain, turned it on him, and fired. Click! The stage gun misfired. The audience rustled its programs. A second click, this time from the offstage gun in the stage manager's hand. It also misfired, and the audience smiled. Thinking quickly, Weismuller plucked his dagger from his waistband, leaped across the stage, and stabbed the villain in the chest, but the knife had a rubber blade and the audience could see it bend against his chest. By now the audience was giggling, and the villain wanted to be "dead" in the worst way. What to do? Looking about him wildly, Weismuller saw the curtains on the window, ripped them down, wrapped them around the bad guy's neck, and started to strangle him, with both actors giving the action a lot of body English. But the curtain was cheesecloth and ripped apart in Weismuller's hands. By now, the theatre was rocking with laughter and the actors were torn between laughing out loud and earnestly finding a way out of the problem. Weismuller was wringing his hands together when he felt the large ring he was wearing. Confidently, he strode to the cowering (and giggling) villain, pressed his ring against the actor's forehead, and said in a full voice, "I keel you weeth my poi-son ring" (Figure 1.2). Applause. Blackout. Curtain.

Figure 1.1 Falstaff's flying fish!

Figure 1.2 "I keel you weeth my poison ring!"

Each of these stories is based on something going wrong, and we find the stories funny because we know how things are *supposed* to happen in the theatre. We know that the theatregoers are supposed to stay in their seats and enjoy the performance, and that they're not supposed to join in—at least not to the extent of tossing fish on the stage. We know that when a character is shot, the actor is supposed to pretend to die. We also know some of the rules of performance, which in the theatre we call **conventions.** A convention is a practice that is understood by all participants, just the way the rules of an NBA game are well understood by all the players and spectators. In a movie, we understand that when the image on the screen dissolves to black and then comes back to a different image, something has happened; either some time has passed or the location has changed. That's a convention of film, and the audience can understand the sequence of events in a film only if it understands that convention. In the theatre, we know that when an actor makes a sound like a sneeze, the character has a cold. That's a convention of the theatre. And we understand that when a blank gun goes off and an actor across the stage bites a blood capsule and lets some red fluid flow out of his mouth, the character is "dead." That, too, is a convention of the theatre. What makes the stories about Falstaff and Tarzan funny is that the conventions were violated—the rules were broken—and the audience and actors knew it.

With these stories in mind, you should be able to define theatre—at least in a preliminary way. Your definition isn't written in stone; it's a sort of "baseline" definition that you can change, correct, and add to as you learn more.

FIRST DEFINITION OF THEATRE

Exercise

Write as complete and clear a definition of theatre as you can.

2

What Is Theatre?

*L*et's look a bit more closely at the two anecdotes in the first chapter. If you study the stories carefully, you can identify at least five things in them that must exist if theatre is to happen.

The Five Essentials of Theatre

1. One or more actors
2. An audience
3. A particular place
4. A particular time
5. A structured event

THE FIVE ESSENTIALS OF THEATRE

Actors

The first essential of theatre is the presence of actors. Without actors, none of the events in these anecdotes could have taken place. Whether the actor was playing Falstaff or Tarzan, throwing a fish or simulating a killing, someone had to be enacting a role, playing a part, imitating an action. Without actors, there is no action, and therefore no performance, and therefore no theatre.

Audience

Equally necessary is the presence and active participation of an audience. Whether they were laughing with the performance or at it, the audiences had to be present to complete each of these anecdotes. Without their participation, the events could not have happened.

Place

Common to the stories is the fact that each happened in a particular place we call a theatre. For the events to happen, there had to be a special space in which this sort of human activity could occur. As you read each tale, you probably envisioned the events; you may have even imagined what the theatre looked like. The Oregon Shakespeare Festival's 1,000-seat outdoor theatre is very different from the tent in which Johnny Weismuller's archenemy nearly died of embarrassment until he could finally "die" to the laughter and applause of hundreds. But both events took place in a special building—a theatre.

Time

A fourth element that these anecdotes have in common is that they took place at a particular time. They couldn't have happened at just any moment, and they couldn't happen more than once. These events happened only at the precise moment at which those particular actors and that particular audience had convened in that particular place to share the experience and to react to the unplanned events.

A Structured Event

The fifth item these stories have in common is that the performances had an organized structure and were rehearsed to unfold in a planned way, and the audience knew when the structure was disrupted.

The Five Essentials Combined

Theatre occurs when these five essential elements combine; if even one of them is missing, theatre can't happen. So what exactly *is* theatre? If you tried to define it by using these five essentials, you might write down something like "Theatre is a structured event that requires actors, an audience, a place, and a time and that depends on everyone's understanding a set of conventions." Though accurate, this definition doesn't convey very much about what it would be like to *experience* theatre.

Here's a description of the theatrical experience that was written by a student at Queens College after his first trip to the theatre.

> Well, I made sure I had my tickets, and I picked up my date and we drove into Manhattan. We were talking about the show—my folks had seen it—and we were pretty excited. We parked the car (you have to pay a lot to park a car in Manhattan!) and we went into the theatre. We sat down in the auditorium where the usher told us. There was a full house, mostly older people, everybody dressed up real nice. Then the lights went down and the curtain went up and the actors came on the stage (I guess) and then the lights came up and the actors moved around and talked. We laughed a lot. I mean, it was really funny! At

the end we clapped, and then we all left—the whole audience. Oh, and the actors bowed at the curtain call. And we went home. On the way home, we talked about how funny the play was.

You'll find ten aspects of theatre in this student's brief description: the five essentials we just discussed plus another five characteristics. Combined, these ten characteristics will increase your understanding of the theatrical experience.

The Five Essentials of Theatre and Five More Characteristics of Theatre

1. One or more actors
2. An audience
3. A particular place
4. A particular time
5. A structured event
6. Communication through all five senses
7. A lasting impact
8. Audience participation
9. The present tense
10. Universally understood conventions

TEN ASPECTS OF THEATRE

Let's review the five essentials of theatre and take a closer look at the five additional characteristics of theatre.

Actors

"The actors came on the stage . . . and . . . moved around and talked," reported the student. Live actors are an essential element of theatre.

Audience

A performance happens in the company of a gathering of strangers. Well, not all are strangers. We frequently attend with friends. "I picked up my date," reported our Long Island student, and with that phrase he reminds us that theatre is a social and communal experience. We might like to watch a film or a TV program on our own because no one can interrupt us or distract us, but theatre is more like a party—we enjoy it as part of a crowd. As herd animals, we humans get comfort and pleasure from being in a crowd of folks who have gathered together for a common purpose.

Most performers would argue that theatre does not happen unless an audience is present. Theatre, they explain, is an event in which a communication happens—from actor to audience and from audience to actor—and without both groups present, theatre does not occur. A rehearsal might happen, but the result is not theatre any more than a football practice results in a victory or a wedding rehearsal unites a couple legally. Talk to any actor who has had the discomforting experience of a "pick-up rehearsal," and he or she will tell you that it's unfulfilling. A pick-up rehearsal refreshes the actors after a hiatus in performances. The actors go through the entire performance without an audience that laughs, claps, or sends waves of energy up to the stage. For the actors, the experience is distasteful, incomplete, and false.

> Is there theatre without an audience? The larger issue behind this question was best phrased by the seventeenth-century English philosopher George Berkeley, who asked, "When a tree falls in the forest and there is no one there to hear it, does it make any sound?" Undergraduate philosophy students ponder this conundrum. How do you validate that the falling tree made a sound when no human was there to hear it and report it? Is a human presence necessary for a phenomenon to occur? When a performance falls in an empty auditorium and there's no audience present, does theatre happen?

Certainly the student's report tells us the audience was an important influence on his experience. "There was a full house, mostly older people," he said. "We laughed a lot," he added. His experience was shaped by the audience's participation in the event.

Place

"We went into the theatre," said the student. Theatre happens in a particular space designed for this activity. Just as religious services are held in churches and hockey games in arenas for ice skating, so theatre is performed in places specially designed to accommodate live theatrical performance.

Time

Like a formal dance, a wedding, or a rock concert, theatre is a special event that happens at a particular time. We go to theatre; it doesn't come to us. Unlike TV, which finds us even in our bedrooms, theatre requires us to go to it. Special planning is necessary. We have to schedule when we are going, and we have to purchase tickets in advance. As with these other events, we go to theatre expecting pleasure. Look back at the student's description: "I made sure I had my tickets," and "we were pretty excited."

A Structured Event

The student's experience began at a specific time, was divided into segments commonly called acts, and ended at a prearranged moment. He reported that things on the stage happened in a prearranged way, that the actors "moved around and talked." They knew what to say and where to move. At the end, there was a ceremony called a curtain call, and then "we all left—the whole audience." One of the things we expect of theatre, just as we expect of a baseball game or a religious service, is that it is an organized event with a careful structure. It has a beginning, a middle, and an end.

All Five Senses

The student described seeing the actors and hearing them. We also smell, taste, and feel theatre; we experience theatre through all our five senses.

You may not realize how completely you understand a performance on the basis of what you see until you try the following experiment. The next time you're watching TV, turn off the sound. Like the student, you will see the actors move around. You will also see scenery and costumes, and you will notice the color and intensity of the lighting. You will see the expressions on the actors' faces. You will see the gestures they make. When you put together all the visual impressions you see, *you create their meaning.* If you use only your sense of sight, you will still have a fairly complete understanding of the performance.

Perhaps the best description of this truth is found in the lyrics that Stephen Sondheim wrote for the Broadway musical *Sunday in the Park with George.* The musical features the innovative nineteenth-century French painter Georges Seurat (Zhorzhe Sir-rot) as its central character, and it deals with the idea that creating a work of art is hard to do. Seurat created paintings made up of thousands of tiny points of color that are carefully arranged in mathematically determined juxtapositions so that—when seen at a proper distance—they create the illusion of a color that is not truly there on the canvas (Color Plate 1). As you look at one of Seurat's paintings, you become an artist because you create colors with your own eye. If you walk up close to *A Sunday Afternoon on the Island of La Grande Jatte,* you will see tiny dots of color, but if you stand away from the canvas, all those dots fuse together in your eye and make a glorious picture. *You* create the picture in just the same way that you create a theatre experience from the many simultaneous sensory stimulations you receive in a performance.

Sondheim's character Georges sings a song titled "Putting It Together" in which he describes how a work of art is created out of bits and pieces. He explains that the art of making art is putting things together:

> Bit by bit,
> Putting it together . . .
> Piece by piece—
> Only way to make a work of art.

Every moment makes a contribution,
Every little detail plays a part.
Having just the vision's no solution,
Everything depends on execution:
Putting it together—
That's what counts.
Ounce by ounce
Putting it together . . .
Small amounts,
Adding up to make a work of art.
. . .
The art of making art
Is putting it together
Bit by bit . . .
. . .
And that
Is the state
Of the
Art.

And that's what *you* do when you experience a play. You see it, hear it, taste it, smell it, and touch it, and your five senses help you enjoy it as a work of art. Just think about how vividly you experience reality through your sense of sight. Sondheim's lyrics to the song "Color and Light" help Georges describe how he is painting:

Color and light.
There's only color and light.
Yellow and white.
Just blue and yellow and white.
Look at the air, Miss—
See what I mean?
No, look over there, Miss—
That's done with green . . .
Conjoined with orange . . .

"Color and light." The sky in the painting appears to be blue, but it is made up, the lyric tells us, of tiny dots of blue and yellow and white. In the nineteenth century, the idea that our eyes could blend dots of color into a recognizable image was new, but today the idea is a commonplace one that we experience every day. When we watch TV or look at the pixels on our computer screen, we put together thousands of dots of color, and our eyes see the image they conjoin to make.

We also experience theatre through our sense of hearing. For a version of "Putting It Together" that Barbra Streisand recorded, Sondheim rewrote the lyric to describe the aural instead of the visual "bits."

The art of making art
Is putting it together
Bit by bit,
Beat by beat,
Part by part,
Sheet by sheet,
Chart by chart,
Track by track,
Reel by reel,
Stack by stack,
By bit,
By reel,
By track,
By stack,
By sharp,
By flat,
And that is the state of art.

Theatre is made up of bits of sound—voices, sound effects, footsteps, slamming doors, and pauses and silences. These sounds are blended together by theatre artists to shape our experience. We sense when the volume is loud or soft, when the tempo is slow or fast, and when the rhythm is regular or erratic. Sounds act directly on our emotions, making a scene exciting, hilarious, or terrifying, and adding the bits of sound we hear to the images we see takes us a grand step toward putting the performance together: bit by bit.

In rare performances, the audience is given actual food to eat, and then the sense of taste is real and not vicarious. We were thrown a biscuit to eat by a cast member of the Broadway hit Nicholas Nickleby.

The two senses of sight and hearing are the most important ones in the theatre, but we also smell and taste a performance. When Ruth Younger cooks breakfast in the first act of *A Raisin in the Sun,* we smell the coffee brewing and the eggs frying. When her husband eats those eggs, we taste them, if only vicariously. These two senses are stimulated in the theatre only rarely, but they *can* contribute to our experience (Figure 2.1).

The fifth of our senses is feeling, or touch. The English language doesn't provide us with appropriate words to separate the various things we mean when we say, "I was touched by him." Do we mean, "He placed his hand on me and I actually felt his touch"? Or do we mean, "I felt sad when he told me his father died"?

As audience members in the theatre, we can feel the arms of our chairs, and we can feel the tension in our necks during an exciting moment in the action. These are physical feelings we truly experience. But we may also feel emotions and be "touched" by the action on the stage; we can cry and laugh. Our experience is called empathy. This word describes the human capacity for participating in another's feelings. In a performance, when a character scalds his mouth from drinking hot coffee, we flinch. We feel what he feels. We empathize with him.

We experience theatre through all five of our senses. It is truly a complete imitation of real life.

Figure 2.1   The audience for this recent revival of *A Raisin in the Sun* could smell and vicariously taste the coffee and eggs.

Lasting Impact

"On the way home, we talked about how funny the play was." Theatre is an experience that stays with us. We have all seen a performance so funny that we remember it when something in our own life happens that's pretty similar. Perhaps you've seen a performance so sad that it pops back into your mind when something in your own life parallels it. At its best, theatre is an experi-ence that has a lasting impact on us.

Here's an anecdote that will illuminate and validate the lasting impact of theatre. Several years ago (this is Tom speaking again), I was artistic director for a resident professional theatre company in Richmond,
(Continued)

(Continued)

Virginia. The patrons who generously helped finance the theatre held an elegant dinner party before each opening performance. It was a formal affair: tuxedos and long dresses, excellent wines in crystal goblets. The purpose of this dinner, over and above celebrating the play and having fun, was to host guests who might be induced to contribute money to the theatre. I was seated across the table from a pleasant man in his mid-forties who revealed that he had not been "to this damned theatre in over a decade!" Putting on my gentlest manner and most diplomatic voice, I inquired why. He told me it was because of "that damned play." I hadn't been running the theatre at the time he had been offended, so I tried to learn what play had set him off—for ten long years. He couldn't remember the title. Nor who had written it. Nor who had acted in it. Nor what it was about. But it had had a lasting impact on him, so I tried to learn what the play was by getting him to tell me what it looked like—what visual images it had left in his memory. "Well, it was about a clown," he recalled. I racked my brain for plays about clowns. "And there were a lot of them and they all looked alike," he added. I began to suspect what play it was. "Did they all talk strangely and in fragmented sentences?" I asked. "YES! That's the one! That damned play drove me out of the theatre!" I realized that the play was a very challenging and fiercely intellectual avant-garde play called *Kaspar,* written by the highly respected Austrian playwright Peter Handke.

Kaspar had a short period of popularity for a very small circle of intellectuals in the late 1960s and early 1970s. It had been broadcast nationally on public television, but I was very surprised to learn that my predecessor in Richmond had produced it in a mainstream theatre. The play wasn't vulgar, but its unusual subject and style made a lot of people who saw it feel stupid.

Over coffee and dessert, I asked the gentleman what he did, and learned he was an architect who designed large office buildings. I saw my opening. "Did you ever wish you could design a building that people would talk about when they walked past it? One that people would remember?" He allowed as that had always been his dream. He lamented the fact that people walked past his buildings without noticing them and never remembered them. I suggested that being ignored must be tough for any creative person, and I sympathized with his frustration. He saw where I was heading. He saw that a work of art that has a lasting impact is something that every artist hopes to create—every Virginian architect and every Austrian playwright. And, when pressed, he admitted that anything that could make him feel deeply, ten years after he experienced it—even though he couldn't remember what it was called, or who wrote it, or what it was about—might have been an important piece of art.

Whatever else theatre is, it's more than a diverting entertainment. It is an experience that can have a lasting impact.

Audience Participation

The student's description includes, "We laughed a lot" and "at the end we clapped." What *we* do as audience members helps shape the experience. Theatre permits us to be more than passive observers; it makes us into the same kind of active participants we are when we chant "DE-fense, DE-fense" at a basketball game.

When we laugh or applaud, we add to the event—our contribution becomes part of the action. Our laughter and applause encourage the actors to do their best, so we have an indirect impact on the performance as well. We also influence how the rest of the audience behaves. We help shape their experience, which helps shape the actors' performances, which helps shape our experience, and so on. The audience members who shuffle through their programs or rattle candy wrappers and the people whose alarm watches chirp and whose cell phones urp can influence the event negatively. Positively or negatively, we are participants in the communal event.

Present Tense

Theatre is a present tense event. It exists only in the present moment, while it is happening. When the audience leaves and the actors go home, theatre ceases to exist. Yes, there can be audio or video recordings of theatre, but these are *past tense* events. Recordings can play back something that happened at an earlier time, but they're not theatre any more than an instant replay of a touchdown is the same as the play that scored six points in the present tense, during the football game. Theatre is live, and anything can happen. And that makes it exciting in a way that no past tense event can hope to be.

Theatre only happens once. It is unique, and each performance is a new event. However similar they may be, the performance you see on Friday night is different from the performance your friend will see Saturday night.

Conventions

"The lights went down and the curtain went up." The student's class report tells us that the audience knew the rules of the game of theatre, the agreed-upon conventions that make it possible for the actors to act and the audience to enjoy the theatrical experience. The audience knew when the virtual reality of the play began and the true reality of the audience was suspended.

We have learned from childhood that when the lights go down in the theatre or when the screen goes black in the movies, a change of place or time is about to happen. When the lights come back up, we understand that the action is taking place in a different place or is happening at a different time, or both. The audience clearly understands the convention that tells them there's been a change in the play's virtual reality.

Figure 2.2   The wrestling match in Shakespeare's *As You Like It* must be carefully choreographed so that the actors don't hurt each other, though the audience can pretend that the characters do. (Shakespeare Festival of Maine)

Here's another convention: "The actors bowed at the curtain call." Who thought up the idea that an audience should show its appreciation of the actors' performances by clapping? And why do actors demonstrate their thanks for the applause by bowing? No one knows the origin of these actions, but the curtain call is a universally understood convention of the theatre.

Two other important theatrical conventions help us enjoy theatre. The first is what the nineteenth-century English poet and literary critic Samuel Taylor Coleridge called the **willing suspension of disbelief.** In an essay, Coleridge describes how theatre works. The audience consciously sets aside its knowledge that what is happening on the stage is a fiction, and it pretends for the duration of the performance to believe that what it's watching is real. The audience *willingly* (knowingly) *suspends* (sets aside) its *disbelief* (its objectivity). The result is that the audience can empathize with the characters in the play and can derive an exciting experience from willingly participating in the event. When the participants don't understand this convention, disruptions are likely to spoil the performance. Excited spectators who don't remember to willingly suspend their disbelief might run up onto the stage to stop the villain from kicking the hero in a wrestling match, which would be like a fan running out onto the field to tackle a football player and prevent a touchdown (Figure 2.2). As audience members, in the theatre or in the stands, we agree to play the game by the rules.

The theatrical experience requires the audience's "willing suspension of disbelief."

— Samuel Taylor
Coleridge

The second important theatrical convention is the convention of "virtual time" and "virtual place." These terms describe our understanding that the action on stage is happening in a time and place that is different from our own. We sit in the theatre from 8:00 P.M. to 11:00 P.M., watching characters in a play who age many years in the course of one short evening. The virtual time of Shakespeare's *Henry V* arcs over many years, and all of it happens in the fifteenth century, while we continue living in our real time in the twenty-first century. We empathize with characters who live in the virtual place we call England while we sit in a theatre in America. Understanding this convention makes it unlikely that we will rise from our seats to intervene in the lives of the characters in Moliere's *The Misanthrope,* characters whose virtual time and virtual place is seventeenth-century France.

The audience must understand the convention of virtual time and virtual place.

If we tried to use all the ideas in the preceding analysis to answer the question "What is theatre?" we might come up with a clumsy sentence such as this: "Theatre is a special event that happens in a particular place in which an audience is present and actors enact a structured event that engages all five of the audience's senses and makes a lasting impact on them because they are participants in the creation of this unique, present-tense event that depends on universally understood conventions."

That sentence may embrace all the ideas we've developed about theatre, but it doesn't describe how much fun it is to go to the theatre. Let's remember that theatre is fun, and go on to learn more about it.

3

The Origins and Value of Theatre

Theatre began long before any records of human activities were written down, but with a little imagination we can speculate about how it probably got started.

As children, we often make up games with our best friends. Our games include the dimension of time—they deal with things that happened yesterday or that we want to have happen tomorrow. And the structure of our games tends to be logical—each action causes a reaction that, in turn, leads to a result. Because we are self-conscious animals, we don't always enact ourselves in our games. Sometimes we represent characters different from ourselves. Best of all, our games tell us stories that have a point to them. Our stories teach us lessons about how we should relate to other people, and they instruct us about ourselves and how we can influence the world about us.

Human beings have been playing games for thousands of years. Our games are reminders of our past triumphs or preparations for the future, celebrations of our glories or rehearsals for our trials. In our games, we create images and fictions by representing people and places and objects, and we started doing this long before there were any written or pictorial records. Playing is a natural human activity through which we try to understand how our universe works and how to prepare for the future. The instinct to play led us to the creation of that activity we call theatre.

THE BEGINNINGS OF THEATRE—PREHISTORY

Among the earliest and the most amazing artistic representations we have are the drawings by prehistoric cave dwellers (Figure 3.1). It seems sensible to assume that if these prehistoric artists could represent oxen and other animals in painted images of hunt scenes or rituals, they also could represent them in

Figure 3.1 This cave drawing from Lascaux, France, shows the kind of bulls that were hunted for food and that were an inspiration for paintings and for the storytelling that was an early form of theatre.

live imitations. They could have "played" at being animals. They could have made theatre.

Let's imagine what prehistoric theatre might have looked like. A clan is huddled around the fire that keeps their cave warm and frightens the wild animals away. No one has eaten for two days and everyone is hungry. Then a man comes into the cave, beaming with pride and dragging after him the hind leg of a huge bull. Everyone flocks to him. Some put the leg over the fire to cook. Others go out to get the rest of the bull. They skin it, hack it into pieces, and present the bull's horns to the hunter as a trophy. Everybody cheers. They eat. And then someone asks the hunter how he killed the bull.

The hunter begins the story of his kill by saying that he streaked his face with berry juice so that he would look fierce. Perhaps he even demonstrates by rubbing berries on his face as he talks. He goes on, probably embellishing the truth a bit, like any good storyteller. He feels exhilaration from the attention he's receiving from his clanspeople, and that guides him to elaborate, to invent, to create a better story than accurate reporting would provide (Figure 3.2).

"It started to get dark, and then out of the shadows of the forest he charged me. There was nothing for me to do but defend myself, so I broke off a branch from a tree, like this *(he picks up a long bone from the pile before him and handles it like a tree branch),* and I ran to a rock and scraped it into a point, like this *(he runs over to a large stone and scrapes the bone against it),* and just then the bull lowered his horns, like this *(he picks up the horns that had been presented to him),* and charged at me *(the crowd gasps with excitement).* In the second before he reached me, I leaped over his horns and plunged my stick deep into his

This story features a man, but it could just as easily be about a woman. Many legendary societies have been run by women, from the Amazons in ancient Greek myths to the land of Xena, Warrior Princess in contemporary TV lore.

Figure 3.2 The hunter tells his story and demonstrates how he killed the bull.

neck. He spun around and there was a horrible moment when I didn't know what he'd do. We were eye to eye. Then a great sigh came out of him, and he dropped where he stood!"

The applause from the crowd is thunderous. The hunter is a hero and a celebrity, and in addition to being a lucky survivor of the deadly bull's charge, he's discovered he's a born storyteller. As he told his tale, he elaborated the details, drew out the suspense, and physically acted out his role, impersonating himself. He used berry juice for makeup, the bull's horns for a costume, and he even used a prop—the bone that represented the branch. His presentation was a very simple form of theatre, for all theatre is impersonation and storytelling.

All theatre is impersonation and storytelling.

In this scenario we've just imagined, you may recognize the five essential elements of theatre. Our hunter was the actor; the clan formed the audience; the event happened at a particular place (before the campfire); the event happened at a particular time (at the end of the day's hunt); and the event had a structure with conventions that were understood by everyone present.

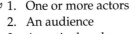

The Five Essentials of Theatre

1. One or more actors
2. An audience
3. A particular place
4. A particular time
5. A structured event

Actors

The hunter did something that is essential to the theatre—he acted a role in a fiction. He created an illusion, and he embellished his storytelling with gestures and vocal inflections. He didn't just narrate his story, he *acted* it, playing out the role when he ran over to the large stone and scraped the bone against it. He acted the other character in this drama as well, the bull, when he held the bull's horns onto his head and said "like this."

Audience

To understand the nature of an audience, whether it's in a theatre, a stadium, or a church, we need to understand two different kinds of human groupings: a community and a collective. In their origins, both theatre and religion served a community. Today only orthodox religions serve a community, while other religious services and virtually all theatrical performances entertain a collective. We currently use the word "community" as a synonym for town, neighborhood, or campus, but there is also a narrower definition taken from the social sciences. **Community** is the name we give to a group of humans for whom the life of the group is more important than the life of any single individual.

In a community, the single person derives meaning from being a part of the community and does not conceive of himself or herself as separate from it. Our fictional hunter was a member of a community, and his entire clan gathered to hear about the kill. For them this presentation was more than an entertaining pastime; this life-and-death event affected their very existence. They understood that the storyteller had risked his life to ensure the life of the community, that the bull's meat was essential to their well-being, and that the hero who saved them kept the tribe alive.

Our modern world still contains communities in this sociological sense. Some of these communities, such as orthodox religious congregations, are valued. Others, such as teenage gangs, are despised. Both are carryovers from an earlier time, and both create challenges for people living in the twenty-first century.

When the hunter told how he killed the bull, he told a life-and-death story to an audience that hung on his every word and gesture because what he told them addressed their essential needs. In the light we imagine flickering on the walls of that cave, the story took on immense importance. It would be remembered and repeated, perhaps the beginning of the oral tradition of the tribe. This first performance was the beginning of theatre, and in its beginnings, theatre's audience was a community.

Theatre's first audience was a community.

Today, we rarely think of ourselves as members of a tribal community. Ever since the days—thousands of years ago—when our ancestors developed from nomadic hunter-gatherers into agriculturalists who stayed in one place and raised their food instead of collecting it, each of us has come to think that, to some degree, we are separate from the group. In the Renaissance, about five hundred years ago, the idea of an "individual" began to take dominance in our understanding of our human condition. An individual is someone who is unique, someone who can exist on his or her own without support from others.

A cluster of individuals who choose to group together in order to achieve some common goal is called a **collective.** Today, we live in collectives. We cluster into cities for the purposes of protection and self-government: to secure good roads, schools, and health care. We feel empowered to move from one city to another, as we wish, and even from one nation to another, changing citizenship with ease. Indeed, America is celebrated as a collective made of people who emigrated from nations in which authoritarian governments denied the individual's inalienable rights.

Today when we gather together for a theatrical performance, we are a very different kind of audience from the prehistoric hunter's community. In contemporary society, we are encouraged by our education and our culture to celebrate our diversity as well as our sameness. We are a collective, not a tribal community. Our tastes in theatre are diverse because we do not always share common beliefs. Indeed, we have different opinions about morality, ethics, politics, and economics, and we even disagree about what gives us pleasure. As a result, we accept the fact that the ideas in our playwrights' stories don't always have a universal meaning, and we don't require the playwrights to tell us universal truths. Although we still need our storytellers to tell us tales that affect our very existence, we usually settle for their entertainments that divert us from our problems so that we can derive pleasure by pretending to escape from "real life."

Today's theatre audience is a collective.

The expectations of a collective's audience are different from the expectations of a community's audience. The community seeks celebration of its achievements and instructions for successfully continuing its communal life. The collective frequently settles for aesthetic pleasure and entertaining diversion.

The function of theatre may have changed as human society has evolved from a community to a collective, but one thing remains certain and unchangeable. Without an audience, there is no theatre. All around our country, theatres fold when nobody attends. Whether we are one thousand tourists clustered in the Winter Garden Theatre on Broadway to see the musical *Cats*, or fifty ecstatic cavedwellers enraptured by a hunter's story, we must be there for the event to happen.

Place

Our prehistoric hunter probably put himself on one side of the campfire and placed his audience on the other. That way, he was well illuminated and could be seen by everyone. The fire was the physical and spiritual center of the clan's life. It was the place where food was cooked, where heat was found, and where light provided security from dangerous animals. Like the hearth in our homes today, the campfire was the spiritual center of life, the place where people gathered to share their knowledge, experiences, hopes, and anxieties.

Time

The hunter performed his theatre at the gathering time, the twilight hour when the clan came together to unite after a day's activities.

A Structured Event

The hunter's performance had an organized story: a structured narrative. It began when he decided to hunt the bull and ended when he brought the carcass back to the cave. When he embellished the facts, when he rearranged the details of his story in order to provide a more exciting experience for his audience, he introduced the notion of narrative. He didn't just tell his clanspeople what he had done, he elaborated and shaped his story so as to bring them the greatest pleasure in the same way that a religious leader elaborates and acts out religious truths with chants, music, and special robes. He turned fact into fiction, and yet he told the *essential* truth in a way that made his group understand its importance. His story provided a lesson to the other hunters in the clan. It provided a central idea, what in theatre we call a theme.

The hunter's story had a point to it. Bravery brings food to the clan, and food is essential to life. Ergo, bravery is a valued behavior. His story told this important lesson in just the same way that religious sermons tell us important lessons.

Over the millennia, theatre's ceremonies addressed the essential concerns of society less and less frequently; instead they began to address such questions as how people should behave toward one another as members of a family and a society. This social function is one that theatre serves today. Although theatre strives to address our most basic questions today, it does so rarely. More frequently, theatre addresses only our social questions, and even more often, theatre settles for providing entertainments that divert us from vital questions. Theatre that is merely entertainment contributes less to our collective welfare than did the theatre of earlier times. Entertainment theatre provides us with less than we truly need, less than we have a right to expect from this most vital form of human experience.

THE VALUE OF THEATRE TODAY

Theatre will involve you in a search for your humanity, for what it truly means to be a human. Theatre provides us with wonderful examples of how people behave in moments of celebration or stress, how they behave in relationship to their families, their societies, their governments, and their deities. From these examples, you may learn to understand the behavior of others and how you should behave. Human behavior doesn't alter much from one age to the next. Just as the knowledge acquired by research doctors in earlier centuries can help today's doctors prevent the spread of diseases like smallpox, so theatregoers can benefit from the lessons presented in theatre past and present. We can learn respect for people of different ethnic backgrounds, for example, from Luis Valdez's *Zoot Suit;* we can learn about the relationships of men and women and how to travel the road to self-fulfillment from classics such as Henrik Ibsen's *A Doll House* (Figure 3.3). The great thinkers of the past who have used theatre as a means of sharing their insights into the human

Figure 3.3
The recent New York revival of Henrik Ibsen's *A Doll's House* revealed that the theme of a woman's journey to self-fulfillment has a powerful impact on contemporary audiences.

condition have taught politicians and scientists, athletes and businesspeople, and they can teach you.

Great playwrights have insights about human life and behavior that we continue to find informative and enriching, and from which we continue to learn vital truths about our own lives. That's why we remember Alexander Pope's observation that "the proper study of mankind is man." We humans have many basic needs, and we have learned how to satisfy most of them. We eat when we need food. We build a house when we need shelter. We find a mate when we need to procreate. We bond into groups when we need safety. These are four ways in which we satisfy some of our basic needs. Here's another. We experience theatre when we need to entertain ourselves and to understand the human condition. Theatre provides us with an experience that makes us intensely alert to the human predicament, its joys and its pains. And perhaps most intriguingly, theatre teaches us about ourselves. Theatre feeds our spirits.

4

Finding Theatre and Getting Tickets

You know where and when the football team plays because there are items in the paper, and you know how to find out what's at the movies and what rock groups are playing at the local night spots. How do you go about finding out what your options are for theatre performances?

No matter where you live, there are eager and informed theatregoers. You might not think, for example, that Salt Lake City is a particularly vibrant theatre town. Yet at 3:00 A.M. on February 2, 1992, the morning tickets were to go on sale for the musical *Les Miserables,* 125 people were already in line at the box office. When the box office opened at 7:00 A.M., there was a rush from hundreds more who had been sitting in their parked cars. In a matter of a few days, all 32,000 tickets for the engagement were sold. Why? Because these people wanted to go to the theatre and because they knew how to find it.

FINDING OUT WHAT'S PLAYING

Theatre is a business, and like a rock concert or a football game, it wants to sell us tickets. Because theatre is only a small business with little money to spend, it places its advertisements strategically, aiming them at the small portion of the public that is interested in theatre, and it relies heavily on free public announcements. With a show that is in hot demand, such as *Les Miserables,* tickets are snapped up, but more often theatres have to try very hard to inform buyers where they are, what they are offering, and how tickets may be bought. Let's explore how and where theatres place ads and announcements so that you can discover how to find theatre where you live.

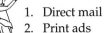

The Four Ways Theatres Advertise

1. Direct mail
2. Print ads
3. Radio and television
4. Telemarketing

Direct Mail

Direct mail is theatre's most efficient and cost-effective way of advertising. Theatres develop lists of persons who are likely to be interested, and they mail attractive brochures directly to those people's homes. Where does a theatre get its lists? It starts with the name and address of everyone who has purchased a ticket to that theatre; that's why, when you buy a ticket for any performance, the theatre strives to get your name and address. Next, it secures the mailing lists of other arts organizations. The theatre swaps its list with the ballet, which swaps its list with the opera, which swaps its list with the symphony, and so on. The relatively small cost of preparing and mailing a brochure generates the largest proportion of a theatre's ticket sales, so this mode of advertising is the centerpiece in a theatre's marketing strategy.

Print Ads

Print ads are comparatively inexpensive, and theatres advertise in many places. Marquees are the most obvious form of print advertising (Figure 4.1), but there are others. Newspapers carry display ads for season tickets just after the Labor Day holiday, when people are settling their schedules after summer vacations; ads for single productions can be found at any time of the year. Commonly these ads are located near the ads for other forms of entertainment, such as the movies. Print ads also appear in magazines that appeal to upper middle income families and in glossy monthlies such as *San Diego Magazine* and *Virginia Today*. Because people who go to one kind of arts performance are likely to enjoy another, theatres commonly place ads in the programs of the ballet or the opera. Billboards and signs on public transportation are yet another place you'll see print ads. Commercial theatres in New York and elsewhere place ads on buses, in subway stations, and on huge billboards that can be seen by commuters (Figure 4.2). You are very likely to have seen a poster, or "window board," yet another form of print ad that theatres use. Posters are aimed at pedestrian traffic, so they are placed in windows that large numbers of people pass by. You may also have seen table tents and handbills. The former are found on tables at restaurants and motels, the latter are handed to you as you walk down the street. Print ads are an inexpensive way to attract the impulse buyer.

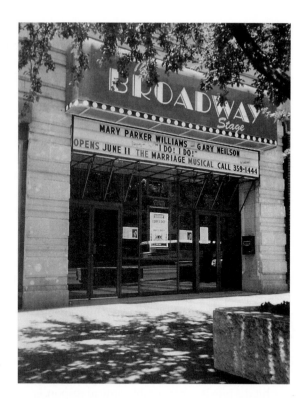

Figure 4.1 This marquee is an obvious form of print advertising for the opening of the musical *I Do, I Do.*

Figure 4.2 A large form of print advertising, this billboard advertises Pioneer Theatre Company's 1996–97 season.

Radio and Television Ads

Radio stations sell ads by time. A thirty-second spot costs less than a sixty-second spot, and an ad broadcast during the evening news costs more than one that airs at 4:47 A.M. Because radio advertising is more expensive than print advertising, many small theatres can't afford to advertise by radio. By contrast, commercial theatre productions like *The Phantom of the Opera* buy a lot of airtime. Have you heard radio ads for theatre? If not, it may be because of the stations you listen to. People who go to the theatre often listen to classical music or golden oldies, so theatres rarely spend their money for ads on stations that play rock, country and western, or New Age music. Theatres would like to advertise regularly on radio, but they can't afford it very often. What is true for radio is even more true for television; you will rarely see TV ads for theatre. The major exceptions are the big commercial productions playing on Broadway or on tour. TV ads are now commonplace in New York, particularly for large musicals that hope to sell $700,000 worth of tickets each week. TV advertising is a relatively new mode of advertising that began with the Broadway musical *Pippin* in 1972 (Figure 4.3).

In 1972, Stephen Schwartz's soft rock musical *Pippin* was not being well received during preview performances, and audiences were walking out at intermission. The gossip in the theatre community was that the show had "flop" written all over it. Rather than close the show and lose all their money when the negative reviews came out, the producers had two brainstorms. First, they omitted the intermission so people didn't have a polite time to leave. Second, they launched a major ad campaign on television. They took their star, Ben Vereen, and made an energetic and colorful TV commercial that showed him singing and dancing. The strategy worked. The show was a box office hit despite its unfavorable critical response.

Figure 4.3 The hit musical *Pippin*, starring Ben Vereen, opened on Broadway in 1972 and was the first to advertise with television commercials.

Telemarketing

We all get those calls asking if we will vote for a candidate, give to a charity, or buy tickets to the symphony. These calls are made by telemarketers, and theatres are among the many businesses that have learned that telemarketing is an inexpensive and highly efficient way to reach their buyers. A theatre builds a list of prospects and engages a group of telephoners who make an appealing sales pitch.

If you have a pleasing telephone voice and are a charming yet aggressive personality, you can make money by working for your local theatre company. The hours are convenient (usually from 4:00 in the afternoon until about 8:00 in the evening) and if you are good at it, you can make a handsome commission on top of your hourly wage. But be certain before you embark on this job that you can take rejection, because you'll get a lot of it. Some people will hang up on you, others will be rude, and more than a few will insult the product you are trying to sell them. "I subscribed last year and I *hated* the shows" is something you'll hear often.

Here's an experience I had when I (Tom) tried to help out with a subscription drive:

—Hello?

—Hello. I'm calling from TheatreVirginia, and I hope this is a convenient time to chat with you. Do you have a free moment?

—Yes, I suppose so . . .

—Wonderful. Well, we're looking through our files and we see that you haven't renewed for next season. We know you won't want to miss out on the seven terrific shows we'll be doing, so we wanted to call and remind you that you could renew *now* and keep the good seats you had this past year.

—Oh dear, I don't know . . .

—Have you been out of town? I notice you didn't return your renewal form when we sent your brochure in the mail last month.

—No, you see . . .

(About here I realized that her voice was very frail and that she was probably quite elderly and perhaps in poor health.)

. . . you see my husband passed away just before Christmas and I don't have any way to get out of the house at night and I can't see to drive very well, and so I don't think I can come to the theatre anymore.

Several hours later, after I'd made the umpteenth call like that, I got very depressed. So many older folks in failing health, with no family or friends, and here I was trying to sell them theatre tickets! I told my managing director that the experience was too depressing and that I was sorry but I just couldn't continue. He laughed heartily. "That's because you're not a real salesman," he teased. "If you were, you'd say

(Continued)

(Continued)

something uplifting like, 'Gee, I'm sorry to hear that you lost your husband, but you know if you'd subscribe to our next season you could meet lots of new folks at the theatre and maybe find yourself a new husband.' " We both laughed, I told him he was a heartless swine, I admitted I wasn't a "real salesman," and I went back to directing plays and let him get on with the business he did so very well—the business of selling subscriptions.

Telemarketing is a major marketing tool for theatres across America. It is used alongside direct mail, print ads, and radio and television spots, and it is the newest of the four ways theatre uses paid advertising to tell you where you can find a performance.

Theatres also post free announcements that tell you where theatre is playing in your city.

The Three Ways Theatres Post Announcements

1. Print
2. Radio and television
3. Internet

Print Announcements

Print announcements are readily found in newspapers, both the large-circulation, mainstream dailies and the weeklies that serve the counterculture community or that promote local businesses. Most papers print a column—commonly titled "Calendar"—that lists events you can attend. Printed announcements usually give you the name and address of the theatre, the phone number to call for tickets, and the names of the plays being presented.

Radio and Television Announcements

All radio and television stations are licensed by the FCC (Federal Communications Commission), an agency of the U.S. government. One of the FCC's regulations is that the airwaves belong to the people, and when a station secures a license to use the public's airwaves—that is, to broadcast—the station must provide a certain portion of its total airtime for use in the service of the public. The announcements it makes are called PSAs (public service announcements), and various stations broadcast different kinds: a lost and found for pets, a listing of school closings, traffic advisories for commuters, or a calendar of arts events. What's true for radio is true for television, but PSAs aren't broadcast as frequently on television as on radio. Although PSAs may assist the theatre in reaching you, they aren't much help when you want to find out the specifics about what's playing.

Internet

The Internet is the newest medium that theatres use for announcements, and it's quickly becoming the most accessible and most current source of information (and for buying tickets). Because the Internet continues to expand rapidly, some of the following information may change by the time you read this, but you surfers know there's a vast ocean of information waiting for you. Dive in!

The longest route is through your preferred search engine. When searching, it'll help if you spell your query using both "theatre" and "theater." That small difference in spelling will result in two completely different sets of hits. The word "theatre" is such a broad query that it will produce more hits than you may want to sift through. You'll stumble into some interesting and unexpected information this way, but here are some time-efficient tips on how to find out where theatre is.

Theatre Web Site Addresses

Theatre Direct International	theatredirect.com
American Theatre Web	americantheaterweb.com
CultureFinder	culturefinder.com
Theatre Central	playbill.com

Large cities, such as New York and London, have specialized sites for cyber-minded theatre lovers who want to stay up-to-date on their favorite plays and players. The home page for Theatre Direct International (TDI) gives you the hottest stage news involving Broadway and Off Broadway productions, as well as productions in London. TDI raises the curtain on a virtual playbill of information, including show openings and schedules, cast members, ticket availability, and even a bit of theatre gossip. Check out this site even if you're not going anywhere. It's amazing to see the number and variety of theatrical offerings in places in which theatrical tourism plays a large part in the local economy.

If you want to find out what the critics said about a play before you buy a ticket, just type in the name of the play in quotes. You'll get lots of unrelated hits, but you'll find the critics' reviews among them. To locate these reviews quickly, look for the word "review" in the address.

Maybe you're not headed for New York or London; maybe you want to find out what's happening in your hometown or during your visit with friends on the Mississippi Gulf Coast. The sites that we've included here list theatre events in nearly every city across the country. These sites invite you to either select or enter the name of a city to learn what plays are available there. The American Theatre Web site, for example, provides listings and links to not-for-profit theatre companies all over the country. Each entry has a summary of the theatre company's work and productions along with a link to the theatre's own Web site for more detailed information. The range is impressive; you can locate information on everything from small community theatres in Texas to the Arena Stage in Washington. Although the big commercial houses of Broadway are not on the site, links to several dozen not-for-profit companies in New York City are listed. Another Web site, CultureFinder, is easy to use and isn't just limited to theatre; it also includes art exhibits and music performances. Search by typing in the name of the city and the range of dates you're interested in.

The last Web site that we listed may be the best of them all. Theatre Central is the *hub* of theatre on the Internet. It gives you information about international theatre and American theatre, and it may even list the plays in your own hometown. The site lists Broadway, regional theatre, national tours, and summer stock. It has fascinating stories, it permits you to buy tickets on-line, and it offers numerous links.

More theatres each day are setting up their own Web sites. You'll need a little luck and some trial-and-error searching techniques to find them because their addresses are often a condensation of the name of the theatre company. When you hit on one, you'll find e-mail and snail-mail addresses, phone and fax numbers, season schedules, performance dates, titles of current productions, ticket prices, and names of the directors, actors, and designers; some sites even list audition dates in case you're an actor looking for a job. A theatre may include on its Web site graphics of its productions, background information about its plays, director's notes, reviews of its productions, or links to related sites.

Go to the Web site for the Colorado Shakespeare Festival (www. coloradoshakes.org). You'll discover that you can watch its productions live while they are being performed. The site does not offer sound, so you can't hear what the actors are saying, and the image updates only every thirty seconds, so it's like watching a badly edited film, but the concept is nonetheless amazing.

Some particularly successful commercial productions maintain Web sites that give you background information about the play. Search by entering the name of the play in quotes. For example, entering "Picasso at the Lapin

Agile" will link you to a site about the very funny play Steve Martin wrote. Many of these sites also tell you the schedule of a production's national tour. Hop on the Internet and find out if the national tour of your favorite musical is headed your way.

TICKET TIPS

Theatres sell tickets to performances in two basic forms: single tickets and season tickets. It's the same practice that is used by basketball teams and symphony orchestras. You can buy one or more tickets for a particular performance, or you can buy one or more tickets to each in the series of productions that a theatre company presents in a season. In the commercial theatre, on Broadway, or in many large cities, theatres produce one show at a time so only single tickets are available.

There are variants on these two forms of tickets that might be of interest to you. You can purchase group tickets for a particular performance at a discounted rate, so if you belong to a sorority, a club, or a professional organization that would enjoy going to a play, you can purchase tickets at a reduced price. Alternatively, some theatres sell a pass as well as a season ticket. Here's the difference. A season ticket admits you to the same seat for each production of the theatrical season. Typically, you select the week of the run and the performance of the week you wish to attend: for example, the second Tuesday night of the four-week run of each production. At the time of purchase, you receive your ticket for each production; you know that you will always have the same seat and that you will always go on the same day of the week. People who attend with friends and make a social or business occasion of their theatregoing prefer this way of buying tickets, and most theatres do three things to make season tickets attractive: they offer you the opportunity to purchase your tickets before single tickets go on sale so that you have an excellent chance of getting good seats; they offer the tickets at a discounted rate; and they offer you the right to exchange your ticket for any other performance of that production. They can't guarantee you a comparably good seat, of course, but you *will* be able to reschedule to suit your convenience. A pass, on the other hand, is good for a specified number of admissions, let's say five. By presenting your pass at the box office, you can get five seats to one performance, or one seat to any five performances, or any variation. Of course, you can only get tickets on a space available basis, so you can't be certain where you'll be sitting. Some people prefer the pass to the season ticket because they can take friends or business associates to selected performances and because they can avoid any production they believe they might not like. Such flexibility is important for people who have strong feelings about what they *don't* want to encounter in the theatre.

How do you actually go about buying your ticket? The surest way is to go to the theatre's box office. Box offices are usually open a full working day, six days a week. The clerks there are more than happy to accept your cash, personal check, or major credit card. If the ad or announcement doesn't tell you the box office hours, a quick phone call will.

The box office usually displays a sign that describes the different prices for seats in various parts of the theatre; the front rows cost more than the back of the balcony, and a seat in the center costs more than one on the side. If you are a student or senior citizen and can produce appropriate identification, you may find that reduced price tickets are available to you. Theatres rarely announce these discounts, so you have to inquire.

Theatre ticket prices are tied to the general economy and can go up and down like the price of gasoline. The highest price yet charged for the best seat at a Broadway show was $100.00 for the hit musical *Miss Saigon,* but most musicals charge $70.00 for the best seats on a Saturday night and as low as $25.00 for back balcony seats on a weeknight. As a rule, musicals cost more than straight plays, and the range for dramas and comedies is from $65.00 down to $22.50. Prices for smaller theatres are proportionately lower and can range from $50.00 down to $20.00.

As you travel about the country, you will find there are no fixed prices for theatre tickets, though some patterns can be observed. Ticket prices in the city we live in are a fair guide to what they are in other cities. For a tour of a major commercial production like *The Phantom of the Opera,* ticket prices range from $70.00 down to $30.00. For the resident professional theatre company, prices range from $37.00 down to $18.00. For local amateur theatre companies, prices range from $25.00 to $12.00. And for plays presented at a university, prices range from $8.00 down to $4.00.

You can see the advantage to buying a season ticket to a theatre that charges $30.00 a seat. Instead of paying $210.00 for the seven-play season, you might pay only $180.00. If you're buying four seats together, you save $120.00. Season tickets—whether for the theatre season or the football season—are as wise a choice for those who attend regularly as subscriptions to newspapers are for those who read one daily.

Sometimes it is inconvenient to go to a theatre's box office. Fortunately, you can purchase tickets by telephone if you are willing to pay a modest service charge and if you have a major credit card. Theatres will mail the tickets to you or hold them at the box office, where you can pick them up just before the performance. In many large cities you can purchase tickets from agencies that are conveniently located in hotel lobbies and department stores. Other ticket agencies can be found by looking under "tickets" in your phone book, and companies such as Tele-charge and TicketMaster will sell you tickets with an added commission. They will mail the tickets to you or have them held at the box office.

For the bargain minded theatregoer, discounted tickets for same-day performances are available in large cities such as New York, London, and Paris at special box offices in central locations (Figure 4.4). In New York, the TKTS booth is located in the heart of the Broadway theatre district. For slightly more than half the face value of the ticket, you can purchase tickets to most

Figure 4.4 The TKTS booth in midtown Manhattan sells discounted tickets for that day's performance of Broadway and Off Broadway shows.

Broadway shows if you are willing to stand in a short line and be flexible about what you want to see. Additionally, most resident professional theatres outside New York offer "student rush" tickets at a greatly reduced price. These tickets are usually available only thirty minutes before curtain time. Student rush seats are usually the same price as a movie—between $4.00 and $7.50—and you might get excellent seats!

You can buy theatre tickets over the Internet for many performances, although this option is only a few years old and not every theatre has a Web site. If you have a credit card, you can select your seat and buy your tickets with a click, and your tickets will be mailed to you or held for you at the box office.

We need to let you know about one final way to buy tickets. Sometimes tickets for a popular show that is sold out can be purchased from people who have extras. Be wary, however, of scalpers who offer tickets at inflated prices. Sometimes their tickets are phony and won't be accepted by the theatre, and their transactions are illegal in most states. But if you are eager to see a popular show, you might take a chance on encountering somebody standing in front of the theatre trying to sell tickets bought for friends whose car broke down.

A ticket is a legally binding contract with the management of the theatre. In consideration of the money you gave them (and the amount is printed on the ticket), they guarantee that you have a particular seat for a particular performance of a particular play. No one else may occupy your seat. But what happens if the management doesn't deliver what they guaranteed you? Then you get your money back.

Here's an unusual instance in which the play did not go on as planned and in which refunds were an issue. The Oregon Shakespeare Festival performs in a 1,000-seat outdoor amphitheatre. While we were watching their performance of *The Taming of the Shrew,* a lightning storm knocked out all the electrical power in the county. After waiting about thirty minutes to see whether power would be restored, the management announced that refunds or exchanges for tickets for another performance were available at the box office. We learned later that because the rains are heavy enough once or twice each season to stop a performance, the management has a rain policy. If the performance is stopped before it is halfway completed, a refund is made. If more than half the performance has been completed, no refund is made. The festival's annual budget includes $40,000 to cover the cost of refunds.

Exercise   WHERE THEATRES ADVERTISE

1. Prepare a list of all newspaper and magazines ads for theatre that you found this week in your city's publications.

2. Prepare a list of all newspaper and magazine announcements for theatre that you found this week in your city's publications.

3. For each radio ad or PSA you heard during this week, describe the length of the spot, what station it was on, what time it was broadcast, and whether it was an ad or a PSA.

4. For each television ad or PSA you saw during this week, describe the length of the ad, what channel it was on, what time it was broadcast, and whether it was an ad or a PSA.

5. Describe how you used the Internet to learn about theatre performances in your city during this past week.

5

Take Your Seat, Please

Once you have your ticket, you're ready to experience theatre. In this chapter, we'll look at a number of things to consider—both before the performance and during it— that will increase your enjoyment when you go to the theatre.

WHEN TO ARRIVE

Broadway performances usually begin at 8:00 P.M. if it's an evening show and 2:00 P.M. if it's a matinee, but many resident theatres outside New York start at 7:00 P.M. on Sunday, and others start at 7:30 P.M. on weeknights. Still other theatres offer shows at 5:00 P.M. and 9:00 P.M. Double check your curtain time. It's printed on the theatre ticket. If your ticket is being held at the box office, phone the theatre or check the ad.

Allow yourself ample time to get to the theatre, and give yourself some leeway if you're traveling by public transportation or if you suspect it will take you a while to park. Unlike the movies, theatre doesn't offer a "next show" that allows you to see the part you missed if you're late.

When is "late"? Performances usually begin some two to five minutes after the announced curtain time. Managements do that on purpose to ensure that the audience is seated before the performance begins, so don't be surprised if your watch reads 8:04 and the house lights haven't yet dimmed. But you are late if you arrive after the performance has begun, and ushers are instructed to keep you in the lobby until some suitable point when your entrance will least disturb those who arrived on time. Some theatres have a video monitor in the lobby so you can watch what you are missing, but more often you will just twiddle your thumbs until you are admitted—which may be as much as thirty minutes into the action. To enjoy the show fully, plan to be prompt.

You will increase your enjoyment if you arrive twenty minutes or so before curtain time. Not only will you have a chance to visit the rest rooms (thereby avoiding the hordes during the fifteen-minute intermission), but you'll also have time to read the program.

The New York Times reported that when Madonna acted in David Mamet's play *Speed the Plow* on Broadway, some of her fans arrived late to the performance. When the play ended, the audience left the theatre, reported the *Times,* but the ushers found groups of fans still in their seats. When asked why, they explained that they had arrived late and were waiting for "the next show."

DECIDING WHAT TO WEAR

You want to dress appropriately: not too fancy, not too casual. If you're not certain what's correct, be comforted. Most theatregoers have faced the same problem.

Fashions and customs change from country to country, from decade to decade, and from theatre to theatre. Not long ago, people wore tuxedos and formal dresses to the Broadway theatre, every lobby had a cloakroom at which gentlemen checked their opera cloaks (not coats, mind you), and every seat had a wire gizmo under it that held the gentleman's top hat. (You'll still find those gizmos under the seats in some older theatres.) America today is an increasingly informal culture, and we tolerate a wide range of dress. We don't expect theatregoers to show up in tuxedos, but even the most tolerant of us is more than a little taken aback when we see something distasteful (like the woman we saw recently at a Broadway show with her hair up in big pink sponge curlers!).

As a rule of thumb, you should dress for the theatre as you would dress to eat at a restaurant, and you should let the price of the theatre ticket and the theatre's location serve as a guide for how to dress. If you are going to an expensive restaurant or if you paid $70.00 for a theatre ticket to a commercial touring production at a downtown theatre, you should expect most of the audience to be dressed nicely: business suits and party dresses. If you are going to a neighborhood restaurant or if you paid $30.00 for your theatre ticket to a summer theatre festival, you should expect the audience to be more casually dressed: open-collared shirts and slacks, blouses and skirts. If you are heading for the local pizza parlor or if you paid $8.00 for your ticket to a college production, jeans and sneakers are the dress of the day. Because we live in a permissive culture, no one will say anything if you show up at a college play in a nice suit or at your city's professional theatre company wearing jeans. But if your goal is to blend in with the rest of the audience so that you will feel appropriate, then common sense, these guidelines, and consultation with friends who are regular theatregoers should provide you with a way to choose which hangers to take out of your closet.

BEFORE THE PLAY BEGINS

At the theatre, you can see the flow of people moving inside. A window at the box office has a sign reading "Reservations" where you would pick up your tickets if they were being held. As you join the crowd heading toward the auditorium, you might be able to check your coat so that you don't have to sit on it or wad it up under your seat. As you move through the lobby, someone takes your ticket, tears it in half, gives you back your ticket stub that has your aisle, row, and seat number printed on it, and points you toward the correct aisle. Finally, an usher hands you a **playbill** and shows you to your seat.

Did you ever wonder why your ticket is torn? Theatre's a money-making business, so careful accounting is important. The director of a Broadway play earns 1.5 percent of the weekly gross, so he or she wants a very precise accounting of what that gross is. Your ticket stub is a part of the accounting process that determines what the director is due. For a hit Broadway musical, the director's 1.5 percent can exceed $10,000 a week.

There are three kinds of information in the playbill: what you ought to read before the play begins, what you might enjoy reading afterward, and advertisements. Playbills come in various sizes and shapes, from the one-page photocopied cast list you might get at your nephew's school play to the oversized and glossy souvenir program you might buy at a summer Shakespeare festival, but they all provide you with some essential information. The most common form is a five-inch-by-eight-inch booklet.

Toward the middle of the playbill you will find the title page, like the one shown in Figure 5.1 from Peter Nichol's comedy *Joe Egg*. The title page tells you the name of the play, the author, and the key artists who created the performance: the director, designers, and other specialists such as the casting director, dramaturg, and stage manager. After the title page is the performance page. It tells you where the action is set, when it takes place, and if there will be any intermissions.

A little further into the playbill is the cast page. This page lists the cast of characters and the actors who play them (Figure 5.2). Here you may read the characters' names, their jobs, their relationships, and other information about them that will help you understand what unfolds on the stage. You can peruse the list of actors' names for any actors you have seen before.

presents

JOE EGG
by Peter Nichols

Directed by
Tom Markus

Set Design by
Ray Recht

Costume Design by   Lighting Design by
Lisa C. Micheels   **Jon Terry**

Production Stage Manager   Stage Manager
Dori Eskenazi   **Harriet L. Sheets**

SPONSORED IN PART BY
The Kingston-Warren Corporation.

*"JOE EGG is presented by special arrangement with Samuel French, Inc."

Theatre by the Sea is a professional company operating on a League of Resident Theatres (LORT) agreement with Actors Equity Association, and is a constituent member of Theatre Communications Group, Inc. and the American Art Alliance.

Figure 5.1 This title page from the playbill for *Joe Egg* at New Hampshire's Theatre by the Sea gives you the name of the theatre company, the title of the play, and the names of the playwright, director, designers, and the other key artistic collaborators.

If you take time to read only the title page, the performance page, and the cast page, you will be marginally prepared to enjoy the show. But the playbill includes much more information that you might enjoy reading before the performance. Most programs contain bios that briefly describe the previous accomplishments of the artists who have created this performance. You

♪ THE CAST

JOE EGG

(in order of appearance)

Bri . . . . .Ian Stuart
Sheila. . . . . .Johanna Morrison
Joe . . . . .Briana Campbell
Pam . . . . .Alexandra O'Karma
Freddie . . . . .David Pursley
Grace. . . . . .Virginia Downing

★ ★ ★ ★ ★

PLACE:

Brian and Sheila's living-room

ACT I

An evening in winter

There will be one intermission

ACT II

Later the same night

★ ★ ★ ★ ★

Figure 5.2 The cast page gives you the names of the characters and the actors. Characters are listed on the left, actors on the right. In some playbills, the cast page also tells you where and when the action is set.

might learn that the lead will be played by an actor you've seen in the movies, that the director's career has taken her to Broadway, or that the costume designer won an Emmy Award. Bios are published to give you some background on the artists, and many theatregoers like to read them. Figure 5.3 shows you some bios for *Joe Egg,* and in reading them you learn that two of

♪ WHO'S WHO

ALEXANDRA O'KARMA (Pam) has appeared in numerous productions in New York City, including *THE HOMECOMING* at the Jewish Repertory Theatre, *KNITTERS IN THE SUN* at the Lucille Lortel (for which she garnered the Villager Award for Distinguished Performance), *I AM A CAMERA* at the American Jewish Theatre, and *A MONTH IN THE COUNTRY, WARBECK, CINEMA SOLDIER* and *A FLEA IN HER EAR* at the Colonnades Theatre Lab. Last spring she created the role of Liz in the world premiere of *FUGUE* at The Long Wharf. Other regional credits include Lady Macbeth at the Tennessee Repertory Theatre, *TO KILL A MOCKINGBIRD* at Indiana Rep , *THE CHALK GARDEN* at the American Shaw Festival, *MAN AND SUPERMAN* at the George Street Playhouse, Terence Feely's *THE TEAM* at the Hartman Theatre, for which she created the role of Selina Proby, and multiple summer stock productions with Michigan's Cherry County Playhouse and Ohio's Kenley Players. Ms. O'Karma appeared on HBO television this past fall as Anna Daley, opposite Tommy Lee Jones, in the BBC production of *YURI NOSENKO, KGB,* and on PBS' American Playhouse series, starring in *REFUGE.*She can also be seen in *TERMS OF ENDEARMENT,* playing a nasty New Yorker named Jane.

DAVID PURSLEY (Freddie) is a veteran of numerous regional theatres including the Virginia Museum Theatre, the Old Globe of San Diego, Seattle Repertory Theatre, Stage West of Springfield, Massachusetts, the Dallas Theater Center, the Arizona Theatre Company, the Barter Theatre, and Nassau Repertory Theatre. His roles have ranged from Horace Giddens in *THE LITTLE FOXES* and Teddy Roosevelt in *TINTYPES,* to Malvolio in *TWELFTH NIGHT* and the bogus aunt in *CHARLEY'S AUNT.* Recently he played the title role in *TARTUFFE* for the North Carolina Shakespeare Festival, and directed their production of *LOVE'S LABOUR'S LOST.* He made his Broadway debut in the Tony-nominated Brecht-Weill musical *HAPPY END,* which starred Meryl Streep and Christopher Lloyd, and he has been in numerous Off-Broadway productions including *PEACE, WINGS,* and *THE THREE MUSKETEERS.* For two seasons he was the Artistic Director of the Cortland New York Repertory Theatre, and has appeared at Radio City Music Hall and at the White House. A graduate of Harvard, he also holds a Master's Degree from Baylor University/Dallas Theater Center.

IAN STUART (Bri) recently spent fourteen months in the comedy hit *THE FOREIGNER* at New York City's Astor Place Theatre, where he gave over 440 performances as "Froggy." Other New York credits include Broadway's *CAESAR & CLEOPATRA,* with Rex Harrison and Elizabeth Ashley; *THE ACCRINGTON PALS* at The Hudson Guild; *MISALLIANCE* at The Roundabout; *COUNT DRACULA* at Equity Library Theatre; *THE JACK THE RIPPER REVIEW* at Manhattan Punch Line. He has extensive regional theatre credits playing leading roles for Hartford Stage Company, Repertory of St. Louis, Pennsylvania Stage Company, Virginia Museum, Delaware Theatre Company, Nassau Repertory, The Barter. He has also played King Arthur in *CAMELOT* and Captain Von Trapp in *THE SOUND OF MUSIC.* Television credits include numerous soaps, most recently "Payson" in *ONE LIFE TO LIVE* and "Dr. Sossaman" in *ALL MY CHILDREN.* Also a director, with more than 30 productions to his credit, he recently staged an acclaimed revival of Pinter's *BETRAYAL* for Connecticut's Boston Post Road Stage Company in Fairfield.

Figure 5.3   Actors' bios in the playbill give you information about their professional careers.

the actors had been seen recently on Broadway and that another was in the movie *Terms of Endearment.*

Toward the back of a playbill you will usually find the staff page, which lists the people who work at the theatre and who helped create this particular production (Figure 5.4). You may not have any keen interest in learning the name of the assistant house manager or the master electrician, but you may be amazed at how many people it took to create the performance you're about to enjoy.

♪ THEATRE STAFF

Artistic Director   TOM MARKUS

ADMINISTRATION

Management Advisor	IRA SCHLOSSER
Administrative Assistant to the Directors	VICTORIA KASABIAN
Development Director	TOM BIRMINGHAM
Administrative Assistant	GAIL McDOWELL
Marketing/PR Coordinator	MICHAEL REZNICEK
Marketing Associate	KAREN A. HEENAN
Marketing Volunteer	PHYLLIS GIGLIO
Business Manager	MONIQUE DI BEASE
Box Office Manager	DRIKA OVERTON
Box Office Assistant	MICHAEL J. TOBIN
Box Office Assistant	CAROL ST. CLAIR
Box Office Assistant	JO ELLEN SCULLY
Box Office Assistant	DOUGLAS D. WERTS
House Manager	JAMIE REYNOLDS
Concessions Manager	SHARLENE HAMMOND
Bartender	MARC CONNORS
Custodian	GARY REYNOLDS

ARTISTIC/PRODUCTION

Production/Facilities Manager	JOHN LAWRENCE BECKER
Production Stage Manager	DORI ESKENAZI
Stage Manager	HARRIET L. SHEETS
Assistants to the Stage Managers	BARBARA ROLLINS
	MELISSA WENDER
Lighting Designer/Master Electrician	JON TERRY
Electrics Intern	MERRITT CROSBY
Properties Director	JOEL PORTER
Properties Intern	MARYANN GORMAN
Costume Shop Foreman/Designer	LISA C. MICHEELS
First Hand	JOY MISSAGGIA
Wardrobe Coordinator	JANE M. CARVILLE
Graphic Design	DIANE DRAPER
Set Construction	BOB SCENIC

Figure 5.4 This staff page from the *Joe Egg* playbill lists the names of all the personnel who worked for Theatre by the Sea. Because this page contains many more names than the cast page does, you can see that theatre is a labor-intensive business.

Theatre is what economists call a labor-intensive industry, which means that it takes a lot of people to create a performance and that automation won't alter how it is done. Indeed, in virtually every part of theatre, there hasn't been much change in how it is done in thousands of years. An actor is still needed to play a role; a dresser is needed to help with quick costume changes; a carpenter is needed to build the set; an usher is needed to show you to your seat. Theatre is like the proverbial iceberg: 80 percent unseen. Although you may remember the actors when you leave, rarely will you give a thought about the fight choreographer or about the props running crew. But without them, the show couldn't go on.

The second kind of information you will find in a playbill is background about the play. This information is usually written by a theatre's **dramaturg.** A dramaturg is a literary consultant whose other work includes translating plays, doing research for directors and actors, and reading new plays that are being considered for production.

The third kind of information you'll find in the playbill is the advertisements. These ads can give you a sense of who will be sitting next to you. If a resident professional theatre company's playbill contains ads for cars and jewelry, then your fellow audience members are probably middle-aged and affluent. If the ads are for bookstores and coffeehouses, expect a younger, university audience. If the ads are for fast food restaurants and toy stores, you'll probably see a lot of children in the audience.

The playbill is your ticket to what the business world calls "added value." If you read the dramaturg's information after you have gone home, you'll get even more value for the dollars you spent on the ticket. If you look through the ads, you may find a restaurant you'd like to eat at after the performance. But even if you look at nothing more than the cover of the playbill, you will get a fundamental image that will help prepare you for the play. The graphic image on the cover of the *Joe Egg* playbill shows the title character as she is seen in her one happy moment in the play (Color Plate 2). From the graphic image on its cover and the written information in its pages to the types of advertisements it carries, the playbill is a valuable tool to assist you in appreciating the experience you are about to have.

About three minutes beforehand, the theatre gives a signal that the performance will begin shortly. In some theatres the lights in the lobby dim two or three times. In other theatres, a bell or buzzer sounds. Some theatres play a recorded voice that asks you to "take your seat, please." If you have been in the rest room, visiting in the lobby, or checking your coat, now is the time to move promptly to your seat.

DURING THE PERFORMANCE

This notion of promptness raises the entire subject of theatre etiquette. There are no absolute laws on behavior at the theatre, though there are some established practices, and common sense should keep you from doing anything that will disturb the audience around you or the actors on the stage. In recent years columns on the subject of audience etiquette have appeared in the theatre sections of newspapers from New York to Seattle addressing the concern that our culture has been weaned on television and that we are in danger of losing our sense of public courtesy. One article described a man who talked back to the characters in the play, and another described a woman who brought her pet chimpanzee to the theatre. The people sitting around her complained because the woman talked throughout the performance, loudly repeating the dialogue to the chimp. The usher asked the woman to leave, but he later admitted it was a shame because the chimp had behaved well. The columnist urged that theatregoers treat actors and audience as they themselves wished to be treated, and she provided a list of rules for good audience behavior. Another journalist adopted Old Testament diction and provided a list of ten commandments for theatregoers. We provide here a variation on their lists.

Ten Commandments of Theatre Etiquette

1. THOU SHALT ARRIVE PROMPTLY. Get to your seat before the performance begins. You don't want to be disturbed by a late arriver, so don't disturb others.

2. THOU SHALT NOT SPEAK DURING THE PERFORMANCE. Laughing at jokes and applauding the actors is encouraged, but don't repeat the dialogue or explain the plot to your companion. You're not at home watching TV. You didn't pay to listen to your neighbors, so don't make them listen to you.

3. THOU SHALT LEAVE THY CHILDREN AT HOME. It's unfair to your children to bring them to a show that bores them or that has language that disturbs them, and their fidgeting is intrusive on those who paid to enjoy the play. Many theatres will not admit children under age five. Save your children's theatregoing for a performance intended for children.

4. THOU SHALT LEAVE THY CAMERA AT HOME. Copyright laws prohibit photographing a performance, so your camera could be illegal as well as bothersome to those around you. The clicking sound is irritating to your neighbors and the flash is dangerous to the actors, and neither is a part of the play.

5. THOU SHALT TURN OFF ALL ELECTRONIC DEVICES. Beepers, pagers, alarm watches, cell phones, CD players, portable radios, and other noisy electronic gizmos have no place in the theatre. If you are a doctor on call, leave your name and seat number with the house manager.

6. THOU SHALT NOT EAT OR DRINK IN THE THEATRE. Unlike a movie, which keeps going no matter what noise you make, the actors on stage are distracted by what they hear in the auditorium. You will contribute to an enjoyable experience if you refrain from rattling wrappers and crunching ice.

7. THOU SHALT NOT PUT THINGS ON THE STAGE. The stage is not a resting spot for your pocketbook or your playbill or your feet. These items are ugly for the audience to look at and dangerous for the actors.

8. THOU SHALT NOT RIFFLE THY PLAYBILL. Do not smack your playbill nervously against your leg, or roll and unroll it, or scrape your teeth with it. Open it in advance to the performance page so you can check for important information if you can read in the dark.

(Continued)

(Continued)

9. THOU SHALT KEEP THY FEET OFF THE SEATS. Don't drape your legs over the seat in front of you, and don't walk on someone else's seat to get in or out of yours.

 10. THOU SHALT REMAIN IN THY SEAT UNTIL THE END. The end means the end of the curtain call. If you are ill or bored and must leave before the play is over, leave as quietly as you can and at an interval if at all possible. It is extremely discourteous to the actors to head for the door before the performance is entirely ended.

After that formidable list of *don'ts,* here's an important *do:* laugh, cry, and applaud! Participate in the event and contribute to the experience. What you do during the performance affects the people around you as well as the actors, and it contributes to your own enjoyment. Remember that the actors can hear you laugh, see you cry, feel your silence. Theatre is a live event, but an unresponsive audience can kill it. You have the power and the responsibility to help create the theatrical experience.

In the final moments before the houselights dim, stop to consider what you hear and what you see. Many theatres prepare you for the performance by playing music that has been carefully chosen to put you in an appropriate mood. If you notice the music, ask yourself what mood it creates and how it prepares you for the performance. At the same time, what do you see? If the stage has a curtain, it will be attractively lighted, though it won't give you any particular information. But if there isn't a curtain, you'll be offered a first view of the stage set—usually attractively lit to express the mood of the play. It can be fun to study the set and guess at the kinds of characters and actions that will occupy it momentarily.

If you look at the people around you, you will discover that the audience is not a truly representative cross section of Americans. A lot of Americans don't go to the theatre. Why? Well, as the famous entrepreneur and show biz mogul Sol Hurok said, "If the people don't want to buy tickets, you can't stop 'em." Many Americans have lost their desire for theatre. Sadly, theatre was once an essential element of human society, but today it has become peripheral to our society, an entertainment that appeals to a minority. Those of us who work in the theatre hope that in the future theatre might regain the prominence it once held in America and the prominence it holds today in more culturally sophisticated nations around the globe.

I remember the first time I went to the theatre, even though it was many years ago (this is Linda speaking). I was five years old when I attended a stage version of *The Wizard of Oz,* and it scared the wits out of me. I remember clearly that I sat about four rows back on the left side of the balcony. I was intensely caught up in Dorothy's adventures.

(Continued)

(Continued)

I laughed at her antics and clenched my fists when she was in danger, but when the flying monkeys swooped across the stage, I panicked and ran shrieking out of the theatre. Happily, I had an adult there with me, or I might be running still.

On that Saturday afternoon, someone taught me how to dress, what to take with me, how to behave, and what would happen when we got to the theatre. That matinee performance set in motion a life-long habit, and now, as an adult, I go to the theatre more than fifty times each year.

GOING TO THE THEATRE

1. List the title of the play you attended, the theatre that was putting it on, and the date and day of the week that you attended.

2. Describe the location of your seat.

3. Describe the audience. What was their general age, how did they dress, and how did they behave during the performance?

4. How many people were listed on the staff page of the playbill? If the page provided a breakdown between the two, how many were on the theatre's permanent staff and how many were connected to this particular production?

5. What did you learn from the bios in the playbill that was of particular interest to you?

6. If there was a director's note or dramaturgical essay in the playbill, give a synopsis of it and explain how it enriched your appreciation of the play.

6

Show Biz Is Big Biz

It's a mistake to describe theatre as "one-size-fits-all." Whether it's in New York or in Des Moines, whether it's on campus or in a warehouse, and whether it's produced on a big budget, or a low budget, show biz is big biz. When you understand how and why theatre is produced, you will have a useful way to decide which kind of theatre *you* want to see. Theatre in America is produced in one of four ways: as a commercial enterprise, as a not-for-profit cultural service, as an amateur activity, and as an educational experience. You will want to know something about all four of these. In this chapter, we'll look at commercial theatre, and we'll explore its alternatives in the next chapter.

When I (Linda) went to my first basketball game, I asked Tom, "Is this like Broadway or more like regional theatre?" He explained that the NBA is the best basketball in the world, that it's like going to the Royal National Theatre of Great Britain. We needed some way to classify the level of entertainment I was about to see, and we used theatre as a measuring stick. Once I was exposed to the best basketball, I became an avid fan, and we know people who have become theatregoers for life after they were exposed to great theatre.

Commercial theatre has a single purpose: to make money. Like any other capitalist venture—a fast-food chain, an automobile factory, or a pharmaceutical laboratory—the people selling the product expect to turn a profit. Commercial theatre producers believe their production will attract ticket buyers in sufficient numbers that everyone in the company will make money. The actors, ushers, and stagehands will earn a salary; the playwright, director, and composer will receive a **royalty;** and the investors will earn a substantial return on their investment. When commercial producers are right, they make a lot of money for themselves and for everyone connected with the venture. When they are wrong, they lose everything. Theatre is a highly risky business.

Though profit is its primary aim, sometimes this highly risky business makes art as a welcome by-product. In its effort to attract ticket buyers, commercial theatre engages the finest talents. Just as an automobile manufacturer hires the most skilled designers, engineers, and workers, the commercial theatre hires the most talented writers, performers, and directors, and sometimes the product these people create is what the world admires and calls "art." And sometimes, it is not. Just as the Ford Motor Company could invest its wisdom and financial resources in the 1950s to develop an ugly, unwieldy, and unpopular car called the Edsel, so the commercial theatre can produce flops such as the musical based on the popular movie *Carrie.* The musical *Carrie* lost the entirety of its six-million-dollar capitalization in one night!

The corporate structure of commerical theatre parallels other businesses. A producer (or producers) comes up with an idea for a product (a play) and convinces people with money to invest in it. A corporation is formed by the producer, who is the CEO (chief executive officer), and by the investors, known by the attractive slang term "angels," who are the stockholders who will make a profit if the public buys the product. The producer engages all the people who will create the product—playwright, actors, stagehands, and so on—and rents the rehearsal hall and theatre in which the product will be presented. When the product is ready, tickets go on sale. If the public buys lots of tickets, everyone makes money. If the public does not buy tickets, the show folds, the corporation declares bankruptcy, the salaried employees are out of a job, the royalty earners don't see a penny, and the angels lose all their money.

How much money? In America today, a commercial theatrical venture capitalizes at somewhere between $1.5 million and $10 million, depending on the play to be produced. A big musical such as *The Phantom of the Opera* spends about $8 million to open on Broadway (Color Plate 3). A small play with four actors and one set must spend around $1.5 million. On top of the capitalization expense is the weekly expense of operating the show, called the "nut." The weekly nut includes the costs of renting the theatre, paying the salaries and royalties, and advertising the production. For a large musical, the nut can be $400,000 a week. Where's the money to cover it come from? From ticket sales. A Broadway musical—again let's use *Phantom* as an example—can sell up to $600,000 in tickets each week, which means the play can turn a profit of around $200,000 a week. How many weeks of $200,000 profit does it take to pay back the $8 million investment? Forty weeks. So near the end of the first year's run of a hit musical, the investors might begin to see some profit. After the angels have recouped their investment, the producer is permitted to keep half the profit, which in our example means that $100,000 is distributed among the investors each week. At that rate, the angels see a lot of profit: more than $5 million a year. The greatest commercial successes run for many years, turning out $100,000 a week profit from the original production. An additional $100,000 a week profit is seen from each touring production—and with

Phantom, sometimes three productions were touring America simultaneously. And on top of national tour profits are the $100,000 a week profit from international productions, and the profits from sales of the original cast CD. More profit is realized if a movie studio buys the right to make a film. And even after the Broadway run has ended and every touring and foreign production has closed, profits can be made from the fees paid by resident professional theatre companies or amateur theatres. In short, the money to be earned from a commercial hit is enough to make the producers and investors very, very rich.

Before you get excited and rush off to invest in a commercial theatre venture, you ought to know that 90 percent of such ventures lose 100 percent of their investment. It is a painful truth to tell, but the wisest producers in the theatre can engage the most proven writers, most attractive stars, and most talented directors and still come up with a flop that closes after one night. Successful commercial theatre is more difficult to achieve than is a basketball team that wins a national championship. Too much can go wrong, and there are no guaranteed formulas to success.

One of the most celebrated examples of a commercial flop was the failed musical *Breakfast at Tiffany's.* The show was based on a popular novel by Truman Capote, which had been made into a successful film starring Audrey Hepburn. The title had name recognition, and people were looking forward eagerly to the musical. Two big stars were hired for the leading roles: Richard Chamberlain and Mary Tyler Moore, both of whom had just completed successful runs in television series and were household names. A team of talented artists was assembled by David Merrick, the most successful producer of his time. The show rehearsed, previewed, and closed. Merrick saw the final preview and announced that the play would not open. He realized it was terrible, and rather than lose more money, he did what many businesspeople do when they discover they have created an Edsel—he cut his losses and folded the corporation.

Commercial theatre can be produced anywhere that somebody thinks money can be made, but you are most likely to find commercial theatre in New York or in a large city with a theatre in which touring productions of Broadway hits are presented.

The Commercial Theatre

- Broadway
- Off Broadway
- Touring Productions

BROADWAY

In America, the center of commercial theatre is **Broadway.** We use the term "Broadway" to imply many different things. To begin, Broadway is the name of a street in the middle of New York City that runs diagonally through Manhattan Island. Most of the commercial theatres in New York are located on or within three blocks of Broadway, between 41st Street and 54th Street or between 6th Avenue and 9th Avenue. This small section of midtown Manhattan—three blocks by fourteen blocks—is the geographic district that carries the legendary name of Broadway. This area has been called the "street of dreams," the "great white way," and the place where "if you can make it there, you can make it anywhere" (Figure 6.1).

Employees of a Broadway show are given an employment contract that the theatrical unions classify as a "First Class Production," as distinct from other contracts that don't guarantee the artists as high a salary. Actors, designers, ushers, and stagehands all earn more money working on Broadway than in any other theatrical job, so for them, Broadway is the best.

Many theatregoers also think Broadway is the best, and sometimes that's a fair judgment. When the finest artists create a successful work, the result can be breathtaking; examples that come to mind include Kevin Spacey in Eugene O'Neill's *The Iceman Cometh,* or the revival of the great American musical *A Funny Thing Happened on the Way to the Forum* that starred Nathan Lane and later Whoopi Goldberg. But a great deal of bad theatre is also presented on Broadway—failures like *Gandhi,* the play Tom acted in that closed after opening night. Nevertheless, Broadway remains in the American consciousness as a synonym for "excellence," and so long as Broadway continues to put on excellent productions, that meaning will endure.

"Broadway" has another meaning. The theatre district, which for decades produced the works of serious playwrights like Williams, Miller, and Albee, has today become a synonym for feel-good theatre. Today, when people say that something is "like a Broadway show," they usually mean the play is lighthearted entertainment. This new meaning has a good economic basis. Theatre tickets cost $70 each, and people who pay that much money want to leave the theatre feeling happy. That is why people go to musicals such as *Cats.*

Specifically, what kind of theatrical production do those ticket buyers wish to see? At the end of a hard day, those shoppers, business executives, and camera-carrying tourists want diversion, not confrontation. They want spectacle and singing and dancing. Also, they want to see what they can't see back home; they want to see what's new on the theatrical scene. American culture values the new over the old. A new model car is more popular than an old one, and this year's new fashion always supplants last year's. In a similar vein, the commercial theatre in New York is dominated by new shows or revivals with big stars. An "all-singing, all-dancing new spectacle" is the pinnacle of American commercial theatre. *Cats, Les Miserables, Guys and Dolls, Miss Saigon, Crazy For You, Rent,* and *The Most Happy Fella* are all perennially popular Broadway musicals.

Ambassador (7) Imperial (20) New Victory (34)
Belasco (30) John Golden (25) Palace (14)
Booth (22) Longacre (10) Plymouth (24)
Broadhurst (27) Lunt-Fontaine (15) Richard Rogers (16)
Broadway (1) Lyceum (18) Royale (23)
Brooks Atkinson (13) Majestic (27) Shubert (29)
Circle in the Square (5) Marquis (17) St. James (32)
Cort (12) Martin Beck (26) Virginia (2)
Ethel Barrymore (11) Minskoff (21) Walter Kerr (9)
Eugene O'Neill (8) Music Box (19) Winter Garden (6)
Ford Center (33) Nederlander (36)
Gershwin (4) Neil Simon (3)
Helen Hayes (31) New Amsterdam (35)

Figure 6.1 Broadway cuts diagonally through midtown Manhattan and is the center of the Broadway theatre district, which reaches from 41st Street north to 54th Street.

The 1998–99 Broadway season included several serious plays: *Death of a Salesman* starring Brian Dennehy, *The Iceman Cometh* starring Kevin Spacey, and Tennessee Williams's *Not about Nightingales.* It is too soon, however, to know if these plays indicate the beginning of a trend or if Broadway will continue to be mostly feel-good theatre.

OFF BROADWAY

The second place you might see commercial theatre is **Off Broadway.** This term describes a kind of theatrical production that began in New York City in the 1950s and that has evolved today as a primary way to present serious drama. For a century, every important new American play began its life on Broadway, but after World War II ended in 1945, the American theatre began to change. Some theatre artists became frustrated by the increasingly popular spirit of Broadway; they wanted to do plays that were artistically rewarding, even if those plays didn't appeal to large audiences. These artists were prepared to earn smaller salaries in order to present plays that nurtured their spirits. A few courageous and adventuresome theatre professionals presented serious plays in small theatres that were not in midtown Manhattan. They sold less expensive tickets to smaller audiences who lived in the neighborhood or who sought out theatre that challenged audiences to think and feel deeply. When Brooks Atkinson, then the critic for *The New York Times*, went to Tennessee Williams's *Summer and Smoke* at a Greenwich Village theatre and then wrote a rave review in the next day's paper, Off Broadway was born. And for the next several decades, Off Broadway was the vital "engine room" for serious American theatre.

It is less expensive to produce a play Off Broadway than on Broadway, so investors risk smaller amounts. The potential earnings from ticket sales are also less, however, so the amount of money to be earned is smaller for investors and artists alike. A common practice today is to open a play Off Broadway, and if it is a success, to move it to Broadway where more money may be earned. The hit musical *Rent* is a good example of this practice (Color Plate 4).

Like the term "Broadway," the term "Off Broadway" has several meanings, the first of which is geographic. It refers to theatres that are *not* in midtown Manhattan. Most Off Broadway theatres are either in Greenwich Village, the section of lower Manhattan below 14th Street that has been the home of artists and writers since the early 1900s, or the Upper West Side, the region west of Central Park and north of 59th Street in which many artists and professionals reside today (Figure 6.2).

Off Broadway is also the name for a specific kind of union contract. The minimum salaries for an Off Broadway contract are lower than for a first class production on Broadway, but they are established by the same unions.

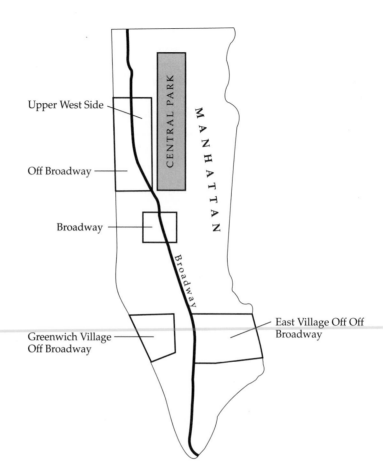

Figure 6.2 Manhattan Island is the center of New York City, and the thoroughfare of Broadway angles the length of the island. This illustration shows the Broadway theatre district in midtown, the Off Broadway theatre districts on the Upper West Side and in Greenwich Village, and the Off Off Broadway theatre district in the East Village.

From your point of view as a member of the audience, Off Broadway is a description for a kind of theatrical experience that is substantive and controversial and that appeals to an intellectually inclined audience. You may recognize some titles that had their start Off Broadway: *Other People's Money* (later a film with Danny DeVito), *Driving Miss Daisy* (later a film with Jessica Tandy), and *Marvin's Room* (later a film with Diane Keaton).

TOURING PRODUCTIONS

You may not be traveling to New York in the immediate future, but some commercial theatre may be traveling to your hometown. Many midsize cities have a theatre that hosts touring productions. Touring productions are plays or musicals that have succeeded commercially in New York and that then go on the "road," as theatre folks call it. The production will be very much the same as it was in New York, although sometimes the scenery has to be simplified to fit into a wide variety of theatres, and frequently the cast is different. A touring production travels from city to city, from theatre to theatre. A "First-Class Tour" travels by plane and stays for three or four weeks in larger cities such as San Francisco, St. Louis, and Philadelphia. First-class tour artists are handsomely paid. A "Bus-and-Truck Tour" travels by bus (with the scenery in a truck) and frequently plays split weeks or one-night stands. Artists in a bus-and-truck tour receive much smaller salaries. The quality of a touring production of a Broadway hit in your city may depend on the kind of tour your city attracts; and the performance may be significantly less impressive than what you would have seen in New York.

People buy tickets to these commercial touring productions for one or more of three reasons. First, some people love theatre and hope for the opportunity to experience excellence in their own hometown. Second, some people may be familiar with a particular show's reputation and are eager to see this newest hit from New York. Third, people want to see the stars. Indeed, to help ensure the success of a commercial tour, producers will engage a star whose name will help sell tickets even if that star is not particularly right for the role. Many stars from the New York stage are unknown to the audiences across America, so producers engage celebrities from television. Sometimes the stars of touring productions are fine actors, sometimes they are not. Because the production will play only a short engagement in each town and will sell almost all its tickets before the local critics and audiences have formed a judgment, the star's name is a major marketing tool in this capitalist venture.

Commercial theatre is only one of the ways that theatre is produced in America. In the next chapter, we'll explore four ways in which noncommercial theatre is produced.

7

More Than Entertainment

In this chapter, we'll look at four ways theatre is produced in America when the primary goal is *not* to make money.

As we saw in Chapter 6, commercial theatre is big business. But in many First World nations, theatre is not primarily a commercial venture. Instead, it is an important part of the cultural infrastructure that people expect their governments to support with tax money in the same way they support education, roads, and fire departments. America is different from other countries because theatre began late in our history and because it started as a form of profitable business. Let us show you how and why theatre developed the way it did in America.

THE BEGINNINGS OF THEATRE—
AND SOME AMERICAN HISTORY

The Puritans who founded the Massachusetts Bay Colony in 1620 believed that theatre was *immoral*. They shared the religious beliefs of Oliver Cromwell, who headed the English government that decreed that it was against the law to perform theatre. The Puritans believed that work was moral and play was immoral, and they equated theatre with the sort of idleness that is "the devil's plaything." Any public activity that took people away from work was immoral, so the playhouses were torn down or nailed shut.

The Puritans, like many Americans today, believed in a very literal reading of their Bible, and they understood that people must be honest. To pretend to be other than what you are is to lie, to be dishonest, and to do the devil's work. Puritans believed that an actor who pretended in a play to be someone else must be lying and was therefore an agent of the devil. This early American belief kept theatre from developing as a part of our cultural mainstream. Indeed, the very first written record of theatre in America dates from a court case in 1665 in which three men were convicted of the crime of performing a play called *The Bear and the Cub.*

But there was a second and conflicting belief held by many early Americans (and by many modern Americans today). They believed that profit demonstrates that the person making the profit is smiled on by God. This belief developed from the Calvinist strain of Protestantism, and it was adopted by many sects in our capitalistic nation. Early Americans who believed that profit was a good thing were eager to enter into businesses that made money, and when they discovered that theatre could turn a profit, they introduced it into the colonies. As early as 1716, a theatre was built in Williamsburg, Virginia (Figure 7.1). (Virginia, you may recall, was settled in the late seventeenth century by English people who were sympathetic to the King and *not* to the Puritan government of Cromwell; these English held different views of morality than did the colonists in Massachusetts.)

These two beliefs of early Americans banged against each other and created the belief that theatre is immoral unless it turns a profit and is therefore a demonstration that God is smiling. This conundrum reveals two enduring truths of American culture: first, a lot of Americans continue to believe that theatre is immoral and should be prohibited by law; and also that the only good theatre is theatre that makes money. Americans approve of *A Chorus Line* because it ran for sixteen years on Broadway and made a huge profit, but disapprove of *Waiting for Godot* because it lost money at the box office, even though our most respected thinkers describe it as a masterpiece. The notion that theatre is something other than a business, that it's something that makes an important contribution to our quality of life, is an idea that is resisted by many Americans, though it is enthusiastically embraced by the citizens of France, Germany, Russia, and Japan, where their leading actors are officially designated as "national treasures."

Happily for those of us who want more from theatre than light entertainment, the concept of theatre as an important cultural resource began to gain acceptance in America during the second half of the twentieth century. With this acceptance, alternative ways of producing theatre developed.

Four Noncommercial Ways Theatre Is Produced

1. A cultural service
2. An amateur activity
3. An educational experience
4. Festival and outdoor drama

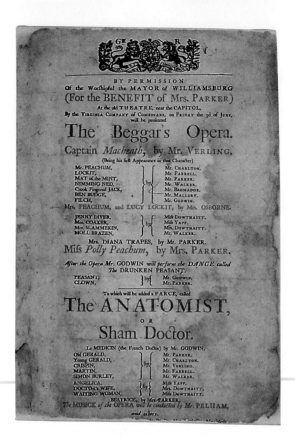

Figure 7.1 This poster announces a performance of *The Beggar's Opera,* a popular English ballad opera that toured to Williamsburg, Virginia, in 1735.

THEATRE AS A CULTURAL SERVICE

Many theatres in America are described as **not-for-profit.** In the 1950s, about the time Off Broadway theatre was getting started, some theatre artists determined to make theatre anywhere but in New York. These artists didn't like the economic pressures that dictated the kinds of plays they could do in the commercial arena, and they didn't like living in New York. So they started theatres in their hometowns. But they didn't want to do amateur theatre with all the qualitative limitations the phrase implies. They wanted to do the great plays from the history of world drama, and they wanted to do them with fine professional artists. These intrepid pioneers wanted to recover theatre from the clutches of commercialism and restore it to its proper function—enriching the lives of the people. These artists founded permanent theatre companies. Whether these theatres are called regional theatres or repertory theatres or resident theatres, they have become a major part of America's cultural landscape.

 In the 1960s, resident theatres organized themselves as the **League of Resident Theatres,** known by the acronym **LORT.** By the 1980s, America had more than 80 LORT companies.

The Alley Theatre in Houston and the Arena Stage in Washington, D.C., were two of the earliest professional theatre companies outside New York, and in a few short years, similar theatres were founded in many cities. Most of these theatres imitated the only model their founders knew—Broadway—and so these theatres were commercial ventures. Rather quickly, their founders discovered that it was almost impossible to make a profit from a resident theatre; most were losing money. About as quickly, they became aware of the many not-for-profit institutions in America: schools, churches, and hospitals. These institutions provide people with services that our society believes are valuable, and they qualify as not-for-profit businesses. When the Internal Revenue Service designates them as qualifying for **501(c)3** status, these businesses may *not* make a profit that is distributed to their stockholders the way that profits from a commercial production may enrich an angel; they do not have to pay taxes; and they may accept charitable contributions. Because these theatres weren't making a profit anyway, it was easy for them to seek not-for-profit tax status.

> 501(C)3 is the Internal Revenue Service's designation for a business that may not disburse profits to its investors, that does not have to pay taxes, and that may accept charitable contributions.

A not-for-profit corporation is governed by a board of trustees. This board is made up of citizens who volunteer their time and expertise to provide guidance to the executive who actually runs the institution—the university president, the hospital administrator, or the theatre's artistic director. The trustees hold the institution "in trust" for the citizens of the community, and they are responsible for its finances and its basic policies.

How much money does it take to operate a not-for-profit theatre? Where does the money come from? Not-for-profit theatres vary widely in size and budget. Small ones such as the New Harmony Theatre in Indiana operate on less than $500,000 a year. Large ones such as the Guthrie Theatre in Minneapolis have annual operating budgets in excess of $7 million. The trustees work with the managerial staff of the theatre to create a realistic budget, estimating how much will be spent and how to bring in an equal amount so that at the end of the season the theatre has a balanced ledger sheet.

The theatre's expenditures are projected by the staff, based on their experience of the true costs of producing the season's plays. The theatre's projected income is divided into two categories: earned income and contributed income. Earned income describes all the money that the theatre gets from the sale of tickets (subscriptions, single tickets, and group sales) and from incidental sources like concessions sales and costume rentals. A rule of thumb is that a theatre must earn about 65 percent of its expenditures and that it must attract the remaining 35 percent in charitable contributions. If a theatre has a budget of $3 million, approximately $1,950,000 must be earned income and

$1,050,000 must be contributed income. Each theatre's success in attracting contributions is different, but two very important questions are: what happens if the total of earned and contributed income exceeds the amount expended, and what happens if the total falls short of the amount expended?

The first question is easier to answer. Because a not-for-profit business is prohibited by federal law from distributing its profits to the trustees, any surplus is either kept in reserve against the shortfall that is likely to occur in some future year, or it is used to purchase needed equipment for the theatre—anything from a new roof to a new computer lighting board.

What happens when the annual report shows that the theatre lost money? The trustees can experience everything from grumbling to panic. In a best-case scenario, the institution makes up the shortfall through an earlier year's surplus, through an endowment, or—in desperation—through gifts from rich trustees or their friends. The normal scenario is that a theatre borrows money from a bank, adds the payments on that loan to next year's expenditure budget, and struggles forward. The worst-case scenario happens when the theatre's loan increases over several years so that the accumulated debt becomes impossible to repay. At that point the trustees may decide that the not-for-profit corporation must go out of business and the theatre's doors must close. A theatre's closure is a sad day for the citizens of that city, but it does happen.

A theatre's crisis doesn't always come at the end of the season. I once served as artistic director for a Shakespeare festival in Maine (this is Tom speaking), and every Wednesday evening the trustees gathered to add up how much contributed income had been donated that week. They had to decide if we could meet the payroll the following day, or if we had to close. We never closed, but it is hard to go about your business calmly when you fear the following week will be your last.

To keep their doors open, the staff and trustees of not-for-profit theatres seek to attract contributions. A not-for-profit theatre has four sources of contributed income.

Theatre's Four Sources of Contributed Income

1. Foundations
2. Corporations
3. Individuals
4. Government grants

Foundations

You have probably heard of the Ford Foundation or the Rockefeller Foundation, but you might not know about thousands of smaller foundations that annually make gifts to worthy causes; some of these smaller foundations support not-for-profit theatres. A foundation is a financial entity that has been created so that accumulations of wealth may be protected from heavy taxation. The foundation's money is used for charitable ends: to support education, medical research, or the arts. A foundation gives away money for purposes that our society views as worthy.

When someone makes more money than anyone could imagine spending, that person usually creates a foundation. In 1997, former basketball player Michael Jordan made $20 million from the Chicago Bulls for playing basketball and more than $40 million from various manufacturers for endorsing their products. Jordan created a foundation that gives money to worthy causes. Now, if only his foundation would contribute to theatre . . .

Corporations

Businesses give money to various deserving causes, and some support theatre. A profit-making corporation has several good reasons to give away money instead of disbursing it to the stockholders. Charitable contributions are in a company's best business interest. To succeed, corporations must have high-caliber persons running them, and corporations recruit nationally for personnel at the managerial and executive levels. One inducement that corporations offer is the quality of life in their city. Corporate executives, like other educated and cultured people, want to live in areas with good golf courses, quality schools for their children, and professional theatre companies.

Corporations also give money to theatres as a form of advertising. When you see that a theatre's production is "sponsored" or "co-produced" by a corporation, you are reading an ad. The corporation has given money to the not-for-profit theatre in exchange for promoting its name to people who might buy its product.

Individuals

Wealthy people can write a check for $50,000 without blinking, but the rest of us can support theatres in smaller ways. Individuals are the largest group of contributors to not-for-profit theatres. Why? Because we are a nation of philanthropists. It is a part of the American ethos that we give our time and money to help those who are less fortunate. Through our churches, through service organizations such as the Red Cross, and as alumni of colleges, we help support our society with gifts of money and time.

You will be asked at some point to contribute to the arts. Perhaps you will receive a phone call from a dance company asking for a donation. Or when you purchase a season ticket to your local LORT theatre, you will be encouraged to round your check up to a higher amount and thereby make a contribution.

Government Grants

In America today, theatres (and other charitable institutions) may receive grants from their city, state, and federal government. Many people argue over whether theatres should be supported with tax dollars, but those of us who work in the theatre believe that not-for-profit corporations that provide a basic service to the community should be supported. The question, of course, is how do we define basic services? Where, if at all, should not-for-profit theatres fall within the list of basic services?

Some large cities award grants to not-for-profit arts organizations as a way of encouraging a tourist attraction that brings lots of tourist dollars into the local economy. State governments frequently have arts councils that make grants to artists and arts institutions. But the federal government's National Endowment for the Arts (NEA) is the most prominent of all government arts agencies. This federal agency was created in 1965, and its function is to disburse federal tax revenues to artists and arts organizations. The law creating the NEA was signed by President Lyndon B. Johnson, and at the signing ceremony he said, "Art is a nation's most precious heritage, for it is in our works of art that we reveal to ourselves, and to others, the inner vision which guides us as a nation."

Government grants for the arts total a surprisingly small amount of money. Our federal government's per capita spending for the arts is less than that of Germany, England, Canada, or France. More of your federal tax dollars are spent each year to support military bands than to support *all* the artists and arts institutions in America. In 1991, the U.S. government disbursed only 67 cents per American to support the arts. In 1996, that sum was cut nearly in half. Today, you pay more for a candy bar than the government disburses per person for the arts.

Even though our government does not support our theatres with much hard cash, the American people have undergone a change in attitude over the past half-century. We are learning to demand theatre as a vital element of society that can be more than entertainment, more than a profit-making business. We are starting to believe what people have known since the first prehistoric hunters gathered together—that theatre is good for the life of the community. America's not-for-profit theatres nurture artists, develop the voices of new playwrights, and serve us all by keeping alive the insights of the great artists of the past.

THEATRE AS AN AMATEUR ACTIVITY

Amateurs are people who do something because they love it. The word comes from the Latin *amare,* to love. There are amateur athletes in your parks, amateur singers in your choirs, and amateur actors performing in community theatres all across America.

"Community theatre" is the term for amateur theatre sponsored by local organizations and performed by volunteers who do it for love, not money. Churches, service clubs, and civic organizations are the major producers of community theatre, and you probably have attended one of their performances at some time in your life. These plays are done for the friends and neighbors of the people putting them on, and most frequently the plays are entertaining old chestnuts that affirm the values of the audience. Community theatre produces the same feeling of goodwill between audience and performers that is produced between the cheering fans and the neighborhood softball team. Everyone knows that the pros play better, just as everyone knows that the Cleveland Symphony plays better than the Friends of St. Michael's Church, but the personal relationship between the audience and the players engenders an excitement that makes it every bit as much fun to go to the amateur performance as it is to go to the softball game. And you may find you'd rather go to community theatre than any other kind.

The cost of producing amateur theatre is very modest because no one is being paid. A few hundred dollars will usually cover the royalties to the playwright, the advertising, and the costs for building the scenery and costumes. These costs are commonly paid by the sponsoring organization, and if a modest admission is charged, that money goes back to the school, the church, or the service club. But amateur theatre cannot be called a business in the same way that commercial and professional not-for-profit theatre must be. It's not a business, it's an activity.

THEATRE AS AN EDUCATIONAL EXPERIENCE

Many Americans' first experience of live theatre is at a school. Most colleges and universities, many high schools, and even some primary schools have auditoriums and present plays (Figure 7.2). "Educational theatre" is the term used to describe plays presented in schools, and educational theatre's primary reason for existence is to provide training to students who wish to study theatre as an academic discipline. Just as students of chemistry need a laboratory in which to concoct evil-smelling potions while they are studying to become researchers in a pharmaceutical firm, so students of theatre need a laboratory in which to botch the classics while they are learning to become professional actors. In many countries this training is offered by vocational schools, but in America students go to universities in which people of varying skills and commitment learn the fundamentals of acting, designing, directing, and playwriting.

Figure 7.2 Elementary school students rehearsing.

Other students study theatre as an intellectual discipline, in much the same way that you may study accounting or history. These students study the ideas of the great playwrights, the political function of theatre in a society, and the history of culture as it has been reflected in written drama and live performance. To serve these students, colleges and universities put on plays. Just as music students must hear music to learn about music, so theatre students must experience theatre to learn about theatre. Theatre as an intellectual pursuit is a second reason why schools do plays.

There's a third reason. Many American cities are too small to support a professional not-for-profit theatre or a commercial touring production, and so colleges serve the population by producing theatre. People in Hattiesburg, Mississippi, or Normal, Illinois, want the enriching experience of theatre, and their local college is best equipped to provide it. Indeed, hundreds of thousands of Americans' primary experience of live theatre is presented by the theatre students at their local college.

The audiences for these plays—whether they are from the student body or from a city's intellectual community—are in quest of enrichment more than diversion, so it is not surprising that a typical season will include plays that are rarely produced in a commercial or a not-for-profit theatre. Instead, educational theatre provides you with a chance to see the classics from earlier ages and the experimental plays of today.

Because educational theatre's two principal reasons for existence are to provide students with a laboratory in which they may learn their craft and to offer a forum in which other students may study the dramatic literature on which this entire field of academic study is founded, educational theatre is—or at least should be—supported by the college or university. The work that students do in educational theatre should not be self-supporting any more than is the work that engineering students do in a computer lab or the work that law students do in a moot court. Unhappily, the administrations of most American colleges and universities fail to provide appropriate financial support for the academic discipline of theatre. Too often, educational theatre is as box-office driven as commercial theatre is and must plan its repertoire with a keen business sense of what will appeal to the ticket-buying public. Much educational theatre has to be self-supporting because of that fundamental dichotomy in American thinking that separates serious work from frivolous play and that judges theatre to be worthy only when it is profitable. The overwhelming proportion of college and university administrators—the very people who ought to understand that educational theatre is education and not commerce—share with the general American public a confusion about the nature, purpose, function, and potential for theatre.

THEATRE AS FESTIVAL AND OUTDOOR DRAMA

A festival theatre can be a commercial venture, a not-for-profit cultural service, an amateur event, or an educational experience. It is defined not by how it does business but by the kind of theatre it presents. Festivals produce plays that celebrate a particular kind of drama or a particular author. Festivals can focus on American drama, on comedy, on musical theatre, or on new plays. The festivals that focus on the works of a single playwright include the many Shakespeare festivals that people flock to in the summers.

> Among the oldest of America's festival theatres is the Oregon Shakespeare Festival, now one of the largest theatre companies in America. It maintains more than three hundred employees, and it produces ten or more plays annually in three theatres for an audience that exceeds 100,000. The Oregon Shakespeare Festival is a multi-million-dollar not-for-profit business that has replaced logging as the major industry in the region. It has spawned dozens of imitators, the most successful of which include the Shakespeare festivals in San Diego and in Montgomery, Alabama.

A festival theatre is also distinguished by its destination audience. Although most theatre audiences are made up of people who live nearby, festival theatre audiences are made up of enthusiastic and dedicated travelers

Figure 7.3   You can see the festive atmosphere here as Revels Company performers Jason Babinsky (left) and Erick Shelly entertain patrons in the Utah Shakespearean Festival's 1999 production of *The Greenshow.* Singers, dancers, magicians, and puppeteers perform preshow events on the Festival's grounds.

who are not concerned with the social importance of being seen at the theatre or seeing the latest Broadway hit. Rather, these theatregoers are there to view the festival theatre's specialty. These people frequently plan their summer holiday around a visit to an out-of-the-way place such as Stratford, Canada, or Cedar City, Utah (Figure 7.3). As a result, festival audiences are the most enthusiastic audiences. They are very knowledgeable but are not unduly critical or demanding. These people are there to have a rewarding time, and they encourage the actors to do their best work by enthusiastic laughter and applause.

Outdoor dramas are a wonderfully American phenomenon, seldom encountered elsewhere in the world, and you may have had a wonderful experience at one. Many Shakespeare festivals are performed in open-air theatres, but outdoor dramas are sometimes based on historical events or religious stories that are performed each summer in open-air theatres all across the country. Outdoor drama includes *The Lost Colony* in North Carolina, which dramatizes the lives of the first English to settle in North America, and *The Hill Cumorah Pageant* in Palmyra, New York (Figure 7.4). Tens of thousands of Americans enjoy outdoor drama each year, and these performances are a vital part of the total picture of America's theatre.

Figure 7.4 *The Hill Cumorah Pageant* in Palmyra, New York, is an outdoor religious pageant that provides both theatrical and spiritual experiences for an audience of 8,000. More than 500 actors are on stage.

IDENTIFYING VARIOUS KINDS OF THEATRES   *Exercise*

Identify each kind of theatre produced in your community in the past year. For each of these items, provide the name of the theatre and the title of the play.

1. A theatre in which commercial productions are presented
2. A professional not-for-profit theatre company
3. An amateur theatre that is not connected to a school
4. A theatre in which student productions are presented
5. A festival theatre in your region

8

Musical Theatre

$\mathcal{M}$illions of people *love* American musical theatre. They love the romantic stories, the astonishing dancing, the gorgeous voices, the dazzling costumes, the spectacular scenery, and above all, the way the music lifts their emotions. Musical theatre makes them feel terrific. Musical theatre is synonymous with the best of American theatre. The ancient Greeks gave us tragedy, the Elizabethan English gave us Shakespeare's verse dramas, the French gave us some wildly funny farces, and we Americans have developed musical theatre to a level where audiences all around the world celebrate it.

HOW DID MUSICAL THEATRE EVOLVE?

The Development of Musical Theatre

1. Prehistory and ancient Greek drama
2. Opera
3. Operetta
4. Ballad operas
5. Musical comedy
6. The musical

Prehistory and Ancient Greek Drama

Musical theatre is older than recorded history. Early storytellers may have sung or chanted parts of their performances, and their friends probably beat on drums to add to the excitement. Archaeologists recently discovered flutes in China more than 10,000 years old carved from animal bones; these instruments may have accompanied stories told around a campfire. Though we

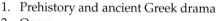

have no written records to prove it, it is highly likely that music and theatre have been joined from the beginning.

We have many paintings and sculptures that illustrate how ancient Greek dramas were sung and chanted, and they suggest how the chorus danced to the accompaniment of a musician who used percussion and wind instruments to maintain the rhythm and underscore the mood with melody. Music contributed significantly to the total effect of ancient Greek drama.

Opera

Opera was invented in the Renaissance. When the theatre artists of fifteenth-century Florence rediscovered the ancient Greek plays, they weren't clear how to produce them. It was obvious that singing and dancing had been part of the performance, but in the absence of written notation, nobody knew what the ancient music sounded like or what the dance looked like. As a result, the Italian artists invented a new form of theatre in which the entire performance was set to music. These operas (the word means "works") were entirely sung, from beginning to end, and the music was considered far more important than the lyrics. Opera lovers go to listen to the music, and if they can't understand the language in which the performers are singing, they often don't mind. Their attention is on the music.

From the beginning, opera was an elaborate and impressive kind of musical theatre. A historian found a diary by an English diplomat who attended an opera in Venice in 1645. The diplomat's description of his experience is amazingly similar to what we might write if we went to see a musical like *The Phantom of the Opera*. He wrote that the performance was accompanied by excellent musicians and singers, the scenery was beautifully painted, and there were machines that flew the actors through the air. He felt it was one of the most magnificent and expensive entertainments the wit of humans could invent.

The greatest operas were written in the nineteenth century by Italian composers Puccini (Poo-CHEE-nee), Rossini (Raw-SEE-nee), and Verdi (VAIR-dee) and by the German composer Wagner (VAHG-ner).

Opera has some obvious traits that will help you distinguish it from other forms of musical theatre. The music is very complex, and only the most well-trained singers and musicians can perform it. The stories of operas are usually set in a distant time and place, and they are frequently based on ancient Greek or German myths. Further, the stories of operas are almost always tragic. The main characters often die, and the operas invoke deep and sad feelings in the audience.

Operetta

As a balance to the sad stories and complex music of opera, composers and writers collaborated to create a kind of light-hearted musical theatre called operetta (the word means "little opera"). Sometimes operetta is described as "comic opera" because the plots include comic characters who make the

Figure 8.1 Kevin Kline, Angela Lansbury, and Linda Ronstadt starred in a Broadway revival of Gilbert and Sullivan's *The Pirates of Penzance*. Typical of operettas, the action is set in a bygone time and in an exotic locale, and each dashing and handsome pirate finds true love with a beautiful maiden in a pretty dress.

audience laugh with their witty lyrics and antic behavior and because the stories end happily. Operettas appeal to a less intense audience than opera because the music is not quite so complicated and because more attention is paid to the lyrics. It's easier to understand the words in an operetta, partly because it's a standard practice to translate them into the audience's language, and partly because some of the words are spoken, not sung. That is, there are brief sequences of spoken dialogue in most operettas.

Operettas became popular in the nineteenth century with compositions by Offenbach, Strauss, and the English team of Gilbert and Sullivan, whose works include *The Mikado, HMS Pinafore,* and *The Pirates of Penzance* (Figure 8.1).

Americans wrote operettas as well. John Philip Sousa is best known as a composer of military marches, but he composed "El Capitan March" for his operetta about the Spanish-American War. Today's musical theatre evolved more from the operetta than it did from opera, but its heritage includes both.

There are some recognizable traits of operettas that distinguish them from other kinds of musical theatre. To begin with, the music is lush and Romantic, and is frequently in 3/4 waltz time. Because an operetta's music is not as com-

The melody for "The Marine Corps Hymn" comes from a comic French operetta by Jacques Offenbach. When they sing "From the Halls of Montezuma to the shores of Tripoli," do you think many Marines know they're singing a song from a stage comedy that featured pretty girls in frilly costumes?

plex as the music for an opera, the demands on the singers and musicians are not as great—and the audience can more readily remember the emotionally pleasing tunes. You may not know where they come from, but you probably know several melodies from operettas, for example, the energetic music for the French cancan.

The stories of operettas are usually set in exotic and Romantic locales—far away places with strange sounding names—and the plots are usually love stories that end happily ever after. Probably the most obvious trait is that operettas include a lot of jokes and comic characters.

Ballad Operas

During the centuries in which opera and operetta developed in Europe and were imitated in America, a separate form of musical theatre became popular in England. This English form also came to America, and it helped shape the kind of musical theatre we know today. In both opera and operetta, music is the most important element, and the **libretto** takes a back seat. ("Libretto" comes from the same word stem as "library"; it's the Italian word for "book," and it is used to mean all the words in a script, including the song lyrics and the spoken dialogue.) By way of contrast, the most important element of English musical theatre was the words, and music was only a secondary embellishment. Quite simply, the English wrote comic plays, inserted some songs into them, and called them "ballad operas."

The songs in a ballad opera were entertaining interludes more than integral parts of the story, and frequently the songs were not composed especially for the occasion. Instead, the authors took well-known popular songs and wrote new lyrics for them, which made the ballad operas audience-friendly because people already knew the melodies. But this practice did not provide an opportunity for music to be specially written in order to help tell the story or to make a major contribution to the ballad opera's emotional impact.

The best known ballad opera was written in 1728 by John Gay. He called it *The Beggar's Opera,* and it is about a dashingly attractive highwayman named Macheath who lives among petty thieves and prostitutes in contemporary London. This provocative setting introduced scandalous characters and made the show titillating and shocking. Sex and violence proved to be big box office attractions, and *The Beggar's Opera* sold out for one hundred consecutive performances, a feat that had never happened before. In eighteenth-century London, theatres normally presented a different play each night, rotating some dozen or more plays so that audiences would return to buy tickets for the different productions. *The Beggar's Opera* introduced the idea of the long run that today finds musicals such as *A Chorus Line* running for fifteen years.

The producer of John Gay's The Beggar's Opera *was named John Rich. The commercial success of the show led a wit to remark that* The Beggar's Opera *"made Gay rich and Rich gay."*

Ballad operas such as *The Beggar's Opera* toured America starting in 1735. The ballad opera form of a spoken play with songs interspersed through it took strong root and joined with the Romantic tradition of operetta to help shape the indigenous American musical theatre.

Musical Comedy

Theatre historians describe the 1866 production of *The Black Crook* as the first example of American musical comedy. *The Black Crook* was a corny melodrama that the producers feared would be a flop if it was presented straight, so they took a big risk and hired a French ballet troupe to appear in the show. Without much concern for their relevance to the plot, the producers inserted songs and dances and turned the corny melodrama into an exciting spectacle that ran for 475 consecutive performances. *The Black Crook,* without anyone's thinking about it in advance, introduced two factors that advanced the ballad opera toward what we now call musical comedy. The first factor was dance. In addition to the songs that the actors sang, *The Black Crook* introduced a chorus of dancing girls. Before too many more years went by, a male chorus was added to the evolving form of the musical comedy. An obvious characteristic of musical comedies now is a large singing and dancing chorus. The second factor, and the biggest attraction of *The Black Crook,* was the appearance of those dancing girls in flesh-colored tights. We might not be titillated by that spectacle today, but in 1866 it was pretty daring. Sex appeal has remained a major trait of American musical theatre ever since.

American musical comedy came into its own in the twentieth century. Writers, blending the light-hearted and Romantic spirit of European operettas with the form borrowed from English ballad operas, invented the **book musical.** A book musical is a play with a plot and characters that tells part of its story through songs and dances. What distinguishes musical comedy from its predecessors is that the authors, instead of inserting songs and dances into an existing play, collaborated with the composers from the outset so that the songs belonged in the play and added to its emotional arc while they helped tell the story and develop the characters. Whereas operettas had made music the most important element and whereas the ballad opera's script was the most important element, the men who wrote the book musicals believed that the story and the music were equally important and that the two could work together to enrich the audience's experience. The best of the early book musicals were the works of composer Jerome Kern and playwrights Guy Bolton and P. G. Wodehouse. They have been called "the fathers of American musical comedy," and their hit musical comedies *Very Good, Eddie* and *Leave It to Jane* are sometimes revived today.

 Watch the 1946 bio-pic about Jerome Kern, *Till the Clouds Roll By.* It may not be accurate biography, but it is a wonderful anthology of Kern's great hits, and it stars Judy Garland, Van Heflin, Lena Horne, and (in a surprise appearance) Frank Sinatra.

Several traits of musical comedy distinguish it from operetta and ballad opera. To begin with, the settings and characters are American. Whether the works are set on a college campus, such as in *Good News,* or in the wild West, such as in *Girl Crazy*, they are filled with recognizable American characters and take place in our familiar world. An even clearer indicator is that the songs are American popular music. They use the 32-bar structure and they're in 2/4 rhythm more often than in the waltz rhythm of European operettas. The songs sometimes embrace the "ragged time" syncopation that came to be called ragtime, and there's a pretty good chance you'll recognize one or more of the old standards and say, "So that's where that song came from." The naive and slightly corny boy-meets-girl plot will end happily ever after—another way you'll recognize a musical comedy. Yet another is that the secondary plot is about broadly comic characters whose jokes and comic routines enliven the show. And the surest sign that you're seeing a musical comedy is that the songs and dances seem to belong in the play. They may not do a lot to help tell the story, but there will be a justification for why they're in the show; they aren't just shoved in or tacked on.

American musical theatre took an important first step toward the kind of show that dominates Broadway today when *Show Boat* opened in 1927 (Color Plate 5). The plot of *Show Boat* is serious even though there is a light-hearted secondary plot, and Jerome Kern's music includes deeply moving songs such as "Old Man River" alongside traditionally light-hearted musical comedy numbers such as "Life upon the Wicked Stage Ain't Nothing for a Sweet Young Girl." The plot deals with interracial marriage, which was a volatile concern in 1927. Indeed, *Show Boat* remains a classic of the American musical comedy. It's been made into films on several occasions and has been revived on Broadway frequently.

The Musical

It's impossible to say when the word "comedy" fell from common use and when the musical comedy matured into the musical, but theatre historians usually cite the 1943 opening of Rodgers and Hammerstein's *Oklahoma!* as the first modern musical. Both descriptive terms are still used today, but there does seem to be a difference between the two kinds of musical theatre.

The major advances that were introduced by *Oklahoma!* include the psychological complexity of characters and the integration of dance as a central part of both character development and storytelling. A dream ballet in the middle of *Oklahoma!* shows the audience the complex psychology of the central characters without dialogue being spoken or lyrics sung (Figure 8.2). The dance sequence also foreshadows the serious events that happen later in the plot. *Oklahoma!*'s replacement of light-hearted tap dance numbers by the more serious dance form of ballet contributed to the maturation process of the musical, and so did the introduction of the sexually repressed character of the villainous Jud, whose dangerous threat to the happiness of the hero and heroine is overcome when he dies in the knife fight that lends a serious tone to the play.

Oklahoma! began what many theatre historians describe as the "Golden Age of American Musicals." In addition to Rodgers and Hammerstein, teams

Figure 8.2 Dance became a central part of both character development and storytelling when musical comedy matured and evolved into the musical, as demonstrated in the dream ballet in *Oklahoma!*

such as Lerner and Loewe or Kander and Ebb were joined by solo composer-lyricists such as Frank Loesser to produce a waterfall of memorable Broadway musicals: *Brigadoon, My Fair Lady, Camelot, Guys and Dolls, Cabaret, Fiddler on the Roof* . . . the list could go on and on.

The two most influential figures in musical theatre of the past three decades have been Stephen Sondheim and Andrew Lloyd Webber. Both men are composers, and Sondheim is also his own lyricist. These two men have stretched the boundaries of musical theatre through their choice of subjects, the complexity of their music, and the sophistication of their theatrical visions. Sondheim's *Sunday in the Park with George* (Figure 8.3) and *Sweeney Todd* introduced intellectual density and compositional intricacy to the musical. Andrew Lloyd Webber's soaring melodies in *Cats* and *The Phantom of the Opera* reintroduced the lyricism of the Italian opera to the modern musical.

Before those two artists arrived on the musical scene, however, a major change had occurred in the late 1960s that expanded the nature of the musical. For decades musicals had provided America with most of its popular songs. Old standards that some of us know today originated on Broadway stages. "Only Make Believe," "Smoke Gets in Your Eyes," "Long Ago and Far Away" are melodies by Jerome Kern. George Gershwin, Irving Berlin, and Cole Porter contributed such hits as "I Got Rhythm," "Alexander's Ragtime Band," and "Anything Goes." But when rock and roll became popular, things changed. Broadway embraced the new musical idiom with the 1968 hit *Hair.*

The dawning of the Age of Aquarius was the dawning of a new era for musicals. Not only did the beat of the music change, but the idea of the book musical was on the way out. *Hair* had no spoken dialogue, and neither did *Jesus Christ Superstar, Cats, Les Miserables,* or *The Phantom of the Opera.* The age of the "sung-through" musical had begun. Isn't it interesting that our modern

Figure 8.3 The pointillist painter Georges Seurat is the central character in Stephen Sondheim's musical *Sunday in the Park with George*. This photo shows Seurat at work while two rich people look at one of his paintings.

musicals share this characteristic with the Italian operas from the Renaissance? Perhaps we have come full circle in our development of the musical.

WHAT IS MUSICAL THEATRE?

A musical is a theatrical performance of a play in which all or part of the text is sung, and in which visual spectacle joins with music and dance to tell the story and to express the characters' larger-than-life emotions.

The musical components of musical theatre are evident, but what about the visual and emotional components? When you go to see a musical, you often say you're going to see a "show," and that means you're excited by the visual spectacle you're about to enjoy. When the helicopter descends in *Miss Saigon,* when the chandelier falls in *The Phantom of the Opera,* or when the kickline of identical dancers reaches the thrilling finale in *A Chorus Line* (Figure 8.4), the visual spectacle in musical theatre becomes of central importance. In just the same way that the seventeenth-century English diplomat was excited by the opera in Venice and the nineteenth-century American audiences thrilled to look at the gorgeous girls in *The Black Crook,* so today's audiences want to be dazzled by spectacle in a modern musical. They want moving scenery and fantastical costumes and a light show worthy of a rock concert. Spectacle has joined music as an equal partner in shaping a musical, as exemplified by the most exciting Broadway show of recent years—*The Lion King* (Color Plate 6).

Together, music and spectacle lead us away from thinking about the problems of our day-to-day lives and encourage us to escape into a virtual world in which the emotions are large and the rewards are rich. A musical's soaring music and sparkling spectacle create a world in which emotions are exalted, and as we enter that world for an evening's entertainment, we know that we're going to feel *terrific* and that we'll have an experience we will remember for a long, long time.

WHY IS AMERICAN MUSICAL THEATRE SO POPULAR?

Why Is Musical Theatre an American Art Form?

- The American spirit
- The artistic melting pot
- The assembly line approach to creativity

The American Spirit

From the times of our earliest settlers, the spirit of Americans has been optimistic, exuberant, expansive, and sentimental. The "new world" of North America abandoned the cynical and tradition-bound thinking of Europe and embraced the future-thinking and democratic optimism that has shaped our culture. The wide expanses of our unconquered continent must have contributed to the development of our national temper, and we have always understood there was a new place to move, a new life to begin, and a brighter future ahead. Americans embraced the concept of "Manifest Destiny" in the nineteenth century as our civilization expanded geographically across the continent. We reveled in knowing that the twentieth century was "The Amer-

Figure 8.4   The cast of *A Chorus Line* performs in unison, and the mirror behind them increases the spectacle.

ican Century," as our economic wealth and military power became unchallenged. As we enter the twenty-first century we embrace the concept of "Space: The Next Frontier." We Americans have an exuberant belief that the future will be better. Our children will be richer and live in nicer homes. New medical discoveries will rid us of disease. The conquest of space will give us new horizons. This optimism also permits us to be sentimental. Because we know in our hearts that everything will work out for the best and that we will all live happily ever after, we are safe to concern ourselves with the plight of others who are less fortunate and to forgive those who trespass against us.

Musical theatre is a quintessentially American art form because the mirror it holds up reflects the world as we want it to be. We look at the stage and see the world that we believe ought to be true, the world that we believe will come true. The Romantic stories acted out by beautiful performers, the elaborate costumes and spectacular scenery, and most of all, the heart-lifting lyricism of the music, all support our inherent beliefs, and we feel good. Musical theatre is celebratory theatre for a culture that thrives on celebrating our emotions.

The Artistic Melting Pot

American culture has absorbed the contributions of the many peoples who have emigrated to our shores, and the musical and visual arts they brought with them have helped shape American musical theatre into a unique form that no other culture could have developed.

Although America began as a European—and in particular, an English—culture, its music quickly expanded beyond the 2/4 rhythm of the

Figure 8.5 The musical *Once on This Island* reflects the color and music of one of the many cultures that make America a unique nation. In this production by The Children's Theatre Company in Minneapolis, actress Paris Bennett dances to the rhythms of her Caribbean home.

Listen to the cast album of A Chorus Line and discover for yourself the variety of musical idiom s in that hit show.

ballad and the 3/4 rhythm of the waltz to embrace the syncopated rhythms from Africa that evolved into ragtime and later into jazz, soul music, and rock and roll. A musical like Scott Joplin's *Treemonisha* could only have been created in America. American musicals embraced the Latin American rhythms of the tango and reggae, and a musical like *Once on This Island* (Figure 8.5) could only have been created in America. The score of a musical today is likely to use all these musical idioms, all these artistic expressions of the peoples who make up the melting pot of America.

Likewise, America's visual arts—though rooted in a European culture of representational painting and sculpture—quickly expanded beyond landscapes and portraits to explore the wonders of traditional art from Africa and minimalist art from Asia. Look at the visual designs for the Broadway musical *Pacific Overtures* and discover for yourself the influence of Japanese art on that show (Figure 8.6). Today, the designs for a Broadway musical reflect an amalgamation of visions and sounds that could only have developed in America.

The Assembly Line Approach to Creativity

Our American genius is best exemplified by the efficient system that Henry Ford introduced for the manufacture of automobiles in the early twentieth century: the assembly line. We may retain a sentimental admiration for the quality that can be produced by "old world craftsmanship," in which one artisan makes a unique object, but that is not the American way. Instead, we fol-

Figure 8.6 The two-dimensional style of traditional Japanese painting was adopted by the scene designer for Stephen Sondheim's Broadway musical *Pacific Overtures. Source: Gottfried, Martin.* Broadway Musicals.

low Ford's lead; we assemble various parts and pieces into our final product, whether that "product" is a new car or a musical. The parts of an automobile are added to the chassis as it moves along an assembly line, and the parts of a musical are added as the show moves through the rehearsal process.

Traditionally, we see artists as solitary workers, as one person in front of a blank canvas, a sheet of paper, a block of marble. We think of a composer sitting at the keyboard waiting for inspiration, then playing the melody, writing down the notation, orchestrating the composition, and finally, playing it before an audience. That practice still exists, of course, but not in the creation of a musical. Musicals are assembled by a team: each person contributes his or her expertise, and each one collaborates with the others so that the final product has been assembled in the same fashion as a new car. Let us describe for you the contributions of each of the experts who helps assemble a musical.

> ## A Musical's Creative Team
>
> - The producer
> - The book writer
> - The composer
> - The lyricist
> - The director
> - The orchestrator
> - The musical director
> - The choreographer (and the fight choreographer)
> - The designers
> - The stars

The producer   The producer launches the project and oversees all aspects of the show from beginning to end. He (or she or, more frequently, a group of producers) decides what show is going to be assembled, raises the capital to finance it, and chooses which artists to hire, where the work will be done, and how and when it will be presented to the ticket-buying public. The producer is the CEO of the corporation that is hoping to make a profit from the venture. The producer overlooks the entire assembly line and makes certain that everything is moving forward wisely and steadily.

The producer's first decision is what is going to be made, what the **property** will be. (A property is anything that can be owned or protected by copyright. A house or other piece of real estate is described in law as "real property," and the book, score, and lyrics of a musical are described as "intellectual property.") Producers may use their own ideas or may accept ideas proposed by someone else, but the assembly line doesn't start until the property is chosen. A musical is rarely based on a writer's original idea, the way a play is. More frequently, a musical is based on an existing source. *Cats,* for example, is based on a collection of poems by T. S. Eliot. *Les Miserables* is based on a novel by Victor Hugo. *Oklahoma!* is based on a play, but *Victor/Victoria* is based on a movie. *Gypsy* is based on an autobiography; *Parade* is based on a real historical event; and *Joseph and the Amazing Technicolor Dreamcoat* is based on the Bible.

Once the property is decided, the producer contracts the project's key creative artists: the book writer, the composer, the lyricist, and the director. In the early stages of a musical's assembly, these four work together to plan the show, usually in a long sequence of meetings. Their work may go on for several years. The producer guides this team to agree on the spirit or tone of the project. Will it be lyrical, like *The Sound of Music,* or cynical, like *Chicago?*

The book writer   In collaboration with the other members of the creative team, the book writer figures out how the story will be told, establishing the main characters and the plot. In collaboration with the composer and lyricist, the book writer figures out where the songs will be placed so they will advance the story and reveal the characters. Later, the book writer writes the scenes of dialogue that help tell the story. (In a sung-through musical, the function of the book writer is absorbed by the lyricist because there is no book.)

The composer   In consultation with the director and book writer, the composer determines the musical idiom for each song and then writes the music. You may wonder which gets written first, the words or the music. If both jobs are done by one person, such as Stephen Sondheim writing *Sweeney Todd,* they are written simultaneously, but when a team writes the songs, it can work either way. When Richard Rodgers worked with Lorenz Hart on *Pal Joey,* the music came first. But when Rodgers teamed with Oscar Hammerstein on *South Pacific,* the words came first.

The lyricist   The lyricist writes the words for the songs and sometimes also writes the book. When separate artists create each of these parts of a show, they have to be certain that the words that are spoken and sung both seem to come from the same character.

It is common for a composer and lyricist to write many musicals together. The assembling of a musical permits and requires a lot of trial and error, and as the show moves along the assembly line, the creators discover that some parts don't fit and should be replaced. Sometimes the creators cut a song from one show and use it in another show years later. On other occasions, they add a song during rehearsals or out-of-town tryouts. Sondheim's famous song "Send in the Clowns" was written after *A Little Night Music* was being performed in out-of-town tryouts, and it was inserted into the show before it opened in New York. This notion of the interchangeability of parts truly illustrates the way musicals are assembled.

The director   The fourth member of the central team of creators is the director. (In chapter 14 we'll look in detail at what a director does.) Through these early meetings, the director leads the book writer, composer, and lyricist toward a common vision of what the show will be like when it opens. The director is a guide in these early stages of the work, but when the property is further along, when the script and songs have been added, the director's work speeds up.

In the second phase of planning, the director becomes the most important person, and he or she supervises the preparatory work of the secondary team of artists: the orchestrator, the musical director, the choreographer, and the designers. The director works closely with each of these artists to maintain a coherence to the show.

The orchestrator   The composer writes the melodies, usually on a piano, but the audience hears the score played by a full orchestra. Because some composers are not trained musicians, the orchestrator selects the instruments that will be included in the orchestra and then arranges the music, writing out the parts.

Irving Berlin couldn't read music, and he composed in only one key. He bought a "transposer" that he fitted over his keyboard so that when he hit the notes in the one key he knew, they were played in whatever key he needed. Berlin was very talented, but he needed an orchestrator to turn his melodies into arrangements that could be played in his shows.

The orchestrator also arranges the music that will accompany the dances in the show. The composer very rarely writes special music for the show's dances, so the orchestrator assembles appropriate melodies from the score and, in consultation with the choreographer, works out the arrangements that will be played.

The music director   The music director teaches the music to the performers and to the orchestra and conducts the performances.

The choreographer   The choreographer invents the dances, teaches them to the performers, and is responsible for a sizable amount of the show's total performance time. Sometimes the director is also the choreographer. Otherwise, the choreographer consults with the director as well as the orchestrator and creates the choreography in a dance studio. The choreographer also consults with the designers to ensure that space for the dances is appropriate and that the costumes enhance the dances. Later on, the choreographer will put the dancers through their paces. If you remember *A Chorus Line,* you have a very good idea what this hard work looks like. Rehearsals are fun to watch, but tough on the dancers.

Some shows have elaborate fights in them, and these are choreographed as carefully as the dances. Think of the switchblade rumble in *West Side Story.* A fight choreographer has a special space on the assembly line.

The designers   The scenery, costume, lighting, and sound designers consult with the four central creative artists (composer, lyricist, book writer, and director), and then they imagine, draw, and supervise the construction and decoration of the show's scenery, costumes, and lights as well as prepare the show's sound design. The scene designer consults with the director to ensure that the visual look expresses the right tone and that it permits the director to stage the scenes and the songs and dances. The costume designer ensures that the costumes express each of the characters correctly, that the colors and textures are harmonious with the scene design, and that the dancers can execute the choreography in those costumes. The lighting designer consults with the director, the choreographer, and the scene and costume designers to determine how he or she can enhance the visual spectacle of the production.

The sound designer shapes what the audience hears, from the singers' amplified voices to the special effects that create aural illusions on the stage. The sound designer, therefore, consults with the director about the desired emotions of each sequence, with the costume designer about placement of microphones, with the scene designer about placement of speakers, and with the musical director about the balance between the orchestra and the singers.

The stars   Sometimes a musical does not have a star. **Ensemble musicals** such as *A Chorus Line, Cats,* and *Rent* (Color Plate 4) have succeeded without the charismatic central performance of a Whoopi Goldberg or a Michael Crawford (Color Plate 7). Audiences, however, love star performers, so early in the musical assembly line process, the producer usually gathers the director, choreographer, composer, and book writer to select the artists who will play the major roles. The producer knows that the popularity of the stars will impact box office sales, and the entire creative team knows that the unique talents of the stars will influence all the preparatory work they are doing. Today, we can't think of the musical *The King and I* without thinking of Yul Brynner, but Brynner was not the producer's first choice for that role. Once Brynner had been engaged, however, all the songs, choreography, dialogue, and designs were adjusted to take advantage of his unique talents and charismatic persona.

When the performers get on board and rehearsals begin, the assembly line really speeds up. For the next four weeks, more and more elements are added to the show. The director guides the actors in the book scenes. The music director helps the singers and musicians learn the songs. The choreographer's dances are added. At the same time, the scene designs are being finished and installed in the theatre. And then the **technical rehearsals** and **dress rehearsals** begin, when all the work of the independent artists—the actors and dancers and musicians, the scenery and costumes and lights, the orchestra and backstage crews—comes together in the final phases of rehearsal. The show gets more complex each day as it races toward opening night. That night, the actors wait backstage, the orchestra plays the overture, and the curtain goes up on this magnificent product of our uniquely American genius.

9

A Guided Tour—
Backstage, Onstage,
and Through the Ages

A theatre building is like an iceberg that's 80 percent hidden under water; there's a lot to it that the public can't see. You'll have a richer appreciation of a performance when you have some sense of what a theatre building is like backstage, so we're going to take a behind-the-scenes tour. Afterwards, we'll take another tour of five different kinds of theatre buildings, and you'll discover how each kind influences your experience. Then we'll take a look at how theatre buildings evolved from their earliest shape to the kinds we find in America today.

THEATRE SPACES

So many people are curious about what's backstage that theatres like the Royal National in London and the Utah Shakespearean Festival in America sell tickets to guided tours of their backstage spaces. Theatre spaces can be clustered into two categories: public spaces and support spaces.

Public Spaces

We call "public" all those spaces that accommodate the audience. Let's start with the box office where you buy your ticket. It's a secured room where a lot of money changes hands, and you can approach it from the street or from the lobby. When you enter the theatre, you're in the lobby, which is a waiting space, out of the sun or rain, where you can sit to read your program or visit with your friends. Theatres decorate and arrange their lobbies to make you comfortable and to put you in a good mood, and their lobbies vary greatly, depending on the theatre's size, when it was built, and whether it was originally designed as a theatre. You might find a place to check your coat or a concession booth for beverages or souvenirs, and there are always rest rooms for your convenience. Some theatres have parking facilities, elevators, and restaurants, and a few newer theatres have special lounges for members, the patrons who have given money to the theatre. Beyond these public spaces is the auditorium.

An auditorium is a "place for hearing." The word has the same stem as the word "audit." When you say "I will audit that class," you mean that you will hear what the professor has to say. When you take your seat in the hearing place, you are an auditor. You are also a spectator who has come to see the play (the same stem as the word "spectacle"). Curiously, the ancient Greeks called the "seeing place" where they sat to watch a performance a **theatron** (THEE-a-tron), but since we use the word "theatre" to describe the whole building, we have come to accept the word "auditorium" for the portion of the theatre where we sit to experience a play.

 Theatre slang also calls the auditorium the "house," and you may hear an usher ask the supervisor (or house manager), "How full is the house tonight?" The term "house" is short for playhouse, and actors will describe an unruly audience as a "tough house."

A lot of words are used to describe different portions of the auditorium, and these words may be useful to you when you are buying tickets. In America we call the main floor the orchestra, and in England it's called the stalls. Most of us use the word "orchestra" to describe a large group of musicians who play classical music. But orchestra originally meant "dancing place," and that's what it was called in the ancient Greek theatre.

The orchestra will have either a solid bank of seats reaching from one side of the auditorium to the other or seats that are divided by aisles into sections (typically, two aisles create a center section and two side sections). The arrangement with the wide bank of uninterrupted seats is called continental seating, presumably because it became popular first on the European continent. The arrangement with aisles is called American seating. To ensure that audiences can leave a theatre quickly in the case of fire or other emergency, federal regulations require that theatres with continental seating must have a space of three feet between rows so that you can pass in front of a seated person easily. Theatres with American seating may have the rows closer together, but no one may be seated more than seven seats from an aisle.

In recent years, and in response to federal legislation, theatres have created places where persons in wheelchairs may be seated. Commonly these seats are at the back or side of the orchestra. If you or your companion uses a wheelchair, specify that at the time you purchase your tickets.

Above the main floor you may encounter the box, mezzanine, loge, dress circle, or balcony. In order to choose (or find) your seats you need to

Figure 9.1 The Presidential Box of the Ford's Theatre in Washington, D.C., provides a limited view of the stage but permits the audience to see the people seated in it. In 1865, Abraham Lincoln was assassinated while seated here, and the assassin leaped from the box down onto the stage.

know the differences among them. A box seat is in a special area that is partitioned off from the general seating. A box seat may be more expensive than a seat in the orchestra, but it might not give you a better view of the stage. Traditionally, a box seat is a better seat *from which to be seen,* and that is why, in bygone times, people were content to pay more for such seats. In the eighteenth and nineteenth centuries, theatregoing was a major social event, and the rich and famous, wearing their most fashionable new outfits, went to the theatre to be seen. The theatres they went to had boxes just under the level of the balcony and placed all around the sides of the auditorium. The boxes closest to the stage were considered the most desirable, even though they provided a very limited view of the stage. Abraham Lincoln was seated in a box (Figure 9.1) when he was assassinated by the actor John Wilkes Booth. There are still boxes in older theatres in New York and London; before you buy tickets to box seats, inquire if they have an "obstructed view," which means they are behind a column or afford only a partial view of the stage.

All seating on a floor higher than the orchestra used to be called the balcony: first balcony, second balcony, and in some theatres a third balcony, or gallery. The slang terms for the gallery include the "nosebleed section," "paradise," or "the Gods" since the seats are so high up that they seem near to heaven. Each balcony was entered from a separate lobby, and the highest balcony was entered from a separate exterior door that led to an entirely separate stairwell. These separate entrances can still be seen in many older European theatres. The gallery seats were originally intended to accommodate only the serving classes, and the snobby upper classes didn't want to mingle with their social inferiors, even while entering a theatre.

Today, the desire to inflate the price of balcony seats has led producers to inflate the words they use to describe various seating areas. The word "mezzanine" used to mean a small balcony halfway up, just under the first balcony, not quite as good a seat as on the main floor but better than one in the balcony. But now the word is sometimes used to describe the first balcony, and sometimes the back rows of the orchestra. The word "balcony" is reserved, in many theatres today, to describe only the very back rows of the upper seating. So when you are considering balcony seats, caveat emptor ("buyer beware"). You can be sure to get the seats you want if you purchase your tickets at the box office, where you can see a seating chart.

The word "loge" comes from an old French word for a comfortable chair, and it is now used to describe theatre seats that are at the very front of the first balcony. There's no widely accepted use of the word "loge," however, and you'll encounter it only occasionally. To avoid confusion, inquire at the box office about where loge seats in that theatre are actually located.

Another term describing the front seats of the first balcony is "dress circle," and it is still used in England and in some American opera houses; you can infer that this term refers to the seats where, in earlier and more elegant times, people "dressed" for the theatre. The elegant women who sat in the dress circle wore floor-length evening gowns, and the gentlemen wore white tie and tails. In the English theatres of the nineteenth century, the dress circle provided the best view of the stage as well as the best view into the royal box. The seats in the stalls on the main floor were looked down on, both literally and socially, and they were entered from a lobby that was below street level, because the entire theatre building was built down into the ground. The entrance to the dress circle was from the street level lobby; the wealthy patrons of the "carriage trade" could get out of their horse-drawn carriages and into the theatre with the greatest of ease, while their coachmen went around to the side entrance to climb the stairs to "paradise."

Support Spaces

The pass door leads from the public spaces to the support spaces. The pass door is different from the stage door, which is the exterior door the actors use to enter the theatre (and where fans wait to get autographs). Once through the pass door, you're backstage. If a theatre was built to present commercial per-

Figure 9.2 A dressing room is equipped with mirrors, bright lights, and shelves for hats and wigs. It is where the actors put on their makeup and change into their costumes.

formances, it probably does not have much backstage space, but if it is a newer building constructed as the home for a not-for-profit company that produces a season of plays, it may have a surprising variety of support spaces.

If you were to walk onstage and look out at the empty seats, you might be surprised by how large the auditorium seems, and you'll get an actor's view of the house. The experience can be pretty intimidating, and it can give you an increased respect for an actor's courage. Would you want to face all those people eight times a week? If you look to either side, you'll see the off-stage spaces from which scenery can be moved onto the stage and from which actors make their entrances. These spaces are called the wings, since they are at the sides of the stage as wings are at the sides of a bird. Over your head, hidden from the audience, is the stage house that encompasses a large empty space called the fly loft, or the "flies," so named because scenery can be "flown" up into the air to hang there on lines of rope or cable and then lowered onto the stage when it is needed. Similarly, scenery can be lowered below the stage through "traps" to an empty room beneath your feet called the trap room. From the trap room, there is access to the orchestra pit, that space below and a little in front of the stage where the musicians sit when they accompany the singers.

Look out at the back wall of the auditorium. In newer theatres there are some very small booths for the technicians who operate the computer boards that control the sound and lights during a performance. In many older theatres there are no booths, and the crews operating the sound and lighting boards are awkwardly placed at the back of the main floor seats.

Let's leave the stage and explore backstage. As you'd expect, there are places for the actors to change clothes in and to rest in while they are offstage. The changing rooms are called dressing rooms (Figure 9.2), and the lounge or waiting room is called the green room. Dressing rooms and a green room may be all there is backstage in a Broadway theatre that was built many years ago. By way of contrast, many newer theatre complexes have a large number of support spaces. These spaces include administrative offices and conference rooms for the staff who do the marketing and public relations work, the fund-raising and development work, and the accounting and educational work as well as the staff who sell subscription tickets. The most prominent of these offices are for the artistic director and the managing director. The former is responsible for the artistic quality of the theatre's productions, and the latter for the company's financial and personnel concerns. Additional offices are needed for the staff who create the productions: the company manager, who cares for the needs of the visiting artists; the production manager, who oversees scheduling and budgets; the technical director, who supervises the building of the scenery; the costume shop manager, who supervises the construction of the costumes; the stage manager, who supervises the rehearsals and performances; and the resident designers, who conceive and execute the productions' designs. As you walk by these offices, you will not be surprised to find them filled with desks, computer stations, and bookshelves, items you'd find in the offices of architects, engineers, and other professionals.

Theatre historians don't agree on where the name "green room" came from, but one widely held belief is that the waiting room in London's Drury Lane Theatre was painted green in the eighteenth century and that actors carried that name for the waiting room with them when they traveled to other theatres. Habit and usage then made it the standard name.

Let's go further into the bowels of the support spaces, further into the 80 percent of the iceberg. There are very large spaces where scenery, properties, and costumes are built and stored, and where lighting and sound equipment is stored and maintained. Of the several spaces in which the production is created, scenery needs the most room. The scene shop is typically a very large and tall open space with room to build large units of scenery from wood, metal, and plastic. As you can see in Figure 9.3, the shop is filled with heavy equipment: saws, drills, welding tools, and so on. The scene shop frequently has a paint frame, a large vertical frame that is attached to a pulley system and on which flat scenery can be fastened so that it may be raised or lowered into a slot in the floor while the scenic artists paint it. Sometimes the areas in which metals or plastics are used are segregated from the main portion of the scene shop because these toxic materials require special ventilation. The prop shop is usually adjacent to the scene shop, because the workers overlap and use many of the same tools. In the prop shop are built and maintained all the items used in the play, from furniture to firearms to food.

In the costume department, you may find a costume shop, a dye room, a crafts room, a fitting room, and a storage room called the racks. Figure 9.4

Figure 9.3   A scene shop is equipped with tools for carpentry and welding and for working with plastics.

shows a typical costume shop, which is equipped with tables on which patterns are made and fabric is cut and with various kinds of sewing machines. Ideally, a costume department also has a well-ventilated dye room where the color of fabrics is altered, and a crafts room in which artisans work with leather, plastics, and other materials to construct footwear, armor, or other parts of the costumes. The fitting room—where the actors try on their costumes—may be nicely equipped with shelves, chairs, and a floor-length mirror or it may be only a curtained-off corner of the costume shop. There may also be a large room called the racks, where costumes are hung and shelved when they are not in use for a particular production.

Then we come to the rehearsal room, the "engine room" of the theatre, where the actors and director work. A rehearsal room is an empty room that is about the same size as the stage. Some are quite tall, to permit actors to stand on platforms, the way they will in performance. If the theatre does musicals, the room usually has a sprung floor so the dancers don't get hurt. Nearby are usually some racks to store the actors' coats and backpacks, and some prop tables hold items the actors use in rehearsal; the floor is typically marked with colored tape that defines what the scenery will be like when the actors move onto the stage.

We've reached the end of this imaginary tour, and you've visited most of the spaces in a theatre. When you take a real tour you may be surprised at the amount of walking you'll do. The image of the iceberg may come back to

Figure 9.4   A costume shop is equipped with cutting tables, dress forms, and a variety of sewing machines. Costumes for each play are made or custom fitted to each actor by the costume shop staff.

you, or you might be reminded of a labyrinth. As you traipse through the corridors and stairwells, you will start to realize the large number of people who work in the theatre and whose labors are unrecognized by the general audience, and you will increase your appreciation of what it takes to create a theatrical performance. Like an army that provides twelve persons to support every combat soldier, the theatre supports actors with a large number of people never seen on stage. One of the reasons theatre buildings are so large is that these workers must have spaces to work.

KINDS OF THEATRES

Each of the five kinds of theatre buildings has its descriptive name, each is best suited to a certain kind of performance, and each provides you with a particular kind of experience. Some may be familiar and others may be unlike anything you've ever seen.

The Five Kinds of Theatres

1. Proscenium arch theatre
2. Arena theatre
3. Thrust theatre
4. Black box theatre
5. Found space theatre

Proscenium Arch Theatre

The most common form of theatre architecture in our time is called the **proscenium arch theatre.** It's a theatre with all the seats facing in the same direction—like those in a movie theatre—and with an ornate frame around a stage that is temporarily hidden from you, usually by a beautiful curtain. Almost every Broadway theatre, most theatres on college campuses, and most large theatres in cities across America are proscenium arch theatres. You have probably been in many proscenium arch theatres. The word "proscenium" (pro-SEEN-ee-um) needs explanation. "Pro" comes from the ancient Greek word meaning "in front." We say we are making "progress" when we are in front of where we were a few moments ago. "Skene" (SKAY-nay) is the name the ancient Greeks had for the free-standing building in which the actors changed costumes or waited to make their entrances. The place in front of the skene, where the actors performed, was called the "proskene." Still later in history, a division was made between the proskene where the actors performed and the auditorium where the audience sat, and the two were separated by an arch. The audience watched the play through the kind of archway shown in Figure 9.5, which we call the proscenium arch.

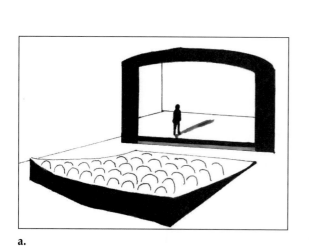

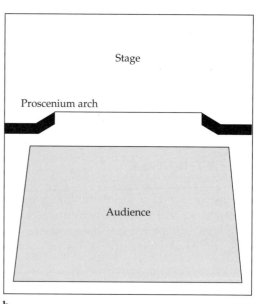

a.   **b.**

Figure 9.5   a. A proscenium arch theatre has a frame around the top and two sides of the stage through which the audience watches the actors on the stage. **b.** A schematic drawing from above is called a "ground plan." This ground plan for a proscenium arch theatre shows how the stage and audience are separated by the proscenium arch.

Figure 9.6 This beautiful old proscenium arch theatre has an ornately decorated three-sided picture frame that separates the stage from the auditorium. You can also see the orchestra pit in front of the stage, the box seats on the side wall, and the mezzanine seats that are in front of and slightly lower than the curved balcony.

When you take your seat, you can recognize that you're in one large space that is divided into two parts: one part for the spectators and one part for the performers. The audience all faces one direction, as you do in a classroom. A proscenium arch theatre might be large enough to seat 3,000, or it might be so small that it seats fewer than 100. Size is not a defining factor, but the stage that the actors perform on is usually raised up a few feet off the ground, and it is separated from the audience by the arch that spans from one side of the stage to the other. This arch creates a sort of three-sided picture frame around the stage, and it hides all the support spaces backstage. The audience watches the performance through a frame, and a proscenium arch theatre is sometimes called a "keyhole stage," to suggest the notion that the audience is peeking through a keyhole into a world that would otherwise be unseen. The proscenium arch theatre was developed in the seventeenth century, and many of the arches reflect the style of those times—decorated with ornately sculptured plaster that is painted to look like a gold picture frame, as in Figure 9.6.

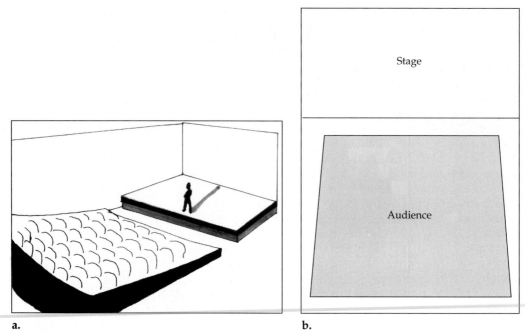

a.   b.

Figure 9.7   a. An end stage theatre does not have a proscenium arch separating
the audience from the stage. **b.** The ground plan of an end stage theatre shows
that the stage is at one end of the space, with the audience facing it at the other
end. There is no architectural separation between audience and stage.

Proscenium arch theatres are best suited to **representational** performances, the description given to performances in which the audience understands the convention of the fourth wall. "The convention of the fourth wall"
is the phrase that describes the situation in which both the actors and the
audience pretend there is a fourth wall to the room represented on the stage, a
wall that has been removed so that the audience can observe the action. In a
representational performance, the actors "represent" believable characters
who live in their own world; the actors do not acknowledge the existence or
presence of the audience. Most of the plays written in the last hundred years
call for representational performances, and that is why proscenium arch theatres are the most common.

Representational performances in a proscenium arch theatre allow
you to identify with the characters and to get completely involved in the
action. You forget yourself for a while, and your experience can best be
explained by the phrase "the willing suspension of disbelief." (See chapter
2 for an explanation of this convention.) It is easiest to pretend that the
drama is *really* happening when we are peeping into the world of the characters, and the frame around the stage—the proscenium arch—helps us to
do that.

Figure 9.8 The scenery reaches to the side walls and ceiling of this end stage theatre. Note that there are no wings or fly loft, and that this end stage theatre has no proscenium arch.

Have you ever been to a theatre that is very much like a proscenium arch theatre but does not have an arch—a theatre where there's no frame around the stage? This theatre is a variation of the proscenium arch theatre, and we call it an **end stage theatre** because the stage is at one end of the space, with all the seats facing it, as in Figure 9.7. Usually an end stage theatre has been built in a space that was not originally intended as a theatre. Virtually all the characteristics of a proscenium arch theatre are found in an end stage theatre, though usually there is very little wing and fly space. End stage theatres lend themselves to representational performances and to the willing suspension of your disbelief (Figure 9.8).

Arena Theatre

When you first enter the Alley Theatre in Houston, Texas, you see that the stage is in the center and the seating is all around it. There is no proscenium arch separating the audience from the actors, and you can look across the stage to see the people seated on the other side, as in Figure 9.9. The **arena theatre** is aptly named. It's the architectural descendent of the ancient Roman arenas where the audience sat on a comfortable ring of seats while the gladiators fought to the death on the earthen circle before them.

The arena is a popular form of theatre today, but it is a development of the twentieth century. For three hundred years the proscenium arch theatre was the only kind of theatre people knew about. Then, around the turn of the

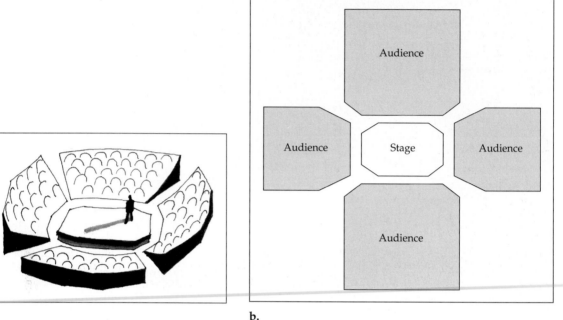

a. **b.**

Figure 9.9 **a.** An arena theatre has seating all around the stage, and the actors enter through the same aisles the audience uses. **b.** Unlike the proscenium arch theatre, in which some of the audience sits far from the stage, all the audience at an arena theatre sits close to the stage.

twentieth century, many theatre artists began to experiment with the impact that theatre might have if different spaces were used. From these experiments came the arena theatre, which became popular in the middle of the twentieth century and became known also as "theatre-in-the-round."

Arena theatres can be square, like the renowned Arena Stage in Washington, D.C., or they can be round or even oblong, like the Penthouse Theatre in Seattle. They can seat many hundreds, like the Alley Theatre in Houston (Figure 9.10), or fewer than ninety, like the arena theatres on many university campuses. Whatever their configuration or size, arena theatres have certain traits in common: intimacy, a proper **aesthetic distance,** and minimal scenery.

Intimacy Intimacy is the most evident trait of an arena theatre. Because audiences are seated on all sides of the stage, and because the actors must be heard by patrons who cannot always see their faces, these theatres-in-the-round are usually quite small. No seat is very far from the stage. The proximity of actors and audience encourages a subtlety in the actors' work that leads the audience to laugh at comic lines or funny expressions. Comedies are very successful when acted in arena theatres.

Figure 9.10   The Alley Theatre in Houston arranges its 296 seats on four sides of the stage.

Proper Aesthetic Distance   The phrase "proper aesthetic distance" describes the condition in which the audience is close enough to the stage to be emotionally involved and yet far enough away to remain physically apart. A demonstration of our natural desire for a proper aesthetic distance is the way we relate to someone telling a story. As we listen to a storyteller—and this is just as true of children in a kindergarten class as of adults listening to a tour guide—we keep a small distance between ourselves and the storyteller. If the storyteller walks away, we move closer, and if the storyteller moves toward us, we retreat. There's a distance at which we feel comfortable, a distance that seems natural. As an audience in the theatre, we want to be physically and emotionally far enough away from the stage to retain our awareness that we are watching a play, and at the same time we want to be physically and emotionally close enough to share the characters' emotional lives. When that happens, we are at the proper aesthetic distance to enjoy the performance. If we are too close, we see the actor's sweat through the character's makeup and we lose our ability to believe, and if we are so far away that we can't see or hear, we also lose our proper involvement. The balance is a delicate one, and for us

The first time you go to an arena theatre, you are likely to be more interested in the audience than what happens on the stage. You will appreciate the action on the stage more completely after you have seen enough arena theatre productions so that the distractions are unimportant. You will become adept at disregarding everything in your line of sight that interferes with your concentration on the play, and you will become skilled at imagining a fourth wall through which you peep at the action on the stage. Only when you are able to suspend your disbelief sufficiently to experience a representational performance fully will you find the intimacy of the arena theatre to be a fair exchange for the illusion that is more easily created in a proscenium arch theatre.

to enjoy theatre most completely, we need the proper aesthetic distance. The fixed seats in most theatres keep us from adjusting our distance from the stage, but arena theatres can often provide the desired aesthetic distance better than proscenium arch theatres, which seat us too close or too far from the stage.

Minimal Scenery   There is very little scenery on the stage of an arena theatre. The audience sees only a suggestion of the play's fictional location from the treatment of the floor, the selection of furniture, and the fragments of hanging scenery that suggest the physical environment. It is almost impossible to create an illusion of a real place when the audience sees that the room has no walls or doors. As a result, the kind of performance that is best suited for this shared space where audience and actors have no arch separating them is **presentational** performance, the opposite of representational performance. Presentational performance describes a performance in which the actors openly acknowledge the existence of the audience and "present" the play to them. Actors speak directly to the

Presentational performance is more common in live theatre than in television or movies. One wonderful exception is the film made from the eighteenth-century comic novel *Tom Jones.* It stars Albert Finney, and if you want to have a good time, rent it from your video shop. You will find that the characters sometimes look directly into the lens and speak or wink directly at you. They break through the convention of the fourth wall that you are accustomed to in movies, and they offer you an example on film of presentational performance.

audience, and frequently they break into song. They wink at the audience on laugh lines and sing to them in musicals. There is no convention of the fourth wall in a presentational performance. The audience does not willingly suspend its disbelief. Quite the contrary: the audience understands that it is participating in a theatrical performance, not peeping into another world.

Paradoxically, representational performances are often successful in arena theatres. Why do you suppose that happens? What is there about theatre that permits audiences to believe in a fiction when there is very little visual support for the illusion? The answer must be that we have learned the conventions of representational performance from our years of seeing plays in proscenium arch theatres and on movie and television screens, and that we are able to imagine a fictional world even when there's little evidence of one. We can see that the room is not a real one, we can see the audience across from us, and yet we can believe in the illusion. We can share in the characters' joys and agonies, but we are never tempted to leap onto the stage and enter their world.

Thrust Theatre

Let's visit The Guthrie Theatre in Minneapolis (Figure 9.11). It's the most celebrated **thrust theatre** in America. When you first walk into the auditorium of The Guthrie Theatre you will see why it's called a thrust theatre. The audience sits on three sides, and the stage thrusts itself into the space where, in a proscenium arch theatre, there would be seats. In the thrust theatre, like in the arena theatre, actors and audience are in a single, shared space. There is no arch separating them, and there's not much opportunity for using scenery to represent the play's virtual place. Instead, the back wall of the stage can be decorated to suggest where the action of the play is taking place. The back wall "suggests" a location rather than "represents" one, as it would in a proscenium arch theatre that has settings with three walls. The actors make entrances and exits through doors in the back wall. Actors also make entrances through the aisles, which pierce the banks of seats in much the same way that the aisles in a football stadium pierce the rows of seats in the grandstands (Figure 9.12). The movement of the characters through the audience's

Aisles in thrust theatres are called "vomitoria," which comes from the Latin word "vomitus," from which we also get our word "vomit." In this case, it describes the way the actors exit, or are "disgorged" from the theatre. You'll hear theatre people speak of a vomitorium by the shortened name of "vom." "Exit through the vom," you might hear a director tell an actor.

Figure 9.11   The thrust stage creates a close relationship between the actors and all 1,441 patrons of The Guthrie Theatre in Minneapolis. The audience sits on three sides of the stage.

part of the theatre increases the sense that the audience and actors are part of the same world.

The plays best suited to a thrust theatre are those classics that were written before the proscenium arch theatre was introduced—before the concept of theatrical illusion became dominant and before representational theatre became the norm. The great classics by Shakespeare and Molière and the ancient Greeks are presentational plays that have a scale to them that can be best achieved in the spacious reaches of a thrust theatre. These plays invite you to help in their creation when the characters speak directly to you. The opening speech of Shakespeare's *Henry V* is given by a character named Chorus, and it captures the excitement of presentational theatre on a thrust stage.

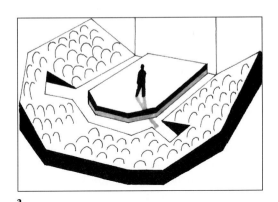
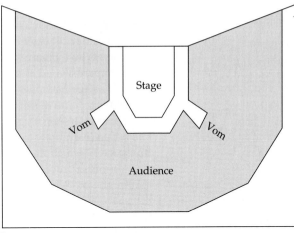

a.   **b.**

Figure 9.12   a. A thrust theatre has a stage that "thrusts" into the area where seats would be in a proscenium arch theatre, and the audience sits on three sides of the stage. **b.** This ground plan of a thrust theatre shows the vomitoria that go under the audience's seats. Actors can enter and exit through these voms.

Chorus tells the audience to pretend, when they hear someone talk about horses, that they can actually hear hoofbeats; he goes on to say that it's the audience's job to imagine how the king is dressed, what the different locations look like, and how much time has passed between scenes. Quite simply, Chorus asks the audience to use their imaginations in creating the performance they will experience.

When you're in the audience of a thrust theatre, you'll experience the same kind of intimacy that you experience in an arena theatre. None of the 1,441 spectators at The Guthrie Theatre is more than fifty-two feet from the center of the stage. Moreover, the audience in a thrust theatre is not divided into small clusters as it is in an arena theatre; instead, it has the same sense that an audience in a proscenium arch theatre has, a sense that it is one, solid, unified mass. The stage thrusts forward into the audience, and the play seems very urgent and immediate.

Black Box Theatre

In the last few decades, **black box theatres** have been built on most university campuses and as a part of the large complex operated in London by the Royal National Theatre. When you first walk into a black box theatre that's all it is: a large empty box of a room that has had its floor, walls, and ceiling painted black. It's well furnished with lighting and sound equipment, but there is no fixed arrangement for the audience's seats or the actors' stage. It's just an empty space until someone decides how to arrange the stage and the seating for a particular production.

Black box theatres became very popular in the 1960s when theatre artists experimented with the nature of theatre. Productions in arena and thrust theatres had proven that the relationship between the performer and the actor could be manipulated with fascinating results, and some artists carried the experiments to great extremes. English director Peter Brook wrote *The Empty Space,* a hugely influential book whose title suggests the value of a neutral space in which the theatrical experience can be studied.

In order to conduct experiments, theatre artists need a neutral space that can be modified to meet the needs of any sort of performance. This neutral space, much like a scientist's laboratory, is a *functional* space in which all sorts of theatre can be created. A black box theatre is usually quite small, rarely holding more than two hundred people, and it can be altered easily so that it can have end stage seating for one performance, three-sided thrust seating for another, and full arena seating for yet another. In more experimental productions, audiences and actors can be placed high up on platforms near the ceiling or down low in pits below the level of the permanent stage floor.

All sorts of plays are well suited to black box theatres, and performance is limited only by the artists' imaginations. Your experience as a member of the audience will be an exciting one because you will be very close to the action, and you may encounter an experimental production that stretches your experience of what theatre can be.

A particularly exciting kind of theatrical experiment conducted in a black box theatre is environmental theatre (Figure 9.13). It was defined by scholar and director Richard Schechner (SHEK-ner) through a sequence of productions he directed in New York in the 1960s and 1970s and in an essay titled "Six Axioms of Environmental Theatre." Two traits of environmental theatre are that multiple actions happen simultaneously and that the performers' and the audience's spaces are continually readjusted. In Schechner's productions several things go on at once, rather like the several acts that take place simultaneously in a circus. Also in his productions, there is no portion of the black box theatre that is exclusively for spectators or performers. All the space is used by both. The actors might perform a scene in the representational manner one minute and switch to the presentational manner the next, not only addressing the audience directly, but actually asking you to move from the platform you've been sitting on so they can act their next scene there. The traditional distinctions between auditorium and stage are violated in environmental theatre. The flow of the action includes the flow of the audience, which could happen only in a black box theatre that has had some imaginative structure of various shapes and multiple levels erected in it so that the actors and audience can continually alter their relationship.

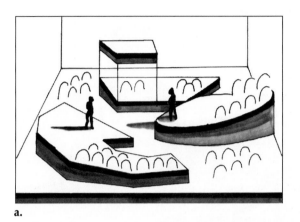

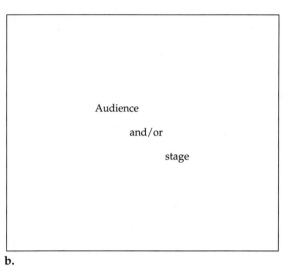

Audience

and/or

stage

a.   b.

Figure 9.13   a. A black box theatre can be arranged many ways. This drawing is for an environmental theatre production and illustrates the variety of levels and platforms used by both the audience and the actors. **b.** This ground plan for a black box theatre shows that there is no fixed location for the audience or the stage. It is an empty room that can be arranged in many ways.

An example of environmental theatre that can be seen on video is Schechner's *Dionysus in '69.* The script is based on the ancient Greek drama *The Bacchae* and tells the story of the conflict between the rational King Pentheus and Dionysus, the god of sexual ecstacy. The actors and audience moved about the black box theatre as the ritual action unfolded. The actors played lengthy sequences in the nude, and many members of the audience chose to join in the action.

Many of Schechner's productions benefited from the work of Latino designer Jerry Rojo, who also oversaw the creation of the Mobius Theatre at the University of Connecticut (Figure 9.14). The Mobius Theatre was named after the eighteenth-century German scientist who gave us the Mobius Strip. It's the ideal image for an impermanent and continually changing space.

As you might expect, most environmental theatre performances have scripts that are created especially for the productions. Should you ever find yourself attending an environmental theatre production, you will be witness to a unique and very unusual theatrical experiment.

Figure 9.14   The Mobius Theatre at the University of Connecticut is a black box theatre in which an arrangement of platforms and stairs has been installed. These spaces permit several actions to happen simultaneously, and the places in which the actors perform and the audience sits may be continually readjusted during a performance.

You can make a Mobius Strip. Tear a one-inch strip from the long side of a piece of paper so that you have a piece that is one inch by eleven inches; hold the two ends together to make a circle, and then flip one end over so that there's a twist in the paper when you rejoin the two ends. Stick the two ends together with some tape. Now put your finger anywhere on the paper and move it around the circle, tracing your path. You'll discover that there is only "one side" to a Mobius Strip. This strip is a subject of significant study in mathematics and is also a useful image for a theatre space in which there is a continual flow of audience and performers from one place to another. The Mobius Theatre was well named.

Another example of environmental theatre is *Orlando Furioso,* an Italian production that toured to New York. It dramatized a famous narrative poem called *Orlando Furioso,* which means "Orlando gone berserk." The poem is an adventure story that is the Italian equivalent of Homer's *Odyssey.* The production took place under a huge inflated tent, the kind that is set up temporarily in city parks to cover tennis courts and is held up by air blown into its plastic walls. It looked like a huge modernistic igloo. Nearly a thousand people were admitted, and inside were three permanent, free-standing stages: one long one at each end and a small square one in the very center that looked like a boxing ring. All three stages were some five feet off the ground so that the audience could see what was happening on them as they walked around the huge enclosure. The story of *Orlando Furioso* follows the hero as he goes through a sequence of wild adventures involving dragons, evil kings, and virtuous maidens. Parts of the play happened on all three stages simultaneously, and the audience walked toward whichever one interested them. From time to time one or more additional stages were rolled into the common space. These square stages were on wheels, and stagehands screamed *"Attenzione!"* as they slammed into the midst of the crowd (that's Italian for "watch out!"). Everyone got out of the way fast, and the relationship of audience to performers to performing space was continually changing. It was a colorful, raucous, and exciting event. It was environmental theatre, and it could only have been produced in the neutral space of a black box theatre—or, in this case, a white dome theatre.

Found Space Theatre

Theatre can be performed anywhere. Audiences could take a seat in the food court of a neighborhood mall, lounge on the lawn of a college campus, or go inside someone's home. Although performances are traditionally given in one of the four kinds of theatres we've already discussed, some performances are given in what is called a **found space theatre.** As the name describes, theatre can be performed in a space that was not intended for use as a theatre: a parking lot, a railroad station, a shopping mall. Why would someone do theatre in a found space? For one of two reasons: to take the performance to the audience instead of the audience to the performance, or to find a rare location that is organic to the performance.

Instead of hoping an audience will buy tickets to an established theatre, some artists take their performances to the audience. We've seen a puppet version of the opera *La Traviata* performed on a subway car in Paris, a mime performance at a cable car stop in San Francisco, and a historical pageant celebrating the fifteenth-century Christian defeat of the Moors on a pedestrian mall in Barcelona. Following their performances, the actors passed the hat for contributions and the delighted crowds gave generously. Not all performances in found spaces are light entertainment, however. Many American theatre artists who take their performances to public places are political activists who believe short and provocative plays are an effective way of engaging people in political debate. These artists hope to change public opinion and influence the policies and practices of their society. This kind of theatre was common in the 1960s and 1970s, when "guerilla theatre" was performed on college campuses and in the lobbies of state legislative buildings. These plays protested America's military involvement in Vietnam, and many people believe that the plays contributed to a reversal of American policy in Southeast Asia. This sort of politically oriented street theatre is not very common today, but you may come across it from time to time.

The second kind of found space theatre is created by artists who believe that conventional theatres do not provide the ideal setting for their plays. One New York group was En Garde Arts, a site-specific company that performed in the ponds and on the bridges in Central Park and that turned the scaffolding on the outside of a Victorian nursing home into a jungle gym and its courtyard into a circus ring. En Garde's producer Anne Hamberger explained, "I believe in going to where people live rather than waiting for them to come to us."

We've never seen a production by En Garde Arts, but we have seen a play about the life of Christ performed on the steps of a cathedral in Spain (Figure 9.15) and have read about a German production of Shakespeare's comedy *As You Like It* that we wish we had seen. The action of the play begins indoors at the court of Duke Frederick, but very quickly it moves outdoors to the Forest of Arden. The director wanted the audience to have the same experience of a forest that the characters would have, so he staged the first part of the play inside a theatre and then, as the characters walked out to the Forest of Arden, the actors invited the audience to follow them into a nearby rustic park. There, the performance continued amid the trees, streams, and glens—moving from place to place in the "forest," as the script suggests. The audience's experience moved from a traditional one in a proscenium arch theatre to an avant-garde experience in a found space.

Found spaces are best for plays that are short and are easily understood and that don't depend on complicated scenery or technology. Your experience at this kind of performance can vary widely. Sometimes you will be delighted by the entertainment, and other times you will be challenged by the political content. In either instance, you'll realize how little is needed for the creation of the theatrical experience. Today, we depend on the sophisticated technology found in proscenium arch, arena, thrust, and black box theatres, but thousands of years ago, when the first actors gathered their tribe together near the campfire to recount the glories of their triumph over the raging bull, they used a found space.

Figure 9.15 The steps leading up to a Spanish cathedral provided the found space for this performance of *The Way of the Cross,* a religious drama. In this scene, Jesus is driven toward Mount Cavalry by a Roman soldier who is wearing a highly theatrical costume. The audience of nearly a thousand stood and sat along the sides of the stairway to witness the performance.

SETTING THE STAGE

The previous descriptions tell you about the architecture of the five kinds of theatres and about the spacial relationships between their audiences and the stage, but you don't usually see a theatre naked, do you? It's usually dressed up with some kind of scenery on the stage. And different kinds of scenery can influence your experience of the performance.

Many plays take place in one location and have a single set. Whether the action takes place outdoors under a tree or indoors in a kitchen, the scenery doesn't change. Other plays take place in a variety of locations. For those plays, the scenery must change several times during the performance, or else the set must be a neutral structure that permits the audience to imagine all the different locations in the action. Theatre has five standard kinds of scenery. Any kind of scenery could be installed in any kind of theatre, but because you're probably most familiar with proscenium arch theatres, we'll ask you to imagine that you are seated in the center of the orchestra, looking at the stage.

The Standard Kinds of Scenery and How They Are Moved

1. Five Kinds of Scenery
    A. Box Set
    B. Realistic Exterior
    C. Two-Dimensional Painted Set
    D. Unit Set
    E. Projections
2. How Scenery Moves
    A. Wagons
    B. Flies and Elevators
    C. Slip Stage
    D. Revolving Stage
3. Hybrid Scenery

Box Set

If you think of a doll's house, you'll know immediately what a box set looks like: it looks like a room with a wall missing. The box set has a ceiling, three walls, and a floor. Many modern plays use box sets, particularly those that take place in a living room or kitchen. When you see a box set, you can expect a representational performance that strives to convince you that you are seeing a "slice of life," because you're being asked to pretend that you are looking into a real room. In some cases, a set won't have a ceiling or the precise right angles you'd find in a real room, but it's still considered a box set. Sets are box sets even when the walls are free standing and slanted so that the audience at the sides of the auditorium can see the whole stage, as is shown in Figure 9.16.

You may have heard the term "drawing room comedy." A drawing room is an earlier name for the room we call a parlor or living room today. It's short for "withdrawing," and it is the room a family withdraws to for privacy, as opposed to the room in which the family receives guests. If you visit older homes in the South or East, you may find a sliding double door between two parts of the living room. The part farthest from the front door is the drawing room. The action of a drawing room comedy is set in a family's private room, hence the name. A drawing room comedy is almost always performed in a box set.

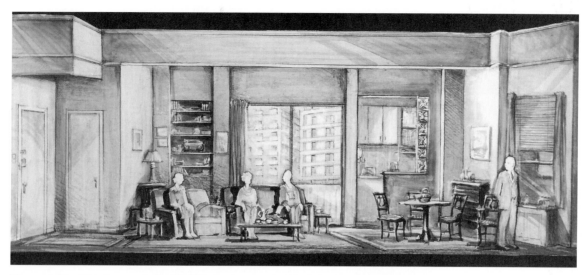

Figure 9.16   This box set is for Neil Simon's comedy *The Prisoner of Second Avenue*. The action takes place in an apartment in New York City. The side walls are on a slight angle so that the audience in the side seats can see the full stage.

Realistic Exterior

The action of some plays takes place outdoors. When performed representationally, those plays require scenery that imitates locations such as the side of a mountain or the countryside next to a lonely road. Whereas the box set is used to create an illusion of an interior, the scenery for this kind of play is built to create an illusion of what you would find in nature. The scenery may be made from wood, muslin, Styrofoam, or other materials, but it is shaped and painted to create a three-dimensional illusion that will help the audience suspend its disbelief.

Two-dimensional Painted Set

Many productions use scenery that is painted to create a decorative background instead of scenery that is built to create a three-dimensional illusion of reality. Two-dimensional scenery is painted on surfaces that are fixed to a frame. Each unit is called a flat. When flats are placed on the side of the stage, parallel with the proscenium arch, each one is called a wing. The wings do not make a solid wall, but they are spaced so the audience cannot see past them. Actors enter through the gaps between the wings, because there is no pretense that the set is a real place. At the back of the stage is a large painted cloth, called a drop. Two-dimensional scenery is frequently called wing and drop scenery, and the drawing in Figure 9.17 illustrates it. The wings and drop might be painted to indicate an exterior (a tree by a road) or an interior

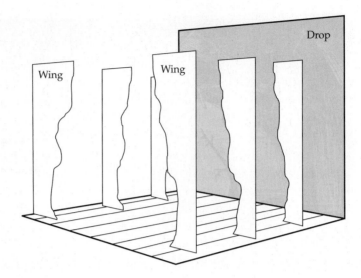

Figure 9.17 This cutaway drawing shows how two-dimensional wing and drop scenery is arranged on a stage.

(a bedroom). When you see a two-dimensional painted set, you can expect a presentational performance that never asks you to suspend your disbelief. Today, two-dimensional scenery is used for ballets, musicals, and plays that were written in earlier centuries when two-dimensional scenery was in fashion.

Unit Set

A unit set is one permanent structure that remains in place throughout a performance and does not represent a recognizable place. It is an architectural arrangement of levels and platforms that provides an audience with a way to imagine whatever location the play requires, as you can see in the design shown in Figure 9.18. When the dialogue says the action is in the king's throne room, the actors kneel before a throne on one side of the unit set and the audience imagines the throne room. When the action moves to a hill overlooking a battlefield, actors place some banners on a platform on the other side of the unit set and the audience imagines the hill. When you see a unit set, you can expect a performance that is presentational at one moment and representational the next. Unit sets are most commonly used for episodic plays such as those of Shakespeare.

Projections

Modern technology has increased the kinds of scenery you can see. Today, you may see images projected onto the front of flat scenery or projected through translucent screens from the back. These projections can create the illusion of a real place or the unrealistic suggestion of a place. Some projections are commonplace and others are experimental, so when you see a set that uses projections, you might be in for an unusual performance.

Figure 9.18   This unit set for a play about Galileo permitted actors to stand on the small platforms at the sides of the stage, but most of the action took place on the large disk in the center. The smaller disk could be lowered so that there was one solid floor, or it could be tilted to create a dynamic playing space, as shown in this photo.

Moving the Scenery

There are very few directions scenery can move. It can move horizontally: off-stage into the wings. It can move vertically: up into the fly loft or down into a trap beneath the stage. It can move in a circle: a big turntable can spin around. Modern theatre uses one or more of these means to change the scenery from what you see one moment to what you see the next.

Wagons   Scenery can be built on wagons that roll off the stage. An entire box set could be put on a wagon, but more frequently a wagon carries only a portion of a set. The horizontal movement of scenery is not very fast, and while wagons are the preferred way of moving heavy scenery, they are usually moved during an intermission.

Flies and Elevators   Scenery can be on elevators that lower into the stage, or it can be rigged to fly upward into the empty space above the proscenium arch, called the flies. The drop at the back of a wing and drop set is commonly flown out to reveal another drop behind it that is painted to indicate the location of the next scene. This vertical movement can happen at the same time that an entire set of six wings is slid offstage, revealing another set of wings in place behind them; these new wings augment the picture on the new drop. A new location is revealed in a matter of seconds.

Slip Stage The floor can be built so that a portion of it slides offstage. Furniture (or actors) can be on it when it moves, and a new location can be created this way.

Revolving Stage A large turntable can be placed in the center of the stage, and new scenery can revolve into view while the old scenery disappears.

Hybrid Scenery

If you can imagine it and if a theatre can afford it, it can be done. You will see productions that put a box set on a turntable and surround it with wing and drop scenery. You will see a unit set that's built on elevators so that the platforms raise and lower as the action unfolds. You will see wing and drop scenery with projections on it that change the imaginary location without the wings ever moving. Popular musicals like *Les Miserables* and *The Phantom of the Opera* thrill audiences with elaborate and innovative set designs that are a hybrid of every imaginable kind of scenery, and the way the scenery moves brings gasps and applause.

THEATRE THROUGH THE AGES

Greek Theatre

The best preserved ancient Greek theatre is at Epidaurus (ep-I-DOOR-us). This theatre is in a rural setting two hours southwest of Athens, and it is still used today for performances of the ancient tragedies. We saw *Oedipus* (ED-i-puss) *the King* there a few years ago, and it was one of the most exciting experiences of our theatregoing lives. On a balmy summer evening the theatre attracts crowds of up to 12,000, just as it did more than two thousand years ago.

The theatre at Epidaurus seems to have evolved from the earthen threshing circles used by farmers (Figure 9.19) that many scholars believe are where ancient Greeks first performed theatre. After completing the harvest, farmers would dance and sing in the threshing circle. From that celebration was born the chorus of Greek theatre.

At Epidaurus you can see that the ancient Greek theatres were not freestanding buildings but were nestled against a hillside. Their major playing space was a circle, and the similarity to the farmer's threshing circle seems

Figure 9.19
From ancient times to today, Greek farmers have built stone rings and filled them with newly cut wheat. When horses or people walk on the wheat, the seeds come away from the stalk. This procedure is called "threshing," and historians believe that the dancing, singing, and storytelling with which ancient farmers celebrated a successful harvest took place in this circle. They conjecture that this threshing circle was the inspiration for the circular orchestra in ancient Greek theatres where the chorus danced and sang.

evident. The seating was carved out of the hillside, and the audience sat in the open air on the benches of the theatron (THEE-a-tron). As you remember, we get our word "theatre" from this Greek word, which meant "the seeing place." The seats followed the natural curve of the hillside and wrapped more than halfway around the performing space, something like the seats in a modern thrust theatre. Most of the action took place on the large flat circle, called the **orchestra** ("the dancing place"), where the fifteen actors who made up the chorus danced and sang (Figure 9.20). In the middle of the orchestra was the altar to the god Dionysus, and it was called the **thymele** (thigh-MEE-lee). Behind the circular orchestra was a free-standing building called the **skene** (SKAY-nay), and in front of the skene may have been a narrow raised platform where the principal actors performed, called the **proskene** (PRO-SKAY-nay). Between the seating in the theatron and the free-standing skene was a large aisle called the **parados** (PAR-a-dose), where the chorus made its ceremonial entrance at the beginning of the performance. (See Figure 9.21 for a clear illustration of this theatre layout.)

The Greek theatre building did not need any scenery, though occasionally some was used. It's obvious that a box set would have been impractical because it would block the view of the audience on the sides. A wing and drop set would have been equally impractical in this outdoor theatre with no fly space for the drops and no wing space to slide off the painted flats at the sides. Accordingly, the permanent architecture of the skene was the background against which the Greeks saw performances.

Figure 9.20 The theatre at Epidaurus, Greece, is one of the best preserved of ancient Greek theatres, and performances are given there every summer. The *orchestra* is a perfect circle, the *thymele* is in the center of the orchestra, and benches for 12,000 patrons are carved into the natural hillside.

 Photos of ancient Greek ruins make everything look white, but that's because the paint has been worn off by rain and wind. Historians assure us the buildings were colorfully painted, and that applies to the theatres, as well. Sometimes pictures were painted on the skene, and those pictures showed the audience where the action of a play was set. In later centuries, when theatres were built indoors and the entire theatre was covered over with a roof, the skene became the decorated back wall. From the ancient Greek skene comes our modern word "scenery."

While Epidaurus's original theatron and orchestra are in fine condition today, the skene is no longer there. When plays are performed there today, unit sets are installed, and they often include a back wall that replaces the missing skene.

The scripts of the ancient plays reveal that the Greeks used wagons and many of the other devices for moving scenery that we continue to use today. One of these devices is the **mechana** (MACK-ee-na), a large crane that could hoist characters into the air above the stage in pretty much the same way we fly Peter Pan in our theatres today. It was frequently used for the actors who played the roles of the gods who resolved the conflict between the mortal characters in the plays.

 A phrase heard frequently today is *deus ex machina* (DAY-ous ex MACK-ee-na). It means "god from the machine." That phrase metaphorically describes the cavalry riding in to save the settlers in a cowboy movie or the friend who helps solve homework problems. An unexpected person or event that comes to the rescue is called a *deus ex machina,* and this phrase for the contrived ending of a play dates back to the use of the crane in the ancient Greek theatre.

Figure 9.21 **a.** This ground plan of a typical Greek theatre includes the names of the important parts of the theatre. The *thymele* (altar) is in the center of the *orchestra* (the dancing circle). The *theatron* (the viewing place where the audience sat) was divided into sections, each shaped like a wedge. **b.** This illustration of an ancient Greek theatre shows the *theatron* where the audience sat (the seeing place), the *orchestra* where the chorus performed (the dancing circle), the *skene* (the stage house), and the *parados* (the passage between the *theatron* and the *skene* that the chorus used for its ceremonial entrance and exit). The *skene* in this illustration has a raised *proskene* (the platform on which the main characters performed). Note how the *theatron* is carved into the natural hillside.

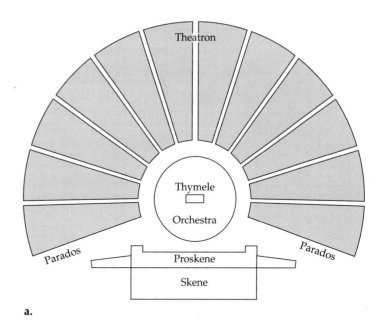

a.

b.

Several American campuses have imitation Greek theatres, and many universities perform ancient Greek dramas in the manner they were originally produced (though the actors speak English, not Greek). There are also modern plays written to be performed in outdoor settings that have circular performing areas in the Greek manner, such as the pageant *TEXAS*, shown in Color Plate 8.

The Greeks established a large colony on the island of Sicily, and the theatres they built there are still standing. In fact, much of Woody Allen's *The Mighty Aphrodite* was filmed in a Greek theatre on Sicily.

Roman Theatre

In the city of Orange, in the south of France, is the most completely preserved Roman theatre. The Romans succeeded the Greeks as the important civilization of Europe, and they must have loved drama because they built theatres everywhere. You could visit the ruins of Roman theatres in Turkey, North Africa, and Spain as well. Roman theatres are very similar to Greek ones. They're still large, and they're still open-air ampitheatres with no roofs. But the Romans built their theatres on flat ground instead of carving them out of hillsides, and they built the seating area as well, as you can see in Figure 9.22. The orchestra is now only a half circle, and the seats are connected to the skene. That makes the theatre a complete and unified structure instead of being made up of parts separated by a big aisle. The skene of this Roman theatre is huge. When it was colorfully painted, it must have been a spectacular backdrop for a play. In front of the skene is a platform big enough for a team of horses and a chariot. This platform is the proskene where the actors performed, and it's the earliest physical evidence we have of what today we call a stage.

When the Roman Empire collapsed, Western European civilization lost its centralized government and unifying culture along with its respect for such intellectual activities as reading, writing, and theatregoing. The advent of the Christian era saw theatre return to its primitive state, as local storytellers and wandering musicians entertained audiences wherever they could

Figure 9.22   The Roman theatre in Orange, France, has an enormous *skene* and *proskene* and a half-circle *orchestra*.

attract a crowd. No permanent theatres were built for a thousand years, and plays were performed on makeshift stages that were set up in a found space, in a town square, for example.

Theatre in the Middle Ages

In the Middle Ages, some plays were performed by troupes of actors and acrobats who traveled in wagons that could be converted into temporary stages. The medieval actors' wagons, as shown in Figure 9.23, were colorfully decorated so that they would attract attention, and they were practical so that they could serve the needs of the performance. A platform could be attached to the side of the wagon for the actors to perform on, and a curtain could be hung off the top of the side of the wagon facing the audience. The curtain could have a street painted on it, and then it could be removed so that a second curtain with a house painted on it could be revealed in very much the same way that a drop is revealed in wing and drop scenery. The characters could exit through this curtain and into the wagon, to rest or to change costumes. The wagon served the same purpose as the Greek skene; it was the backstage area that became known in later centuries as the tiring house.

Names can be misleading. Don't mistake a tiring house for a house where actors go to "tire" themselves out. The term "tiring house" comes from a shortening of the word "retiring" and suggests that actors exit, or "retire," when their characters go offstage, in the same way a family retires to the "withdrawing room" when they want privacy.

Figure 9.23 Wagons like this one were used in the Middle Ages by actors who traveled from town to town. The side of the wagon could be lowered and used as a stage, and the inside of the wagon became the changing room, or tiring house. The curtain at the back of the stage could be painted to suggest a particular place.

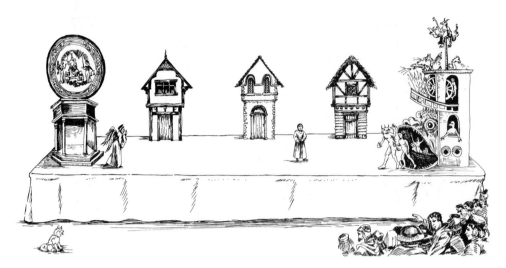

Figure 9.24 A mansion stage could be set up in a town square. It had a wide platform for the actors to perform on, and at the back were houses that could be either two-dimensional painted scenery or three-dimensional structures. Each mansion (or house) suggested a particular location. The characters could enter from one of these mansions, and the wide platform was a neutral area that permitted the actors to move about without being limited to the space in front of a particular mansion. This drawing shows the mouth of hell (and the devils coming out of it) at one end of the stage and an angel coming from heaven at the other. In the middle is the character symbolizing humankind.

In the later Middle Ages, the traveling actors' wagons, now called pageant wagons, became very elaborate; think of them as the ancestors of the parade floats you see on New Year's Day. The audience would gather at various point throughout the city, just as people today stand on street corners to admire the parade floats as they roll by. The pageant wagons would drive up to a designated place, and the actors would set up their platform stage, roll down the painted backdrop, and give a short performance; then the wagon would roll on toward its next destination while a subsequent wagon would roll up to take its place. Each wagon's performance was one scene in a long play that told a story, and the audience would remain in one place waiting for the next wagon to arrive with the next scene. The performances were presentational, as the actors would speak directly to the audience and sometimes hop off the stage and intermingle with the spectators.

If you have ever seen the end of a homecoming parade, you will have some idea of how another popular form of medieval stage might have developed. The parade concludes in a parking lot, and all the floats are lined up end to end. In the Middle Ages, all the pageant wagons may have ended up in the town square, where the largest gathering of people could admire them, and they lined up side by side so that their individual platforms combined into one very long platform. The players from each of the wagons did their

Figure 9.25 This temporary platform stage was set up in the town square of Bratislava, Slovakia. The curtain has been painted to represent a house, and the actors standing backstage, at the rear of the platform, wore costumes from the fifteenth century.

sketches, one after another, using not just their own small platform, but the entire length of the platforms that were lined up alongside each other. This kind of theatre is called a **mansion stage.**

Today the word "mansion" is used to describe a very large house, but "mansion" used to be the medieval French word for house, so the term "mansion stage" described a long stage with a number of separate houses attached to the back of it, each depicting a unique location. These houses could be built of solid materials and give the illusion of being three-dimensional, or they could be painted on the curtains at the backs of the pageant wagons. Because all these houses were visible to the audience at all times, some people describe a performance on this sort of stage as "simultaneous staging" and describe the stage itself as a "simultaneous stage," though "mansion stage" is the more accepted term. Figure 9.24 shows you what a mansion stage might have looked like.

You are not likely to see a mansion stage today, but the idea of performing in a town square is still alive, as you can see in Figure 9.25. The photo shows the temporary stage we saw in the town square of Bratislava, Slovakia, in 1995; you could also see one if you visit Oberammergau, Germany, where *The Passion Play* is presented every ten years. If you'd rather stay closer to home, you can visit Eureka Springs, Arkansas. Each summer, *The Great Passion Play* is performed there, and in its twenty-five years, more than six million people have attended (Figure 9.26).

Elizabethan Theatre

The newly built Shakespeare's Globe Theatre in London is a round wooden building with an uncovered courtyard in the middle, and from above, the theatre has the shape of the letter "O." Shakespeare's Globe Theatre is built along the lines of the theatre Shakespeare acted in, and we call it an Elizabethan

Figure 9.26 A modern mansion stage is used for *The Great Passion Play,* a religious drama presented to tens of thousands of spectators each year in Eureka Springs, Arkansas. All the different settings for the play are visible to the audience throughout the performance.

public theatre. Color Plate 9 shows a performance in this theatre. Many Shakespeare festivals across America perform in theatres based on what we think the Elizabethan public theatres were like. Two of the best known are at the Oregon Shakespeare Festival and the Utah Shakespearean Festival.

None of the original Elizabethan theatres are still standing, so no one knows precisely what they were like, but scholars do agree that these theatres were very different from the Greek and Roman theatres and from the mansion stages of the Middle Ages. The primary sources for an imaginative reconstruction of an Elizabethan public theatre include a rough sketch by a seventeenth-century tourist, a business contract that lists the dimensions of a theatre, and the texts of the plays, since they imply certain things about the stage. For example, when Shakespeare describes the theatre as a "wooden O," it's fair to guess that the original Globe Theatre was round. The drawing in Figure 9.27 may help you understand our description. You can also watch the first portion of Laurence Olivier's Academy Award–winning film version of Shakespeare's *Henry V* or the delightful Academy Award–winning movie *Shakespeare in Love.* These films give you vibrant illustrations of theatregoing in Shakespeare's time.

Elizabethan public theatres were freestanding buildings of wood and plaster. They were either round or multisided, and in the center was a large courtyard that was open to the elements. This openness meant that the

Figure 9.27 This drawing shows what an Elizabethan public theatre may have looked like.

audiences were vulnerable to the sun and rain, just the way you are today if you go to a football game. The buildings were three stories tall, and protruding into the center of the courtyard was a three-sided stage about five feet tall. The stage had at least one trapdoor in it so that characters could enter from below, and high above the stage was a sheltering roof that gave the actors some protection from the sun and rain. The roof was beautifully painted to suggest the sky, and it was called "the heavens." The poorer members of the audience who paid only a one-penny admission charge stood on the ground to watch the performance. They were called "groundlings" and were presumed to respond loudly to coarse humor and lots of action. The richer members of the audience paid a second or third penny for admission to the seats on the second or third floors, where they were protected from the elements. The platform stage thrust itself into the center of the open courtyard, creating the exciting relationship between actors and audience that we have today in a thrust theatre.

The platform stage was set up against one side of the courtyard so that there was a back wall for the actors to use for entrances. This wall had two or three doorways in it, and there was probably a small, elevated stage above the center doorway that could serve as a balcony or to suggest that the characters were standing on a hill. What is most unusual about the stage of an Elizabethan public theatre, compared to our modern theatres, is that the architectural facade remained neutral throughout the performance. The theatre building itself was a unit set that didn't require any decorative scenery. All parts of the architectural stage were continually in the audience's full view, but no part of it suggested a particular locale. Instead, the dialogue described where the action took place, and the audience imagined whatever particular location the characters said they were in. For example, when Romeo wooed Juliet, she was standing on the balcony, and the audience imagined an Italian courtyard. Indeed, Shakespeare's plays do not depend on an illusion created by scenery, costumes, or lighting. Their performance conventions were quite different from ours. To change the location of the action, one set of characters exited and another set entered through a different door. The audience immediately understood that the scene had changed. A presentational performance on an Elizabethan stage is very exciting, and once you have experienced the performance of one of Shakespeare's plays in the kind of theatre he wrote for, you will truly appreciate how exciting his plays are.

Shakespeare died in 1616; in 1642 there was a civil war in England during which the king was beheaded and the victorious Puritan government made theatre illegal. All the wood and plaster theatres fell into disuse or were torn down, and by the time King Charles II was restored to the throne in 1660, there were no more Elizabethan public theatres. This unique and functional theatre that had served Shakespeare so well was not seen again until the twentieth century, when scholars began to research what it had looked like. That research led to the construction of many Elizabethan-styled theatres in America and to the 1996 opening in London of Shakespeare's Globe Theatre.

Renaissance Theatre in Italy

About the same time that the English were building their wood and plaster theatres, the Italians were rediscovering the glories of ancient Rome. In literature, painting, and architecture, the Renaissance was in full flower. Architects saw the ruins of ancient Roman theatres all around them, and they rediscovered *De Architectura* (ar-key-tek-TOO-ra), a book by a Roman named Vitruvius (vi-TROOV-ee-us) that included lengthy descriptions of what ancient Roman theatres were like. It was translated from Latin to Italian in 1486, and in the next few years a lot of new theatres were built. Instead of slavishly imitating the ancients, however, the Italian architects made what they believed were improvements. To begin, they built their new theatres indoors so that the rich nobles who paid for them didn't have to sit outside in the rain or sun. Then, they made the new theatres smaller because they weren't open to the general public. Just as the White House in Washington has a small movie theatre for the exclusive entertainment of the President's guests, so these Italian theatres were for the exclusive entertainment of the nobleman's guests.

Just north of Venice, in the town of Vicenza (vi-CHEN-za) is the Teatro Olympico (tay-AH-tro oh-LEEM-pee-coe). It was built in 1580 and designed by the famous architect Palladio (pa-LAH-dee-oh), and it is in perfect condition

Figure 9.28 The Teatro Olympico, built in 1580, remains in perfect condition today. The theatre is indoors and very small. It has an ornate facade at the back of the stage and a half-circle orchestra.

(Figure 9.28). The ornately decorated theatre looks like it's made out of white marble, except for the ceiling, which is painted to look like the sky, complete with fluffy clouds. The theatre is small, yet it's similar in some ways to that Roman theatre in southern France. The seating is in a half circle, and so is the space in front of the stage. And the small stage is slightly raised off the floor. You couldn't bring a horse and chariot onto it, but then this whole indoor theatre seems like a miniature.

The facade of the stage is covered with columns and niches and statues and architectural details. The Teatro Olympico is more ornate than any theatre we've discussed thus far. The Greeks used to paint the front of their skene, and the Romans made the skene very ornate; now the Italians have added something new. They've let you see *through* the facade! The three archways in the skene are open, and you can see into the distance. The doors are like picture frames, and the vistas take your eye to the horizon. The facade and the stage in front of it in the Teatro Olympico are an unchanging unit set, just like the ancient Greek skene and the facade of the Elizabethan public theatre. But the painted vistas seen through the archways in the facade are changeable scenery.

Renaissance Italian painters were fascinated with the theory and practice of perspective drawing. We are so accustomed to perspective drawing today that we can't imagine drawing in any other way. But Renaissance artists like Palladio were captivated by the new idea that mathematically precise rules of spatial relations could enable the artist to draw something that appeared to have depth. And what better way to present the illusion created by perspective drawing than to put the painting in a frame! As with drawing, so with theatre. The archways in the facade of the Teatro Olympico are like the frame on a painting, and they permitted Palladio to create a vista in which two-dimensional scenery painted on flat canvas could represent a three-dimensional "real world" that we spectators could peep into.

If we moved from one seat to another, we would discover that the center arch reveals three different vistas, so that we look down a long street no matter where we sit (Figure 9.29). The floor is on an incline and the two-dimensional painted scenery on those streets gets smaller and smaller as it gets further away from the audience. This device, called forced perspective, makes the distance seem great. By making things progressively smaller, the artist can make them seem further away. If you were to walk up the central street shown in Figure 9.30, you would look like a giant, since you would be taller than the buildings.

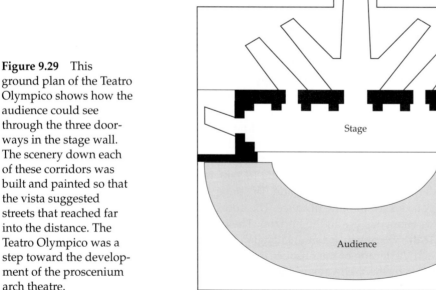

Figure 9.29   This ground plan of the Teatro Olympico shows how the audience could see through the three doorways in the stage wall. The scenery down each of these corridors was built and painted so that the vista suggested streets that reached far into the distance. The Teatro Olympico was a step toward the development of the proscenium arch theatre.

Figure 9.30   The classically inspired ornate facade of the Teatro Olympico has three archways; this photo shows the vista beyond the central arch. Notice that the floor is raked upward and that the scenery along the corridor grows smaller so that the illusion of great distance is created.

In Parma, the Teatro Farnese (far-NAY-zay) was another experiment by the Italian architects, and it is famous for having the first proscenium arch in theatre history. It's also an indoor theatre, but it's a little bigger than the Teatro Olympico. The Duke of Farnese probably wanted to outdo the Duke of Vicenza. The Teatro Farnese was built in 1618, and originally it was as ornate as the Teatro Olympico. But Parma was bombed during World War II, and the theatre was badly damaged. There are some photos of what it looked like before 1945, but today only a few parts of the walls retain their ornamentation. The rest is a plain wooden structure.

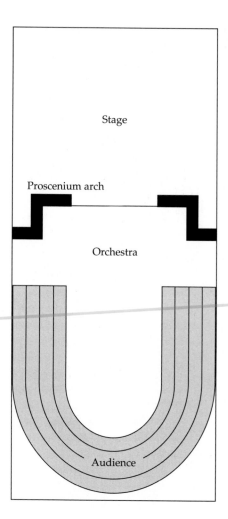

Figure 9.31   This ground plan of the Teatro Farnese shows the horseshoe seating for the audience, the large orchestra that could be flooded for mock sea battles, and the stage with its proscenium arch. Perhaps seats were placed in the orchestra, facing the stage, for performances that took place on the stage.

The seats in the Teatro Farnese and the large orchestra in front of the stage are in a horseshoe shape (Figure 9.31). On some occasions, seats may have been placed in the orchestra so the audience could see a performance on the stage; on other occasions, the orchestra was flooded and used for mock sea battles. The major feature of the Teatro Farnese is the proscenium arch that separates the stage where the actors performed from the auditorium where the audience sat. It's as though the central door in the facade of the Teatro Olympico had been made larger, and the audience was asked to watch the play through the frame around it (Figure 9.32). The scenery on the stage of the Teatro Farnese would not have been a box set, since that wasn't invented until the nineteenth century. It might have been a unit set on some occasions, but most frequently it would have been wing and drop. We know that because of the existence of drawings that show where the wings were placed. The proscenium arch was used with wing and drop scenery that was painted in perspective to create illusions that prepared the way for today's realistic theatre.

Figure 9.32 Italy's Teatro Farnese, built in 1618, was the first theatre to have a proscenium arch. Much of the ornate decoration shown here was destroyed during a bombing raid in World War II. The large orchestra in front of the stage may have been flooded for the presentation of mock sea battles.

Baroque Court Theatre

The proscenium arch theatre quickly became the only kind of theatre in Europe. Everybody loved the idea of peeking through a picture frame into the magical world on stage. The rich lord of almost every castle had a proscenium arch theatre built for his family and friends, and the merchants of almost every town built one for the townspeople's entertainment. A couple of elegant court theatres remain in perfect condition today, nearly two hundred years after they were built. The one in Cesky Krumlov (CHES-ski KROOM-lov), the Czech Republic, is particularly exquisite.

The theatre is so beautifully decorated that you feel like you're in a museum. This theatre was built in the eighteenth century, during a period that art historians call the Baroque, meaning that everything is covered with elaborate ornamentation, as you can see in Color Plate 10. The ceiling has angels flying through the sky, and the walls are painted to look like sculptured marble. So is the proscenium arch, the railing of the balcony, and the lord's box, which is in the center of the balcony. You'll notice that the orchestra in front of the stage is small and filled with benches for the audience. Over the centuries the full circle of the orchestra in the Greek theatre became a half circle in the Roman theatre, and now it's used for the audience, not the actors. The half-circle or horseshoe shape is still used for the balcony, but the main floor is now filled with seats facing the stage—the better to see the action through the picture frame of the proscenium arch. The floor of the auditorium is flat, and the spectators who sat on benches might have had trouble seeing over one another, so the stage floor is on an incline, raked upward away from the audience. As the actors moved **upstage** (away from the audience), they stood higher above the ground and could be seen by the people seated on the flat floor of the orchestra.

A large portion of the stage, called the apron, sticks out in front of the proscenium arch. In this theatre the apron is flat at the front, but in many theatres it is curved. Before the days of electric light, theatres were lit by candles, and if the actors walked very far upstage it was hard to see them. So they did most of their acting close to the audience, on the apron.

The scenery at Cesky Krumlov is wing and drop. There still exist beautifully painted wings and drops that depict outdoor and indoor scenes, and on occasions performances are given on this stage in the manner they were given two centuries ago. The theatre is lit only by candle, the actors use the ornate costumes and the wing and drop scenery of that era, and the performance creates a kind of theatrical magic that gives you goose bumps.

10

Theatrical Styles

*A*ll theatre imitates reality, but there are many ways to do that. In this chapter, we'll present six different ways that theatre imitates reality; each of these is a **style.**

"Style" is the word we use to describe *how* an artist imitates reality, and each style is based on the artist's understanding of truth. Some artists imitate reality the way a camera records it, while others imitate it abstractly, showing how they *feel* about reality. Twentieth-century artists, such as the great painter Pablo Picasso, showed us surprising ways to see reality (Figure 10.1), and they introduced us to Modern Art, the name used for much of the artistic expression of the twentieth century.

All artists are dedicated to telling us the truth as they see it, and the six styles presented in this chapter are based on six different perceptions of truth. The most familiar style, Realism, is based on the belief that we see the truth when we look at the world with a scientist's objectivity and recognize things by what they look like. Realistic theatre shows us how things appear, and it imitates "apparent reality." What you see and hear on stage imitates the world as you know it. In the theatre, you know the scenery and actors aren't real, but you pretend they are real because they imitate apparent reality. We are particularly fond of theatre that accurately replicates the world as we see it because such apparent reality is familiar. It doesn't confuse us. In fact, when we like a play, we describe it by saying it's "real." What we mean is, it's good. We judge things to be good when they appear to be real.

There are additional ways of seeing reality. When you dream, images look strange because you're seeing their subjective reality. The way you *feel* about things influences the way they look. In a nightmare, things appear distorted and threatening. In a happy dream, things seem beautiful. Those images express subjective reality, which is every bit as true as the objective reality you see when you are awake. There's a third way to perceive reality. In your imagination, you can improve on reality. You can imagine an idealized

Figure 10.1   This drawing in the style of Picasso shows the profile and the front view of a woman simultaneously. As you look at it, you can imagine that you are facing the subject or standing to the side of her. Stylized art of this kind does not seek to imitate apparent reality. Rather, it shows what the artist believes is the essential truth of the subject.

reality in which the world looks the way you wish it looked. Idealized reality shows you a third kind of truth. When theatre imitates subjective reality or idealized reality, it shows us something that does not look like apparent reality. We call those kinds of theatre stylized. Stylized theatre is not better or worse than Realism, it's merely different. When you become familiar with it, you might find that subjective reality and idealized reality show you a more compelling truth than the truth of Realism, and you might say a play is good because it's "true."

We think of stylized theatre as the opposite of Realism, but Realism is just the most familiar of the six styles. We name the six styles by the same names used in describing literature, painting, and music, and we cluster them into three groups. The first pair imitates objective reality, the second pair imitates subjective reality, and the third pair imitates idealized reality. We have used line drawings of a house to illustrate each of the six styles. The house used as a model is shown in the photograph in Figure 10.2. Each of these styles is based on a philosophic premise that leads to a theory of how truth can be shown, and each has traits you can recognize. We'll point these traits

Figure 10.2   Realism on stage would require an exact replica of this real house.

out for you so you can understand why a production looks the way it does and so you can judge how well the playwright, director, and designers have accomplished what they set out to do.

The Six Theatrical Styles

Two styles imitating *objective* reality

1. Realism
2. Theatricalism

Two styles imitating *subjective* reality

3. Expressionism
4. Surrealism

Two styles imitating *idealized* reality

5. Classicism
6. Romanticism

Most of the examples of style in this chapter will be from a play titled *Waiting for Godot*. ("Godot" is pronounced go-DOUGH by Americans, but the English and French stress the first syllable: GOD-oh). There are two productions of *Waiting for Godot* available on videotape, but those of you who have never read it or seen it will find the following description helpful.

Waiting for Godot was written by Samuel Beckett, an Irishman who lived in Paris and wrote in French. It was a strange and avant-garde play when it first appeared in 1953, but in only a few decades *Waiting for Godot* has become a classic that many people describe as the most important play written in the twentieth century.

The play takes place on a country road. The stage directions don't say which country, nor where the road leads, nor what the climate is, nor the time of day. The only distinguishing things the audience can see are a rock that's big enough to sit on, and a tree. The ground is flat, and the sky is clear. The play takes place in a barren wilderness that could be almost anywhere, as you can see in Color Plate 11.

There are five characters in the play. They all dress in old-fashioned clothes that suggest the years around the turn of the twentieth century, but their derby hats are dusty and their suits are worn and wrinkled. Their clothes make them look like bums or like the comic characters from old silent movies played by such actors as Charlie Chaplin, Buster Keaton, or Stan Laurel and Oliver Hardy.

The two main characters are Vladimir (known by his nickname, Didi) and Estragon (Gogo). Vladimir is intellectual and analytical. He continually tries to figure out where he is, what he is doing, and what things mean. He speaks in long and complex sentences, and he sometimes grows morose and despondent. By way of contrast, his companion, Gogo, is optimistic, yet very emotional and immature. He responds excitedly to whatever happens around him, and he speaks in short phrases. The two men appear to have known each other for a long time. They are waiting for another man, named Godot. They have a vague recollection that they are supposed to meet him, but they are not confident they're in the right place, nor when Godot said he would arrive, nor what he looks like. While they are waiting for Godot to arrive, they pass the time by playing games, by discussing their religious beliefs, by remembering events from their past, by looking for food, by doing exercises, by telling jokes, and by quarrelling about who Godot is and whether or not they should continue to wait for him. None of their activities brings positive results. Nothing they do leads to Godot's arrival, and they never understand why they are waiting for him or who he is. Yet they go on waiting.

Two other men arrive. One is named Pozzo (POT-zo). He carries a whip, speaks in stern commands, and thinks he is important. He is preceded by a very, very old man named Lucky. Lucky carries an armful of luggage, including a picnic basket, and he staggers under the weight of his burden. He has a noose around his neck, as you can see in Figure 10.3, and the end of the rope is held by Pozzo as if it were a leash and he is walking his dog. These two strange men arrive, and Didi and Gogo at first think that Pozzo might be Godot. When they learn he is not, they question him about a number of things, but Pozzo has no answers that make sense to them. To pass the time, they ask Pozzo to have Lucky perform for them. Lucky begins a bizarre dance, and then is given the command, "Speak." He launches into a very long speech that sounds like gibberish. Though there are phrases we can understand, there's no apparent logic to his ramblings. When he is finished, Pozzo and Lucky continue their journey. They don't know where they are headed any more than they know where they have come from. They only know they must stagger on. They leave, and Didi and Gogo are alone again. They grow

Figure 10.3   The four main characters in *Waiting for Godot.* Front row, Gogo and Didi; back row, Lucky and Pozzo.

sad. The day is ending, and Godot has not come. What should they do? Where should they go? Suddenly a young boy arrives with a message. Mr. Godot won't arrive today, but surely will tomorrow. The boy leaves as night falls and the moon rises. Didi and Gogo, having nothing else to do, talk about leaving, but just sit on the ground to wait. That's the end of Act One.

Act Two follows much the same pattern, though it is quite a bit shorter. Didi and Gogo are still waiting for Godot. They engage in pastimes that alternately entertain and depress them. Pozzo and Lucky return, but this time Pozzo is blind and Lucky can no longer speak. They stay for a much shorter time, and then stagger onward, leaving Didi and Gogo alone again, morose and dejected. The boy arrives with a similar message. Godot won't come today, but surely will tomorrow. Didi and Gogo are alone, and night falls. What should they do? They consider hanging themselves from the tree, but discover they can't. They agree to leave, but they don't. At the end of the play, they are just where they were at the beginning—alone in the wilderness, waiting for Godot.

Much of this play is very funny. Some of it is very sad. All of it stirs scholars and critics to ponder its mysteries and meaning. And in the theatre, it has fascinated and entertained audiences for half a century. Because *Waiting for Godot* has been produced in a variety of styles, it provides examples that will help you understand the six styles of theatre.

OBJECTIVE REALITY

Realism

Realism has been the dominant theatrical style of the past century, and you may never have noticed any other style. Realism is based on the philosophy called Determinism. In the late nineteenth century, scientists increased their knowledge of human biology and social scientists learned about the socio-economic pressures that influence our behavior. Their combined knowledge led to the belief that people are "determined" by forces beyond our control and that we are the product of our environment and our genetic inheritance. Our bodies and our intelligence are determined by the genes of our natural parents. Our behavior is determined by the socio-economic circumstances in which we were raised. Determinism celebrates logic and science, and it discards two ideas that had been believed for centuries: the idea that we are foreordained by God and that he has determined our nature, and the idea that we have free will and can make ourselves into whatever we wish. Rather, Determinism sees us as the victims of both natural and social forces beyond our control. Playwrights accepted Determinism as the truth of human nature, and audiences believed that they could learn the truth by studying how characters behave in a play. Like the scientist with an objective eye who looks at an insect under a microscope, an audience looks at an imitation of life through the intensifying frame of a proscenium arch. By imitating apparent reality, theatre presents examples for us to study. We analyze the characters' behavior to learn *why* they behave as they do, and that helps us understand why *we* behave as we do. Scenery and costumes imitate the rooms and clothes we see about us because these are the environmental influences that shape us. Dialogue imitates the speech of real people who have been shaped by their genetic inheritance. Realism imitates apparent reality in order to show us the truth.

You will also hear the term **Naturalism.** Realism and Naturalism are used interchangeably today, though a century ago they had slightly different meanings. Some scholars continue to insist there is a difference between the two styles, and that Naturalism imitates apparent reality in absolute detail and focuses on the ugly, unpleasant, and commonplace in our lives, while Realism imitates life selectively and may focus on the pleasant aspects of life as well as the dreary. For our purposes, both words are correct and the term "Realism" is used more frequently.

Almost all the dramas we see in the movies and on television are Realistic and imitate the world we know. We can imagine ourselves talking with the characters, driving in the cars, living in a house like the one in Figure 10.4. But

Figure 10.4 This line drawing of the real house shown in figure 10.2 is an artist's indicator of the style of Realism.

Figure 10.5 An overweight Gogo and a baldheaded Didi are dressed in realistic clothes and stand before a realistic tree in this *Waiting for Godot.*

Realism is not limited to imitating the world we live in. It can also imitate the world of an earlier time, as shown in Color Plate 12, or of an exotic place we have never visited. Realism is the style of historical dramas such as *The Lion in Winter,* where people live in houses very different from ours. Realism is the style of dramas that take place in exotic lands, such as *The Last Emperor,* where people wear clothes that are different from ours. So long as we believe that what we are seeing exists now, or existed once, or exists somewhere, the style is Realism (Figure 10.5).

> ### Reality Check of the Three Traits by Which Realism Can Be Identified
>
> - Does it look like a world you know or that you believe existed at some earlier time or in some exotic land?
> - Do the characters speak in a language that you believe people speak now or spoke at some earlier time or in some exotic land?
> - Do things happen for reasons you can understand, and is there a logic that explains why things happen the way they do?

Theatricalism

Theatricalism is based on the belief that, as Shakespeare said, "all the world's a stage and all the men and women merely players." Theatricalism shows us the truth of our world by imitating our objective imitations of it. That is, Theatricalism imitates the way theatre imitates life. Theatricalism recognizes that we are self-conscious creatures who perceive our own actions as part of a performance. We know we're acting in our everyday life, as seen in the self-conscious photo in Figure 10.6. Theatricalism shows us the truth of the self-conscious performance we call "living."

Theatricalism became a popular style in the mid-twentieth century, and a famous example of it is Thornton Wilder's play *Our Town*. In it, a character

Figure 10.6 The style of Theatricalism is demonstrated in this self-referential photo of Tom taking a photo of Linda taking a photo of Tom. Note that we are both wearing modern clothes, but that we are reflected in a mirror with an ornate rococo frame.

If this idea of life as a performance interests you, you will enjoy reading a book by Neal Gabler titled *Life the Movie*, published in 1998. It uses films such as *The Truman Show* and *EDtv* to prove its theory that we are all performers, self-consciously performing our own lives. Gabler's argument is a fine introduction to the basic idea of Theatricalism.

named The Stage Manager talks directly to the audience and tells them who the characters are and where the action is taking place. The audience sees the objective reality of an empty stage, but is asked to imagine the kitchens and the drugstore that The Stage Manager describes in words, while the actors walk about on stage, miming doors, newspapers, and ice cream sodas. The objective reality is a theatre, and the performance imitates the way theatre imitates life.

At one level, the performance is about theatre, and Theatricalism shows us how theatre creates the illusion of objective reality; that's why the stage setting in Figure 10.7 reflects the audience. The truth that Theatricalism shows us is that it's as difficult to separate illusion from reality as it is to distinguish between a real event and a theatrical imitation of it. To make this point clear, Theatricalism shows us how theatre makes its illusions: scenery is changed before our eyes, actors put on their costumes while we watch, and characters speak directly to us, explaining when they are "in" the play and when they are not. Theatricalism boasts of its self-consciousness; it is illustrated in the drawing of a house in Figure 10.8.

The description of the opening moments of a play we saw recently is a very clear description of Theatricalism:

The stage was a raised platform, and there was no curtain, so we could see "backstage." The lighting instruments, props, and furniture were in full view, and some costumes were draped on the set. The stage manager was sitting at his worktable, in full view.

The actors were wandering about, greeting us, chatting with each other. They seemed to be wearing their own clothes, not costumes. After a while, as we sensed the performance was about to begin, the actors gathered in a huddle and played spin the bottle. The man that the bottle pointed to was apparently "it," and he spoke the opening lines of the play as some of the other actors started putting on their costumes and some stagehands moved the furniture into place. The speaker told us that the actors were going to act out an old and familiar story, and on behalf of the playwright, he thanked us for being there.

Figure 10.7 Josef Svoboda is one of the most influential modern scene designers, and he created the scenery for this *Waiting for Godot* in the style of Theatricalism. The action was set in a theatre. The stage design repeated the architectural boxes of the auditorium, and the back wall was a multipaneled mirror that reflected the actors, the tree in the center of the stage, the auditorium of the theatre, and the audience.

Reality Check of the Four Traits by Which Theatricalism Can Be Identified

- Is the action set in a theatre?
- Do the characters play roles in a play-within-a-play?
- Does the production show you how the theatre works: how scenery moves, and how actors assume their characters?
- Does the play demonstrate how hard it is to distinguish between illusion and reality?

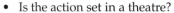
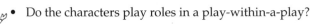
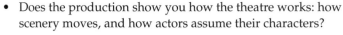

SUBJECTIVE REALITY

Expressionism and Surrealism both imitate *subjective* reality, and in order to explain them, we first need to describe the intellectual and historical context in which they evolved. The same curiosity that led some scientists to seek for truth by studying our objective experience led others to seek it by studying

Figure 10.8 The real house shown in figure 10.2 is drawn here in the style of Theatricalism. See how the house announces that it is a house.

our subjective experience. In the final decade of the nineteenth century, about twenty years after Realism was established as the dominant theatrical style, doctors such as Sigmund Freud began to study the way dreams reveal the truth of human experience and how our conscious actions are influenced by our subconscious desires. At about the same time, even though they did not have the doctors' scientific research on which to base their observations, playwrights such as August Strindberg began to write strange new dramas called "dream plays." A few decades later, these scientific and theatrical innovations inspired German playwrights to develop Expressionism and French playwrights to develop Surrealism. These playwrights were part of what is called the Modernist Movement, a development in literature, music, and the visual arts that dominated the first half of the twentieth century. Modern Art describes the arts that express the unconscious, the primitive, and the irrational instead of a faith in human reason as a tool for revealing the truth of the human condition.

Why is Modern Art dissatisfied with the truth of objective reality? These playwrights abandoned Realism because they wanted to show us the deeper truth that outward appearances hide. Expressionism and Surrealism both show us how the artist *feels* about the essential truth of the world, instead of what the artist thinks about the objective appearance of the world. Both these styles show us a distorted picture of the world and express the profound truth that the artist knows—the truth that you may have never recognized or that you have tried to ignore.

The difference between the objective and subjective realities is the subject of *The Picture of Dorian Gray,* a wonderful story by Oscar Wilde that was made into a fine movie. Dorian Gray is a handsome and honorable young man who has his portrait painted. When he sees how admirable he looks, he wishes he could remain like that forever and that the painting would change. He gets his wish. To the astonishment
(Continued)

(*Continued*)

of everyone, Dorian never changes in his outward appearance. But as he becomes more and more debauched and evil, the painting changes. It shows his inward truth, which is very different from his outward appearance. Dorian hides the painting in the attic, and at the end of the story he stabs it. The painting reverts to show the handsome and pure young man, but Dorian turns into the grotesque and bloody monster that he is in truth. Only then is his subjective reality seen by others. Until then, they have been deceived by the appearance of his objective reality.

Expressionism

Expressionism is a style that developed in early twentieth-century Germany after doctors discovered that we can learn the truth by analyzing the images in our dreams. Expressionism is based on the belief that dreams reveal the truth that we hide from ourselves in our waking state. The wildly distorted images that we see when we dream are what we truly feel (Figure 10.9). Dream images are our honest perception of reality. When we are able to analyze the distorted images of our dreams, we learn the truth.

Expressionism depicts violent and extreme emotions because it developed at a time when artists felt frightened by the way big government and big industry were using people. The average human was being turned into a cog in a big machine that produced money but oppressed individuality. Expressionists were angry, and they created theatre that showed their terror of the way humankind was losing its freedom. As a result, Expressionistic theatre

Figure 10.9 The real house shown in figure 10.2 is drawn here in the style of Expressionism. The distorted shape and severe angles suggest the artist's emotional reaction to the house.

Figure 10.10   The 1919 film *The Cabinet of Dr. Caligari* is an excellent example of Expressionism. Note the sharp angles in the design, the high contrast in the black-and-white composition, and the actors' exaggerated makeup. This picture shows the moment in the story when the dummy is discovered in the box.

has an angry tone and a shocking manner. It shows the world as a terrifying nightmare, as you can see in the still photo from the classic film *The Cabinet of Dr. Caligari* (Figure 10.10). Expressionists feared that a conflict between capitalist businesses would lead to war and that war would crush the average person. When World War I broke out in 1914, they saw that their nightmares had come true.

The painter Edvard Munch wrote this description of the experience that led him to paint the famous Expressionist painting *The Scream:* "I walked along the road with two friends. Then the sun went down. All of a sudden the sky became blood. I stopped, leaned against the railing, weary to death. Over the dark fjord and the city lay clouds dripping with blood. My friends went on, I remained behind, trembling, with an open wound in my breast, and sensed a surging cry throughout nature." *The Scream* shows how Munch felt subjectively instead of what he observed through his objective eye.

Expressionism was born when theatre developed the techniques for showing subjective truth in objective form. The first technique of Expressionism is to show the world through the eyes of the central character. Since

Figure 10.11 This Expressionistic scene design for *Waiting for Godot* has sharp angles and stark contrasts; it creates a world that presses dangerously on the place where Didi and Gogo wait.

Expressionists viewed people (and therefore their central characters) as the victims of an oppressive industrial society, their central characters saw a world that threatened them. This view led to scenery, costumes, and makeup that used highly contrasting or extremely intense colors (reds and oranges and blacks) or that had sharp angles that seemed about to stab the characters, as in Figure 10.11. A second trait is that only the central character is psychologically complex. All the other characters are seen through the central character's eyes and are symbols with a single trait. Their names describe their jobs (The Doctor, The Policemen) or their relationship to the central character (The Friend, The Seducer). A third trait is that the dialogue does not sound like real speech. Instead, it is filled with angry descriptions of violence, and it is frequently compressed so that it sounds like a message you'd find on a Post-it note: "DOWNER NEWS. MALL. BACK 7. DINNER OUT." You can reconstruct the entire message from these fragments and understand what was meant: "I have received some very distressing news, and I have gone to the mall. I will be back around seven o'clock. Why don't we plan to have dinner at a restaurant instead of eating at home?" In Expressionism, a character's emotion is often so extreme that he or she cannot speak in grammatically complete sentences.

A fine example of Expressionism is *The Cabinet of Dr. Caligari,* a silent film made in Germany in 1919. It begins with a young man named Francis sitting on a park bench, talking with another man. A young woman, apparently a sleepwalker, walks past in silence. Francis explains she is his fiancée and adds that the couple has had a terrible experience. He tells their story to his companion.

Though you may not realize it until the final moments of the film, what happens next is shown from the young man's point of view. The

(Continued)

(*Continued*)

strangely distorted houses and streets, the exaggerated makeup on the actors, and the events of the plot are all shown through Francis's eyes. You are seeing his subjective view of the world.

As the story unfolds, you learn that Francis is engaged to the young woman and that they visit a fair where one of the exhibits is run by an evil-looking man named Dr. Caligari. For a fee, Dr. Caligari shows people a man named Cesare (CHEZ-ar-ay) who has been asleep for twenty-three years. Caligari keeps Cesare in a box that looks like a coffin. For an additional fee, Caligari awakens Cesare so people can ask him questions. Cesare knows the future and predicts that Francis's close friend Alan will die before the next morning. The prediction comes true. Indeed, it is the second mysterious death in two days, and the police suspect Caligari and Cesare. Francis begins his own investigation of the murders. The next night, Caligari sends Cesare to murder the young woman, but when he stands over the sleeping girl, Cesare can't go through with it. Instead, he carries her away through the angled and darkened streets. Cesare is captured, and the girl is rescued. Everyone converges on Caligari's home, but they find Cesare is still there, sleeping in his box. Then they discover that the body in the box is only a dummy. The real Cesare is still on the loose. Caligari escapes and is chased into a large building that is an asylum for mental patients. As Francis and the police search for Caligari, they discover a 200-year-old book by a Swedish doctor named Caligari who wrote about conducting experiments to learn whether someone who has been hypnotized can be commanded to do something that would be against his or her will when awake. Francis and the police realize that Cesare had been hypnotized and that the evil Caligari, who has been conducting the same experiments, is actually the chief doctor of the insane asylum who has adopted the name Caligari in imitation of the Swedish doctor. Francis and the police continue to search for Caligari, but when he appears, he looks dignified, like the head of the asylum should. All the nurses and guards respect him.

You suddenly realize that the events you have just seen are Francis's version of the truth. Francis is actually a patient in the asylum, and the entire story is his paranoid version of the world. The young woman is not his fiancée, she is merely another patient. The chief doctor is not an evil man. Francis's subjective reality has been given objective form.

You are not likely to see an example of Expressionism in the theatre today, but you'll find an Expressonistic sequence in the film *Casino Royale*, a spoof of James Bond movies. And some violent video games are Expressionistic. In them, you see the world subjectively, as the villains come to get you, and the garish colors, sharp angles, and distorted proportions of the virtual world are nightmarish. Expressionism is no longer the startling theatrical innovation that it was eighty years ago, so if your local college revives an Expressionistic play such as *The Adding Machine,* take advantage of the opportunity to see it. You may be excited to discover how this fascinating style affects you.

Reality Check of the Four Traits by Which Expressionism Can Be Identified

- Are the scenery, costumes, and makeup distorted, and do the designs use intense colors and sharp angles?
- Do the characters speak in short and fragmented dialogue?
- Do most of the characters have names that describe what they do rather than individualized names?
- Is the tone of the play angry, and does the central character seem to be a tormented victim?

Surrealism

Surrealism developed in France in the peaceful years following World War I. Surrealism is based on the belief that the images in our subconscious reveal the truth and that the truth can be beautiful, lyrical, and sometimes very funny. Instead of rendering the dark nightmares of Expressionism, Surrealism puts on stage the fantastical and whimsical images from our subconscious (Figure 10.12).

Surrealists did not seek subjective truth exclusively in dreams. They also believed that they could release the images in their subconscious when

---

Alfred Hitchcock made a suspense film with Gregory Peck and Ingrid Bergman called *Spellbound,* and in the middle of it is a dream sequence based on the designs of Salvador Dali, a famous Surrealist painter. Dali's visual rendering of the dream complements the explanation in the dialogue of how a psychoanalyst helps a patient understand the meaning of a dream; the sequence provides us with a wonderful demonstration of Surrealism. We see how the dreamer turns a ski slope into the roof of a house, how a revolver is seen by the dreamer as a wheel, and how the psychoanalyst's analysis of the dream images helps the dreamer understand the truth in just the same way that an analysis of the clues at a crime scene helps a detective find a murderer. We urge you to watch *Spellbound.*

Figure 10.12 The real house shown in figure 10.2 is drawn here in the style of Surrealism. The artist has shown a dreamlike and playful attitude in which the chimney becomes a human form, the window winks at you, and the stairs have turned into a long tongue.

they were awake if they could find a way to keep their conscious minds from intervening or censoring the creative process. Surrealists sought ways to put themselves into a trance that would permit their subconscious to express itself directly. Some tried hallucinogenic drugs, some tried fasting, others tried staying awake until their minds lost their rational controls. In these states of heightened sensitivity, many Surrealists tried "automatic writing," writing down on paper whatever came directly from their subconscious. Painters tried the same sort of activity, putting on canvas images that seem jumbled or strangely juxtaposed. These efforts produced some of the most exciting art of the twentieth century. Figure 10.13 shows a production of *Waiting for Godot* that was conceived in the Surrealist style.

Surrealism has five recognizable traits. First, Surrealism's dream images are curves, not angry angles, and they are usually in pretty, pastel colors. Second, the pressure of space and time is relaxed, and things happen slower and

Surrealism has a playful tone and a lyrical manner, and many of the plays written by Surrealists defy staging. Consider this stage direction from a play called *En Gggarrrde!* (Pernod with Sugar is a licorice-tasting alcoholic drink that is very popular in French cafés. Naming a character Pernod with Sugar is like naming that character Gin and Tonic.)

The individuals on the raft stand on their heads—The Pernod with Sugar, discreetly, disappears inside a sea gull, whistling an obscene tune. An animated cartoon could show this but it's impossible to stage this action in the live theatre. The author of this play was joking around, entertaining his readers by stimulating their imaginations, but he never expected this stage direction to be realized on stage.

Figure 10.13 Note the curved lines, uncluttered space, and whimsical mood of this Surrealistic design for *Waiting for Godot*. The unrealistic costumes and scenery are painted to intensify the surreal style.

seem to have more space around them than they do in objective reality. Surrealism's dream images are cheery and unthreatening. Third, images change into other images right before our eyes. Just as in a dream, a beast can turn into a handsome prince. There is a playfulness to the metamorphosis of objects in a Surrealist's dream.

A fourth trait of Surrealism is the transformation of words into pictures, usually in a whimsical way. The saying "time hangs heavy" can be rendered visually as a clock hanging heavily off the edge of a table. Salvador Dali painted many pictures exploiting this verbal-visual joke; color plate 13 shows you the best known.

One day Linda was working in her studio, and the sun was streaming in the window. She asked me to draw the blind. Instead of pulling the cord, I scribbled something on a piece of paper and handed it to her. I had transformed words into pictures. Figure 10.14 shows you how I had "drawn the blind."

Figure 10.14   My drawing of the blind.

The fifth and final trait of Surrealism is that its logic is associative as opposed to causal. Logic is the word used to describe the relationship of ideas or events. Causal logic describes a relationship in which one thing causes something else to happen: you fail a test because you did not attend class or read the assignments. Associative logic, by way of contrast, describes how your mind moves from one idea to another through the associations between the two ideas instead of through direct causation. You think of the state of Utah, and you associate Utah with Mormons, and you associate Mormons with Brigham Young, and Young with children, and children with toys, and toys with games, and games with sports, and sports with television, and television with commercials, and commercials with beer. Whoa! How'd you get from thinking about the Mormons in Utah to thinking about beer? By associative logic. Associative logic is the way a creative mind works, and causal logic is the way an analytic mind works. The sequence of events in a Surrealistic play may puzzle you at first because one event is not caused by another. Instead, one event is associated with another, and that association leads to a plot that is very much like the sequence of events in a dream. To understand the plot of a Surrealistic play, you have to analyze the play as a whole just the way a psychoanalyst must consider a dream as a whole. The dreamer is the key to the meaning of the symbols in a dream, and the playwright is the key to the meaning of the symbols in a Surrealistic play.

You are not likely to see any pure examples of Surrealism in the theatre today, but you'll see it in other arts. Surrealism may no longer be the startling innovation in the theatre that it was sixty years ago, but you'll see it almost every day in music videos, in TV movies like *Alice in Wonderland*, and even in ads in magazines.

 An ad for Grand Marnier, the after-dinner liqueur, is in the Surrealist style. It shows a forest of large trees and very large oranges on the ground that seem to be six feet tall. The tree in the center has a woodpecker sitting on it that has pecked away a large portion of the trunk to reveal a bottle of Grand Marnier inside. The tree has been transformed into a bottle, and the oranges suggest the liqueur's flavor by associative logic.

Reality Check of the Five Traits by Which Surrealism Can Be Identified

- Are the scenery, costumes, and makeup distended into curved and swirling images that have unusual proportions, and is there a lot of open space in what you see?

- Do people or objects change their appearance before your eyes, and turn into other images?

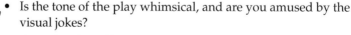

- Is the tone of the play whimsical, and are you amused by the visual jokes?

- Does the play offer an altered sense of time, with some events happening faster or slower than they do in life?

- Does the logic of the sequence of events seem very difficult to follow?

Postmodernism is a term that describes the innovations in artistic expression in the years since Modern Art lost its vogue. In the theatre, Postmodernism is a development that blends some of the characteristics of both Theatricalism and Surrealism, and it has three very recognizable traits. The first of these traits is that the scenery is done in an abstract manner, similar to Surrealism, that is called imagistic design. The second trait is that the costumes are an eclectic mixture of historical eras and national dress that are reminiscent of Theatricalism because these costumes could coexist only in the theatre. The third trait is that the performance distorts our sense of time and creates a self-consciousness that keeps us aware that we are seeing a performance and should not suspend our disbelief. We'll elaborate on each of these three traits so you can recognize Postmodern theatre when you encounter it.

For those American theatregoers who are middle-aged and grew up viewing Realism, the scenery of Postmodern theatre is weird and confusing. But for theatregoers who grew up viewing MTV, it should be very welcome. Consider this TV commercial. You see a close-up shot of a chain-link fence. Through the fence, you see a cement slab. In the background, you hear New Age music and the muffled sounds and voices of men playing a sport. In slow motion, some water swooshes across the screen. You hear the reverberating sound of a basketball going through a net, followed by the distant cheers of a crowd. The Nike swoosh appears on the screen. This commercial is an example of imagistic design. You never hear a voice selling you a product; you never even see a basketball shoe. Your mind assembles this sequence of aural and visual images. The sounds tell you that a basketball game is being played, and you realize that the water mov-

(Continued)

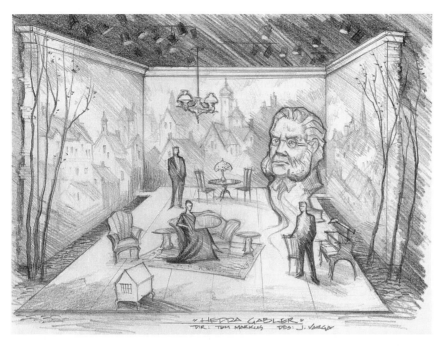

Figure 10.15 An imagistic scene design for *Hedda Gabler.* The floor of the room seems to swirl out of the oversized statue of playwright Henrik Ibsen, and the painted cityscape surrounding the room reinforces the dreamlike quality of the production.

(*Continued*)

ing in slow motion is the sweat from a player. The Nike swoosh puts the image of a basketball shoe in your head. Imagistic design is easiest to use on film and video, but it can be used on the stage as well.

The second trait of Postmodernism is that the costumes are a jumble from many historical eras and from many different cultures. A Japanese samurai warrior appears alongside a twentieth-century European business executive and a Native American in traditional buckskins. Some characters wear clothes that mix eras and cultures together: an Egyptian galabiya, a Roman military helmet, and Nike running shoes. This jumble creates a visual world that never existed, a world that exists only now, in the theatre.

The third trait of Postmodernism is that time unfolds more slowly or more quickly than it does in "real" life. One character might move in slow motion while others move at a normal rate. The tension between their tempos makes the audience aware that actions can be experienced in different ways simultaneously.

Here's a description of a production of Henrik Ibsen's *Hedda Gabler* that Tom directed and for which Linda designed the costumes. The play is traditionally produced as an example of Realism, with a box set representing a sitting room in Norway in 1890 and with the characters wearing the appropriate clothes of the period, speaking in everyday language, and behaving in a normal way. But Figure 10.15 shows that the setting for our production had a raked floor with sparse furniture
(*Continued*)

(Continued)

and no walls. Surrounding the floor was a sepia-toned painting of a city. The setting included a ten-foot-tall statue of General Gabler instead of the painting of Hedda's father that the script describes and that traditional productions have hanging on a wall. Although the statue was referred to as General Gabler, many in the audience recognized that it was in truth a sculpture of the playwright Ibsen. While all the other characters ignored the statue, Hedda saw it as the same huge object that the audience did. At moments, while other characters were speaking normally, Hedda would move toward that statue in slow motion as though she were living at a different tempo. This action altered the audience's perception of time. Although most of the dialogue was spoken in a traditional manner, sometimes a short sequence of lines was spoken over again, as though there had been a time warp. The audience's sense of time was disrupted. At selected moments in the production, the characters—instead of speaking to one another in the representational manner—would continue their dialogue while facing straight toward the audience in the presentational manner. The characters were lit in eerie green spotlights that took them out of the world of the play and into their own minds at the same time that the dialogue continued as though the audience was not seeing what it imagined it was seeing. The audience experienced several actions simultaneously. To further disrupt and alter the audience's perceptions and to move the audience from an intellectual to an emotional experience of the play's dramatic action, the characters were costumed in an eclectic manner. Some were dressed as though the action was taking place in 1890, and others as though the year was 1990. One wore a suit from the 1920s with running shoes from the 1990s.

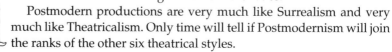

Postmodern productions are very much like Surrealism and very much like Theatricalism. Only time will tell if Postmodernism will join the ranks of the other six theatrical styles.

IDEALIZED REALITY

Before the Expressionism and Surrealism of Modern Art, even before the advent of Realism in the late nineteenth century, artists showed us the truth of idealized reality. The two styles that prevailed from ancient Greek times to the mid-nineteenth century were Classicism and Romanticism.

Classicism

Classicism is based on the belief that we can learn the truth if we use our powers of reason to create an ideal world. A first step in that path is to adhere to the motto of the ancient Greeks: "moderation in all things." Classicism rejects excess, whether in human emotions or architectural design, and it celebrates the control we can assert by using our reason. Classicism approves of balance and proportion in all things, including architecture, human behavior, or forms of government. Those items that are proportionate and in balance are good, those that are out of proportion and balance are not. Classicism believes that the truth of an idealized reality can be known when we use our willpower to create an ideal world, and the first step in doing that is to achieve perfect moderation and balance. Take a look at Figure 10.16 for an illustration of classical architecture.

Classicism leads painters and sculptors to display the ideally proportioned human form. All those statues from ancient Greece that we see in museums were sculpted to show idealized humans whose heads are exactly one-eighth the height of the total figure. Although the sculptors knew we humans aren't perfectly proportioned, they made art that showed the ideal we aspire to. Classicism also leads architects to use mathematically precise proportions in designing their buildings, citizens to form a government that resists the centralization of power, and playwrights to demonstrate how disaster befalls characters who are guilty of extreme behavior. Excessive pride—the Greek word for it is **hubris**—was wrong, the Greeks believed. The central characters of Classical drama struggle to maintain rational control over their natural impulses, and the plays teach a moral: moderation is the path to happiness.

In design, Classicism is a formal and austere style that evokes the essence of ancient Greece. Classicism's scenery employs the vertical columns and horizontal steps associated with ancient Greek architecture, and the purest Classical design has perfectly symmetrical balance. Color Plate 14 shows classical costumes that evoke the long lines and draped garments worn in ancient Greece. Even new plays done in the style of Classicism will make us think of ancient Greece.

The language of Classical drama is elevated in tone and form. Instead of imitating the everyday speech of Realism, the characters speak in formally structured sentences in order to demonstrate how people *ought* to speak. If our willpower directs our minds, we will speak in an idealized manner and engage in philosophical debates. Classical dialogue frequently takes the form

Figure 10.16   The real house shown in figure 10.2 is drawn here in the style of Classicism. Note the exact symmetry and the formal use of columns, triangular pediments, and perfectly proportioned rectangles.

> ## Reality Check of the Four Traits by Which Classicism Can Be Identified
>
> - Do the scenery and costumes remind you of ancient Greece? Are they formal? Do they approach symmetrical balance?
> - Do the characters speak in formal language, and do they engage in intellectual debates?
> - Is the central character asserting willpower in an effort to control basic impulses?
> - Is the tone of the play austere and intellectual?

of an intellectual debate between two characters who express opposing ideas, and the ideal is the moderate point between their positions.

Classicism originated in the fifth century B.C.E., and we associate it with the art and thought of ancient Athens. But Classicism has remained a popular style down through the centuries, and it has risen in prominence whenever people believed they could improve on nature by shaping the world to their own vision of moderation and balance. In seventeenth-century France, playwrights wrote plays of perfect balance about characters from Greek mythology. In nineteenth-century America, architects returned to Classicism, and many university administration buildings are in the Classical style.

Classicism's quest for an idealized reality was challenged in the eighteenth century when the concept of the unique individual captured our imaginations. The unique individual is free to pursue his or her natural self and is not constrained by reason. During the Renaissance, people began to think that the willful constraints of Classicism opposed the natural freedom of the individual, and they began to suspect that Classicism did not reveal the truth. Rather, truth could be found by throwing off the intellectual straitjacket of Classicism and celebrating the ecstasy of the quest for perfection.

Romanticism

Romanticism is based on the belief that truth is shown in our idealized image of perfection. The truth we experience in everyday life and the truth that Classicism offers are the result of thought and are very different from the image of perfection we *feel* is true. We feel that people should be beautiful and happy, that we should all speak elegantly, and that our houses and our clothes should be beautiful. Like Classicism, Romanticism shows us an idealized reality, but it's an image of perfection that is based on our emotions, not our reason.

Romanticism sets its stories "long ago and far away," in bygone historical eras or in mythical times and magical locales where things are the way we *want* them to be. Romantic stories take place in the long-ago time of Gandhi or in the imagined future of Luke Skywalker; they take place in King Arthur's mythical court or the magical palace in Sinbad's Bagdad. The objective reality of our own world is disappointing, so we escape to the idealized truth of a better time and place.

Because we feel that the average human is a compromiser and is not as admirable as a hero who seeks perfection, Romantic playwrights create characters who are exceptional. Romantic heroes never give up their ideals, even when common sense says they'll fail. Their actions are motivated by emotion, not rational thought, and we're swept up in their emotions. Romantic heroes act to "do good" for society and others, and they are not interested in personal gain. When Romantic heroes suffer, we admire them and wish we had their courage. Some Romantic heroes are based on historical people, but the myth overshadows the real biographical details, and we know them only through their legend. The real Roman slave named Spartacus may have kicked his dog for all we know, but the Romantic hero that Kirk Douglas played in the movie *Spartacus* lived and died for the noble cause of freeing the slaves.

Romantic heroes seek to be unique, to be true to themselves no matter the cost; a good example of a Romantic hero is Don Quixote in the musical *The Man of La Mancha* (Figure 10.17). We admire his quest for perfection even when we know he cannot attain his goal. The effort to achieve the ideal embodies the truth of Romanticism: that the image of perfection is the most valuable truth we have.

In Romantic tragedies, we admire the effort of the heroes who fail to attain the ideal. In Romantic comedies, we identify with the heroes who get what they go after even though we know that in the real world they would not succeed. Indiana Jones finds the Holy Grail only in a Romantic story, for we know that in reality he would have been killed. Luke Skywalker can kill the embodiment of evil only in a Romantic tale.

 The pinnacle of Romantic theatre may be the song "The Impossible Dream" from *The Man of La Mancha.* Listen to that song again, and think about the lyrics.

The supporting characters in Romantic drama are perfect in their own ways. Some are perfectly heroic and so they are handsome; others are perfectly evil and so they are grotesque; still others are the villain's perfect victims and so they are entirely vulnerable. The supporting characters in Romantic drama are closer to stereotypes than to individuals because they show us the idealized reality by which we can quickly know their truth.

These idealized characters speak in idealized dialogue, and the language of Romantic theatre is the opposite of the vulgar language of Realism. It is "elevated" over the everyday prose you and I speak because it includes beautiful visual images and artfully balanced diction; sometimes it is in formal poetry. Some of the greatest professions of love are those Cyrano speaks to Roxanne in *Cyrano de Bergerac,* a glorious example of Romanticism.

Figure 10.17 Don Quixote is the title character in *The Man of La Mancha.* When he sings, "To dream the impossible dream," he sings the central message of Romanticism.

Instead of the formal and mathematically precise architecture of Classicism, the architecture of Romanticism builds out of curved lines that swirl toward heaven, like the spire atop the drawing of the house in Figure 10.18. Instead of plays written according to rational guidelines, Romantic plays are thrilling adventures that jump from one location to another, that have several subplots, and that flip-flop between happy and sad scenes, ultimately soaring to great emotional heights. These sprawling and swirling plays show us that truth is found through a quest for the ideal.

Figure 10.18 The real house shown in figure 10.2 is drawn here in the style of Romanticism. Note the ornate decoration and the swirling spire that reaches toward heaven in this artist's notion of an idealized house.

Reality Check of the Four Traits by Which Romanticism Can Be Identified

- Is the action set in an exotic and distant historical era, or in a mythical time and magical locale?
- Do the characters speak in "elevated" language?
- Is the central character striving toward an ideal that he or she could never achieve in reality?
- Are you swept up in the thrilling emotions of the story?

IDENTIFYING THEATRICAL STYLE

Recognizing the traits of the various styles helps us understand how a play affects us and how the playwright sees the world. Begin your analysis of a play by asking yourself if the play was an example of Realism or if it was intentionally stylized. If it was stylized, think through the various styles to see which best describes the play. Use the reality checks we've provided throughout this chapter; Figure 10.19 may also be helpful. Once you have identified the play's theatrical style, you can decide whether the production succeeded or failed in what it set out to do. You will be able to understand why you liked the play or why you didn't. By the way, very few plays are done purely in one style. Theatre mixes styles the way a chef mixes the ingredients of a stew.

Realism

Theatricalism

Figure 10.19 Realism on stage would require an exact replica of this real house. The line drawings surrounding this photo illustrate each of the six styles.

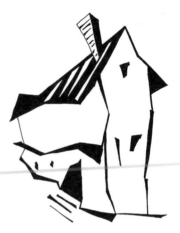

Expressionism

Romanticism

Surrealism

Classicism

Not one of the six artistic styles is any better than the others; each is merely a distinct way in which artists strive to present the truth. Some artists imitate objective reality and create works in the styles of Realism and Theatricalism, some imitate subjective reality and create in the styles of Expressionism and Surrealism, and some imitate idealized reality and create in the styles of Classicism and Romanticism. Still other artists create using more than one style in a single play.

The more you know about the varying styles, the more you can open yourself to the unfamiliar and potentially exciting truths of the performance unfolding before you.

ANALYZING STYLE   *Exercise*

Choose a theatrical production that you have recently attended, and provide the title of the play and the names of the director, the scene designer, and the costume designer. Name the theatrical style that *best* describes this production. Discuss three or more traits of that style that you recognized in the scene design or costume design and that support your choice.

11

The Elements & Principles of Theatrical Design

The language of design begins with the names of the four **elements of design**—color, line, mass, and texture—and continues with the names of the five **principles of design**—focus, balance, proportion, rhythm, and unity. These familiar words have very specific meanings in the language of design and are used by more than theatre designers. These elements and principles are used by fine artists who give us pleasure through their paintings and sculptures, by fashion designers, and by architects who design the houses we want to live in.

In this chapter, we provide you with an understanding of how design influences your theatrical experience. We will be using the set design for the play *Waiting for Godot* that is shown in Color Plate 11 as a basis for our explanations of the four elements and five principles of design, because this design is very bold and provides very clear illustrations.

The Four Elements of Design

1. Color
2. Line
3. Mass
4. Texture

The Five Principles of Design

1. Focus
2. Balance
3. Proportion
4. Rhythm
5. Unity

ELEMENTS OF DESIGN

Color

Nature wrote the first guidebook to color; nature contains bright colors and dull ones, common colors and rare ones. Some combinations of colors are more pleasing to us than others depending on what colors have surrounded us in our lives. People in the tropics have learned to like the combination of red and orange because of the brightly colored flowers and birds there. Those colors may seem garish to Scandinavians, who may prefer the tasteful combination of pale violet and pastel yellow that they see on the wild flowers in the parks. Nature has taught us that some colors go well together, but others don't. When theatrical designers use this first element of design, they know how to manipulate it to influence how we think and feel about what we're seeing on the stage.

We respond to color both physiologically and psychologically. Physiologically, the wavelengths of the various colors have a direct impact on our optic nerves. The longer the wavelength, the more agitating the color; the shorter the wavelength, the more soothing the color. Blue and green have short wavelengths, and that's why bedrooms and hospitals are painted blue or green. The long wavelengths of the color red agitate us as much as the piercing sounds from a shrieking car alarm. We respond physiologically to colors without knowing it.

Our psychological responses to color have been learned from childhood. We associate certain ideas or emotions with each color. There's a marvelous song from the musical *Pal Joey* that deals with this idea. It's titled "That Terrific Rainbow," and here are the lyrics:

> My life had no color
> Before I met you.
> What could have been duller,
> The times I went through?
> You lowered my resistance
> And colored my existence.
> I'm happy and unhappy too.
> I'm a red hot mama,
> But I'm blue for you.
> I get purple with anger
> At the things you do.
> And I'm green with envy
> When you meet a dame.
> But you burn my heart up
> With an orange flame.
> I'm a red hot mama,
> But you're white and cold.
> Don't you know your mama
> Has a heart of gold?

Though we're in those gray clouds,
Some day you'll see
That terrific rainbow
Over you and me.

The "terrific rainbow" that shapes our psychological responses is the first and most important element of design: color.

Most of us associate the color red with anger, or passion, or violence, or danger—but we don't imagine a bride getting married in a red dress. In India, however, red is a common color for a wedding dress. The color red has a very different connotation for people from that culture than it has for those of us from a European or North American background. Your psychological responses to color are learned from your culture.

Scientists have discovered three colors that cannot be created by mixing other colors together. These colors, called the primary colors, are red, blue, and yellow. The color wheels in Figure 11.1 and Color Plate 15 show only the three primary colors, but of course many other colors exist. Red can be manipulated to make colors ranging from pastel pink through deep burgundy, for example, and yellow can be manipulated to make colors ranging from eggshell to brown. For a better understanding of color and how it influences our response to a theatrical performance, let's look at the three properties of color.

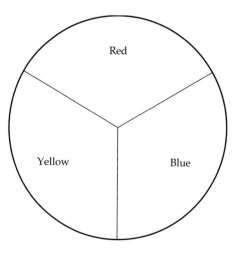

Figure 11.1 Color wheel: the three primary colors of red, blue, and yellow.

The Three Properties of Color

1. Hue
2. Intensity
3. Value

Hue   Hue is the name of the color: red, for example, or blue, or yellow. Each hue describes a scientifically precise manipulation of that color. Every hue has a precise wavelength, which is how the eye distinguishes it from another hue. Each pixel on our computer screens has a hue that has been determined by a precise measuring of its wavelength.

Here's a wrinkle: black and white are not hues, though we commonly speak of them as though they were. If you take an artist's box of paint tubes and make an equal dab from each color on a blank piece of paper, one hue on top of another, the result will be black. If you don't make any dabs from any of the paint tubes, the result will be a pristine page: white. White is the absence of hues, and black is the presence of all hues.

An infinite range of hues can be achieved by mixing hues. When we mix equal amounts of two primary hues, we make a new hue. Red mixed with yellow creates orange; red mixed with blue creates violet; blue mixed with yellow creates green. These three hues are called the secondary hues (Figure 11.2 and Color Plate 16).

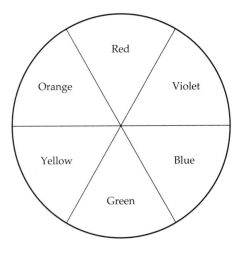

Figure 11.2   Color wheel: the secondary colors of violet, green, and orange.

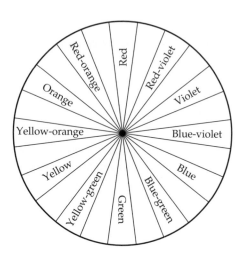

Figure 11.3 Color wheel: twenty-four hues.

We can make a new hue by mixing any two adjacent hues, and it is named by hyphenating the names of the hues we mixed. For example, if we mix the primary hue of yellow with the secondary hue of green, we get a hue called yellow-green that looks like the hue of a Granny Smith apple. We could expand the color wheel indefinitely by mixing new hues, but a wheel with twenty-four hues is the most common one (Figure 11.3 and Color Plate 17).

For centuries, people gave colors whatever name they wanted. A dress that was the same color as the round tropical fruit was said to be the color orange. Another dress that was the same color as a jack o'lantern was said to be the color pumpkin. These names were imprecise, because what you see as pumpkin may look like orange to me, and who can distinguish between scarlet, vermillion, and fire-engine red? If you've ever brought home a navy blue coat and discovered that it didn't match your navy blue slacks, then you know how confusing color names can be.

Early in the twentieth century, artists realized the value of a standardized way to describe hues, so they established a codified system in which only the primary and secondary hues have identifying names: red, orange, yellow, green, blue, and violet. All other hues are given the hyphenated names of the hues they were made from: red-orange, for example, or blue-green. Although imprecise names like puce, chartreuse, and peach are still used to market products in the fashion and automobile industries, serious artists have abandoned such vague descriptions and use only the precise name that defines a particular hue that has been created by the exact manipulation of the primary colors.

Certain hues grab our attention more than others. We describe red or orange as "warm" hues, and blue or green as "cool" hues. When we see them next to each other, warm hues seem to advance toward us while cool hues seem to recede. The scene designer for *Waiting for Godot* used the warm hue of red-orange for the earth and the cool hue of blue for the sky so that the ground would seem close to the audience and the sky would seem distant.

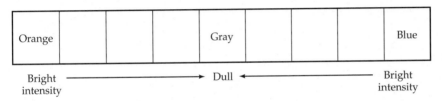

Figure 11.4 Intensity bar.

Intensity Intensity describes the relative brightness or dullness of a hue. A hue is at its brightest intensity when it is pure. A pure hue becomes duller when it is mixed with the hue that is exactly opposite it on the color wheel. The pure hues that are directly opposite one another on the color wheel are called opposite hues. If we add equal amounts of the opposite hues of blue and orange, for example, we will get gray. Figure 11.4 and Color Plate 18 show that as the two opposite hues of blue and orange are mixed in progressive amounts, their intensity is reduced and they seem duller.

Because the intensity of a hue can have an impact on us, the designer of *Waiting for Godot* selected intensities that guided the audience's emotional response. The earth has a hue of red-orange, but it has a dull intensity because the red-orange was mixed with its opposite, blue-green. Consequently, the earth looks grayed out and muddy, whereas the blue sky has a bright intensity and seems more exciting.

Value Value describes the relative lightness or darkness of a hue. The value of a hue is *raised* when white is mixed with it and *lowered* when black is mixed with it. When black is added to blue, the hue of that blue is lowered toward what a layperson would describe as navy blue; when white is added to orange, the hue of that orange is raised toward what nonartists would describe as peach (Figure 11.5 and Color Plate 19).

"Tint" and "shade" are words that describe the modification or changes that are made when the value of a hue is raised or lowered. As white is added to a hue and the value is raised, designers say the hue has been tinted. As black is added to a hue and the value is lowered, designers say the hue has been shaded. The higher the value, the cheerier our response; that's why designers of comedies regularly use high values for their sets. Lower values are commonly used for tragedies because they make us feel somber. The designer for *Waiting for Godot* used a high value for the sky and a medium value for the ground to guide the audience to a cheerful experience.

Our Responses to Color Designers work with mathematically precise formulas to create a hue (e.g., 71 percent of the hue of orange plus 21 percent of the opposite hue of blue to reduce the intensity plus 8 percent of black to lower the value). We laypeople might look at that hue and call it "brown" because most of us describe hues by using adjectives that provide a recognizable reference: robin's-egg blue or fire-engine red. The descriptive name or the mathematical formula is only important as a tool for communication. If you want to buy

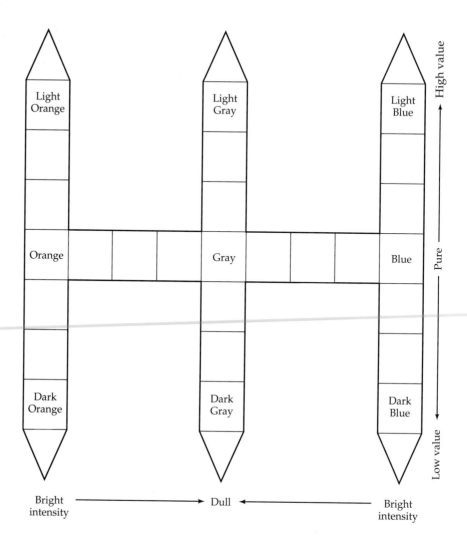

Figure 11.5 Value and intensity bars.

 Now that you understand how the value and intensity of a hue can be changed, you will recognize that many advertisements use only one hue. The designer, through the use of a wide variety of values and intensities, creates a picture that has great vitality. Designs that use only one hue are called monochromatic and are common in advertising; on rare occasions you may see a monochromatic theatrical design, as shown in color plate 20.

paint for your bedroom, you might use a descriptive adjective; if you want to analyze your response to a theatrical performance, you will find it helpful to understand how color is modified or manipulated, and you will find the precision of the designer's terms easier to use: hue, intensity, and value.

So, how did the designer manipulate the audience responses to color in the set for *Waiting for Godot*? The hues of red-orange and blue are in nearly equal proportion. The red suggests heat, vitality, and passion. The orange suggests a natural environment that is stable and friendly. Together, they create the hue of a place that is natural and friendly, yet one where passionate events could happen. The red-orange earth is contrasted strongly with the blue of the sky, which is close to the blue-green that is the direct opposite of red-orange. That contrast helps create the illusion of distance and open space, and the opposing hues create a tension between the lower half of the stage picture, where the actors must stand, and the upper half, where their ideas may soar. The sky has a brighter intensity than the earth, so it seems to be the more desirable place. The blue sky also has a higher value than the red-orange earth, which increases the tension between the reality of where the characters find themselves and the ideal where they'd like to be.

Line

When the curtain went up on *Waiting for Godot*, the audience, whether they realized it or not, saw and responded to a lot of lines. In somewhat the same manner that color shapes our responses to what we see, so does line. Some scene designs are made from scaffolding and are composed primarily of line, so their lines are easy to see. Lines in other designs are obscured by other elements, and we have to work hard to see them. Figure 11.6 shows a schematic of the set design for *Waiting for Godot* reduced to lines.

You may understand that a line is the shortest distance between two points, and you may have drawn doodles in lines and circles and ellipses and angles. You may not, however, be aware of the six properties of line: path, width, continuity, sharpness, length, and direction.

The Six Properties of Line

1. Path
2. Width
3. Continuity
4. Sharpness
5. Length
6. Direction

Figure 11.6 A schematic of the scene design for *Waiting for Godot* reduced to its lines.

Each of these six properties has an impact on us physically and psychologically. Each gives us the illusion of some physical feeling, and each is associated in our minds with certain emotional qualities. Let's look more closely at these two ways in which each of the six properties of line affects us.

Path   Path describes the *way* a line moves from one point to another. All lines start from a point. When you put your pencil on a piece of paper you make a point, and when you move your pencil you make a line. If you use the graphics program on your computer, wherever you put your cursor is a point, and when you drag it with your mouse, you create a line. Whether the line that you've created is straight or curved, the way that it goes is its path. A line can take three paths: a straight path, a zigzag path, and a curved path.

Figure 11.7 is a line that takes a straight path. This line gives us the physical feeling of control. We sense that we are looking at something planned, something created by humans, since experience teaches us that nature has no straight lines. A railroad track that runs straight across an uneven terrain gives us a sense of importance and control: humankind has asserted control over nature. Psychologically, we associate straight lines with masculinity, assertiveness, and directness.

Figure 11.7 Line: a straight path.

Figure 11.8 is a zigzag line that makes us feel queasy. There is something indecisive and uncertain about this line's continual change of path. The driver who zigzags down the highway is a danger to us. Psychologically, we associate zigzag lines with excitement, nervousness, and danger.

Figure 11.8 Line: a zigzag path.

Figure 11.9 is a curved line that makes us feel calm and at ease. The grace and fluidity of the line is relaxing to look at because it seems to belong in nature. Psychologically, we associate curved lines with femininity, youth, and subtlety.

Figure 11.9 Line: a curved path.

When we look at a design of a dress, a book cover, a car, or the scenery for *Waiting for Godot*, the path of its lines will guide us to physical feelings and psychological associations.

Figure 11.10   Line: thick and thin lines distinguish these two houses.

Width   Width describes the thickness of a line. Physically, a thick line gives the illusion that we're seeing something heavy, and a thin line gives the illusion that we're seeing something light. Which house in Figure 11.10 looks as though it "weighs" more?

Psychologically, we associate a thin line with delicacy, serenity, and passivity. We associate a thick line with masculinity, forcefulness, and aggressiveness. What are your responses to the width of the lines in the design for *Waiting for Godot* shown in Figure 11.11?

Continuity   Continuity describes the consistency of a line's movement on its path. Is the line a solid, continuous one, as in Figure 11.12, or is it an interrupted, broken line that has no continuity, as in Figure 11.13?

Physically, the continuous line gives us the feeling of security, whereas the interrupted line makes us feel uneasy. Its irregularities are unpredictable, and they disrupt our sense of security. Psychologically, we associate constancy, faithfulness, and smoothness with a continuous line, while a broken line gives us the associations of playfulness, informality, and flexibility. What are your responses to the continuity of the lines in the design for *Waiting for Godot* shown in Figure 11.6?

Figure 11.12   Line: a continuous line.

Figure 11.13   Line: a noncontinuous, interrupted line.

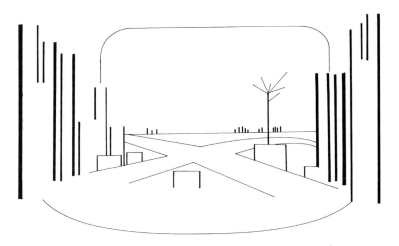

Figure 11.11   Line: both thin and thick lines are seen in this design.

Figure 11.15   Line: We have different responses to long and short lines.

Figure 11.16

Figure 11.17

Figure 11.18

Sharpness   Sharpness describes a line that is precise, as opposed to a line that is fuzzy. Images with fuzzy lines make us feel that something is far away or soft. Images with sharp lines give us the feeling that something is close at hand and hard. Psychologically, we associate boldness and sharpness with the precise line, and gentleness and indecisiveness with the fuzzy line. Which of the two dogs in Figure 11.14 looks softer to pet?

Length   A long line gives us the feeling of calm because it is unchanging and has a sense of purpose and direction to it. Short lines make us nervous and agitated because they are always changing, always requiring us to guess where they are headed. Psychologically, we associate grace and stability with long lines, and bustle and irritation with short lines. The long and short lines in Figure 11.15 illustrate the difference. What are your responses to the length of the lines in the design for *Waiting for Godot* shown in Figure 11.11?

Direction   Direction describes where a line is headed in relation to the base of a composition, whether that base is the earth we stand on, the bottom edge of a painting, or the floor of a stage. Lines can move in one of three directions: vertical, horizontal, or diagonal. Physically, a vertical line excites us because it seems to defy gravity and soar upward (Figure 11.16). Psychologically, a vertical line is associated with strength and austerity.

A horizontal line calms us physically because it has the same gravitational pull all along its length (Figure 11.17). It is stable and seems to repeat the line of the horizon. Psychologically, we associate a horizontal line with tranquility and serenity.

A diagonal line agitates us physically because it fights gravity in an unpredictable and energetic manner (Figure 11.18). Psychologically, we associate a diagonal line with dynamism, instability, and surprise.

Our Responses to Line   Each of the six properties of line influences our response to a design. As you grow expert in recognizing these properties and analyzing your response to them, you will grow increasingly skilled at understanding theatre. This chart will help you.

Figure 11.14   a.   **b.**

*A Quick Guide to the Physical
and Psychological Effects of Line*

Property	Physical Effect	Psychological Association
1. PATH		
STRAIGHT	Control	Masculinity, assertiveness, directness
ZIGZAG	Queasiness	Excitement, nervousness, danger
CURVED	Calm	Femininity, youth, subtlety
2. WIDTH		
THICK	Weight	Masculinity, forcefulness, aggressiveness
THIN	Lightness	Delicacy, serenity, passivity
3. CONTINUITY		
UNBROKEN	Security	Constancy, faithfulness, smoothness
BROKEN	Uneasiness	Playfulness, informality, flexibility
4. SHARPNESS		
PRECISE	Close and hard	Boldness, sharpness
FUZZY	Distant and soft	Indecisiveness, gentleness
5. LENGTH		
LONG	Calm	Purposefulness, grace, stability
SHORT	Agitation	Change, indecisiveness
6. DIRECTION		
VERTICAL	Uplifting	Dignity, strength, austerity
HORIZONTAL	Calm	Tranquility, repose
DIAGONAL	Agitation	Dynamism, instability

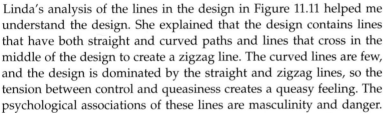

Linda's analysis of the lines in the design in Figure 11.11 helped me understand the design. She explained that the design contains lines that have both straight and curved paths and lines that cross in the middle of the design to create a zigzag line. The curved lines are few, and the design is dominated by the straight and zigzag lines, so the tension between control and queasiness creates a queasy feeling. The psychological associations of these lines are masculinity and danger.

Most of the vertical lines are thick, which creates a feeling of weight in the design, reaffirming the associations of masculinity and forcefulness.

(Continued)

(Continued)

Many of the lines are broken—even the long horizon line is broken by the vertical lines of the distant rock formations—so they create a feeling of uneasiness but also of flexibility and playfulness.

Most of the lines are precise and not at all fuzzy, so the design seems close up and has a hard feeling that creates a sense of boldness.

Most of the lines are long and create a calm feeling, and their psychological associations are purposefulness and stability.

The direction of the lines is a dynamic combination of the calming horizontal line of the horizon, the uplifting vertical lines of the rock formations, and the agitation of the diagonal roads.

The overall response to this set design is one of tension and uncertainty. To illustrate how the lines of this design influenced her, Linda made this list of the adjectives and descriptive terms she used in her analysis.

Physiological Impact	*Psychological Responses*
Control vs. queasiness	Masculinity; danger
Weight	Masculinity; forcefulness
Uneasiness	Flexibility; playfulness
Close and hard	Boldness
Calm	Purposefulness; stability
Calm; uplifting; agitation	Dynamism; dignity; tranquility

This list reveals that the design is of a masculine, hard, and heavy world that creates in the viewer a tension between calmness and agitation, between forcefulness and irregular playfulness. The designer's use of line helped make this set design an appropriate one for *Waiting for Godot*.

Mass

Mass describes the apparent weight of an object. Our assessment of the mass of an object is determined by measuring its volume and by describing its shape.

The volume that an object occupies is three-dimensional and is determined by measuring its height, its width, and its depth. The word "size" is often used as a synonym for "volume," but "volume" is a better word because it implies three dimensions.

The shape of an object describes its form: a sphere, a cylinder, a cube, or "the shape of a tree." A shape can be regular, like a cube, or irregular, like an anthill. A shape can be something seen in nature, like a tree, or something that

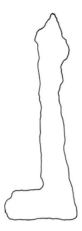 

Figure 11.19 A two-dimensional and a three-dimensional drawing of a hoodoo.

is manufactured, like a suitcase. A shape can be immediately identified, like a carrot, or it can be amorphous, like a whirlwind. Mass communicates to us immediately because it uses recognizable shapes most of the time.

As we look around us in the theatre (and in "real life"), we see only three-dimensional shapes. Because we see these shapes as distinct from their surroundings, we sometimes think of them as having edges; we sometimes define a shape by its outline. When we draw a shape on a flat piece of paper, we either abstract it down to two dimensions (e.g., we draw a circle as a symbol for a sphere) or we use the technique of perspective drawing to communicate the three-dimensional shape we wish to describe. Figure 11.19 shows two-dimensional and three-dimensional drawings of the rocky formations in the design for *Waiting for Godot.*

An object's mass gives us both physical responses and psychological associations. We respond physically to an object's apparent weight. We don't want an elephant to sit on us, but we welcome a puppy. We can, however, be fooled by appearances. For example, those large boulders that fall on characters in the movies are made of plastic foam and weigh very little. The rock formations on the set for *Waiting for Godot* were made of Styrofoam and were easily lifted by the stagehands. But the rocks *appeared* to have great weight, and that is what the audience responded to in the theatre.

Figure 11.20   This drawing illustrates mass. Compare this drawing to the drawing of line in Figure 11.6, and you will see a bold difference. Instead of showing only the outline of the shapes, this drawing shows you their mass.

Psychologically, we respond to the familiarity of a mass. An unfamiliar mass might be a composite of human, animal, and reptile parts (the monster from the movie *Alien*) or it might be a gelatinous ooze (the flowing enemy in the movie *The Blob*). As the shape of that unfamiliar or amorphous mass grows or shrinks in volume, our response adjusts accordingly.

Figure 11.20 shows the mass, rather than the line, of the set design for *Waiting for Godot*. A first glance tells us that there is a great amount of weight in the masses in this design. The heavy rock formations give us the physical response of being earthbound. We recognize some familiar masses that seem appropriate in respect to their space and shape: the tree, the roads, the large rock in the center. These shapes augment our comfortable response. But then we must make sense out of those nearly amorphous masses at the sides. Anyone who has visited southwestern America will recognize them and know they are called "hoodoos," and will feel comfortable with them. But those who have never seen the hoodoos in Bryce Canyon might think we're looking at some imagined planet's barren landscape, and our anxiety level might go up significantly. Our response to mass depends on the life experience we bring to the theatre.

Texture

Texture describes what something feels like when we touch it (or what we imagine it *would* feel like *if* we touched it). Think of a building, and you will quickly understand this concept. Is the building made of rough stone or smooth glass? Architecture provides wonderful examples of texture, and as you walk about in the next few days, make note of the wide variety of textures on the buildings you see.

Texture can be rough, medium, or smooth. Each one gives us a physical response and a psychological association. The design for *Waiting for Godot* gives us a very strong sense that if we were to touch the set it would feel rough. The scene designer chose rough textures for *Waiting for Godot* specifically to elicit certain physical and psychological responses to those textures.

A rough texture is perceived as irregular and as reflecting very little light. We associate roughness with such psychological concepts as natural, coarse, poor, and sporty. Both the rocky landscape and the woolen clothes of the characters in *Waiting for Godot* are rough.

A smooth texture is perceived as hard and as reflecting a lot of light. Our associations with smoothness include sophistication, cleanliness, wealth, and order. When the moon rises in the final moments of both acts of *Waiting for Godot,* it appears smooth and we might sense an order in the skies that does not exist for the characters stuck on earth.

A medium texture, of course, is relative to the extremes. We perceive it as firm to touch and as being moderately reflective. We associate a medium texture with maturity, conservativeness, and stability.

A quick analysis of the textures in the design for *Waiting for Godot* reveals that the earth is rough and the distant sky is smooth. The rough earthiness of the place where the characters walk is irregular; we expect casual and primitive things to happen on it, and we expect poor characters to inhabit it. The smooth sky is hard and shiny, and it suggests an order and cleanliness that the characters can see but cannot reach. Perhaps of greatest interest is that the set has no middle, it has no medium texture. We see only the tension between the rough and the smooth.

Creating a design is like making a cake. A visual artist mixes the four elements of design in much the same way that a chef mixes the ingredients of a chocolate cake: flour, sugar, butter, chocolate. Those same ingredients might be mixed to create cookies, or brownies, or a variety of other choice edibles. The ingredients become a chocolate cake only when they are mixed according to a particular recipe.

PRINCIPLES OF DESIGN

Five principles of design are used to organize the four elements into a coherent composition. Let's look more closely at each principle.

The Five Principles of Design

1. Focus
2. Balance
3. Proportion
4. Rhythm
5. Unity

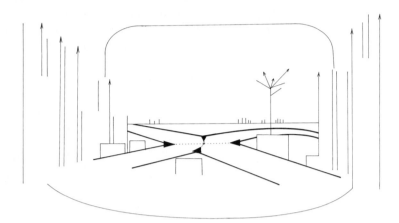

Figure 11.21   The lines in this set design have been simplified so that you can see how they create focus.

Focus

Focus describes how the elements of design are arranged so as to guide our eye to look where the designer wants us to look. Focus can be accomplished through any of the four elements of design, but it is easiest to achieve by the manipulation of line. Line can point us to what is important to look at.

If several lines in a composition point to the same place, our eye will follow those lines and look there. Figure 11.21 shows how the lines in the design for *Waiting for Godot* guide our eye to the central place of the stage, the place where the two roads cross. That central place has focus; it is even *underlined* by the line at the top of the boulder in the middle of the stage.

We like designs that have focus because we feel comfortable and secure when we know where we are supposed to look. A composition that does not guide our eye and has us looking every which way makes us uncomfortable and we will probably dislike it. We humans want to know where to look, and that's why a designer will arrange one or more of the four elements to guide our eye to focus on a specific place.

Balance

Designers arrange the element of design called mass according to the principle of design called balance. The word "balance" describes the equal distribution of apparent weight on the two sides of a composition's center line. Think of a child's seesaw. If it has a chubby ten-year-old on one end and a thin four-year-old on the other, the board won't balance.

Balance is achieved by manipulating the element of mass. A composition may have symmetrical balance, it may have asymmetrical balance, or it may be imbalanced. Figure 11.22 illustrates each type of balance. We'll also use the set for *Waiting for Godot* to clarify the differences.

A designer achieves symmetrical balance when the two sides of the center line are a mirror image of each other and the apparent weight on each side of the design is identical. Theatre designers rarely use symmetrical balance

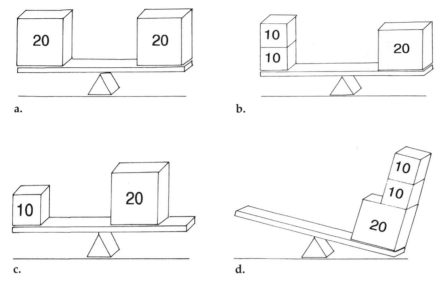

Figure 11.22   a. Identical twenty-pound blocks on each end of a board is a demonstration of symmetrical balance. **b.** An example of asymmetrical balance is a twenty-pound block at one end of the board and two ten-pound blocks at the other. **c.** Another example of asymmetrical balance is a twenty-pound block on one side, close to the central axis, and a ten-pound block at the extreme end on the other side. **d.** If all the weight is on one side, the board falls to that side and the composition is imbalanced.

because it creates a very formal and artificial arrangement of mass that seems unlike the world we see in nature. For most plays symmetrical balance would create too arbitrary and constricting a design. Symmetrical balance might be appropriate for a production of a classical Greek play such as *Oedipus the King* because that play comes from a culture that believed in humankind's potential for imposing order on nature. If the designer for *Waiting for Godot* wanted a truly symmetrical design, the line and mass would have had to be arranged like Figure 11.23. That set is very rigid to look at. It seems artificial, not something we expect to find in nature. This set design seems appropriate only for the production of a play in which the characters are as formal as the symmetrical balance is. A symmetrically balanced design for *Waiting for Godot* would be an inappropriate choice by the designer.

Figure 11.23   A perfectly balanced, symmetrical design for *Waiting for Godot.*

Figure 11.24 This design feels balanced even though the mass is not identical on each side of the stage. This set is a demonstration of asymmetrical balance.

Figure 11.25 An imbalanced design makes the audience feel uncomfortable. A design like this one might be used for a brief scene in an Expressionistic play, but it would rarely be used as the only setting for a play.

Asymmetrical balance is achieved when the apparent weight on the two sides of the center line feels equal although the masses are not identical. Asymmetrical balance is the most common sort used in theatrical design. The design for *Waiting for Godot* shown in Figure 11.24—the one that we've been examining all along—is a fine example of asymmetrical balance. The weight of the tree and the slightly longer road on the right side of the center line feels equal to the weight of the greater number of hoodoos and the slightly off-center placement of the central boulder on the left side. The masses are not identical—they are not a mirror image of each other—but the design feels balanced.

Figure 11.25 shows an imbalanced set design for *Waiting for Godot;* the set appears to tip heavily to one side. A designer will arrange mass to achieve imbalance only when the goal is to cause the audience to feel greatly agitated.

Color Plate 1 George Seurat's *A Sunday Afternoon on the Island of La Grande Jatte* is an example of pointillism; the painting was the subject of Stephen Sondheim's Broadway musical *Sunday in the Park with George*. This painting must be viewed from a distance, because if you stand close to it you will only see dots of color and not the objects or shapes that they create. Your eye "creates" the picture in the same way you "create" a theatre performance.

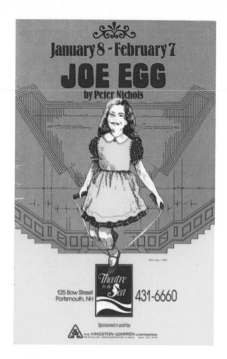

Color Plate 2 The cheery cover of the program for *Joe Egg* at New Hampshire's Theatre by the Sea prepared the audience for a lighthearted evening so that they would enjoy the comedy in the early part of the play, before the mood turned sad.

Color Plate 3 The cost of producing Andrew Lloyd Weber's *The Phantom of the Opera* was more than $6 million because it required a large cast and expensive scenery and costumes. Big production numbers such as this one excite audiences but are costly to produce.

Color Plate 4 *Rent* began Off Off Broadway in the late 1990s, but audience demand for tickets prompted the producers to move it to Broadway. This picture shows the cast singing "La Vie Bohème," one of the musical's most rousing numbers. The touring production of *Rent* entertained audiences across the United States.

Color Plate 5 *Show Boat* has been a hit each time it was revived on stage or in the movies, and the Broadway production in the 1990s proved that the 1927 musical by Jerome Kern and Oscar Hammerstein II is still great entertainment. *Show Boat's* serious theme of interracial marriage is still pertinent today.

Color Plate 6 *The Lion King* is based on the animated movie, but director and costume designer Julie Taymor found visually exciting ways to show both the live actors and the animal characters they play. Here, the dancing zebras demonstrate the power of spectacle in musical theatre.

Color Plate 7 Michael Crawford's face was half hidden behind a mask in *The Phantom of the Opera,* but his star power and his performance of the song "The Music of the Night" helped make this one of the most successful musicals in Broadway history.

Color Plate 8 *Texas,* an historical drama with song and dance, is presented annually in an outdoor theatre that resembles an ancient Greek theatre. The natural setting and the circular acting space remain as vital today as they were 2,500 years ago.

Color Plate 9 Shakespeare's Globe Theatre is a new open-air theatre in London. It is located near the site of the original Globe Theatre where Shakespeare's plays were first produced, and it is designed to look like an Elizabethan public theatre. Note the "groundlings" standing on three sides of the stage, the three galleries for seating, and the colorful decoration of the stage house. Performances in this theatre give today's audience an exciting introduction to what theatre was like in Shakespeares's time.

Color Plate 10 The baroque court theatre in Cesky Krumlov, the Czech Republic, has an ornate proscenium arch, a beautifully painted ceiling, and a horse-shoe shaped balcony that provided excellent seating for the noble family that built the theatre. The backless benches in the orchestra provide a good view of the stage, but are less comfortable. The five wings that are painted to suggest trees and the painted drop at the back of the stage are original eighteenth-century scenery.

Color Plate 11 Realism is the style of the scene design for this production of *Waiting for Godot*. The scenery created the illusion of a real location in nearby Bryce Canyon.

Color Plate 12 *The Hatch Family*, by nineteenth-century American painter Eastman Johnson, is an example of Realism because it looks like a world that you can believe existed at some earlier time. The details are accurate and complete, and although the painting is of real people in a real room, it could just as easily be a painting of characters in a box set for a realistic play.

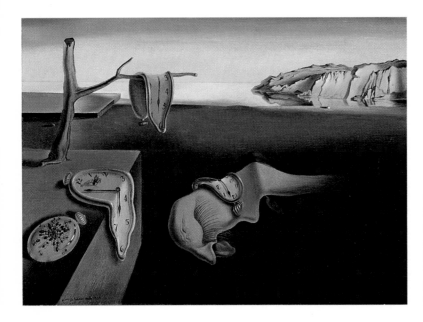

Color Plate 13 Salvador Dali's *The Persistence of Memory* is a demonstration of how words can be turned into visual images. Dali turns the phrase "time hangs heavy" into a picture that captures the surreal truth of the words.

Color Plate 14   The costume designs worn by the chorus in *Oedipus the King* use long lines and draped garments to remind the audience of ancient Greek sculpture.

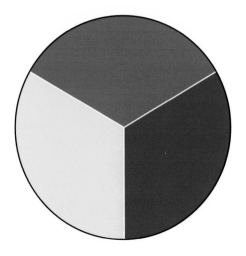

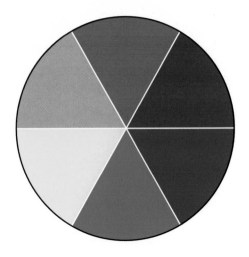

Color Plate 15 Color wheel: the three primary colors of red, blue, and yellow.

Color Plate 16 Color wheel: the secondary colors of violet, green, and orange.

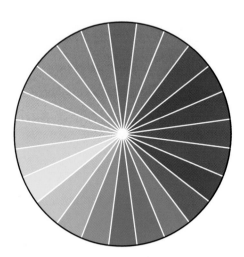

Color Plate 17 Color wheel: twenty-four hues.

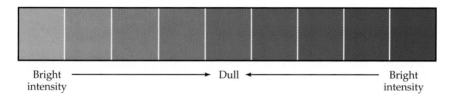

Color Plate 18 Intensity bar.

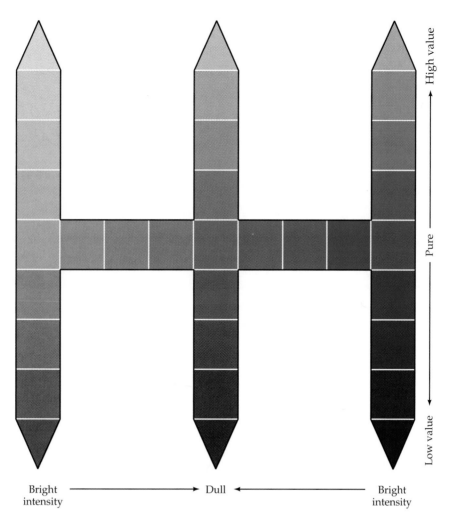

Color Plate 19 Value and intensity bars.

Color Plate 20 This monochromatic design for the musical *Quilters* was rendered on a computer so the intensity and value of the hue could be precisely manipulated. Both scenery and costumes are the hue of orange. The intensity of the hue is brighter in some places and duller in others, and the value of the pure hue has been tinted higher in some places and shaded lower in others. Although the design is monochromatic, the feeling is of a very "colorful" design.

Color Plate 21 Note the unrealistic style of this design for *Waiting for Godot*. The sky is three squares, the ground is raked and has lines that create the illusion of great distance, the entire environment is walled in, and the only color in the world of gray is the green grass and the leaves on the tree.

Color Plate 22 The costume is realistic, and its color, line, mass, and texture tell you a great deal about the character of Gogo before you hear him speak the first words of *Waiting for Godot*.

Color Plate 23 Lighting design created the illusion of time of day, location, and mood through the use of color, direction, and intensity in this production of *Waiting for Godot*.

Color Plate 24 Neil Simon's *The Sunshine Boys* is about two old vaudeville comedians who have worked closely together for years but who hate each other in private life. Their success as a comedy team depends on their precise timing and shared business, and if the actors know each other well they find these roles easier to play. (New Harmony Theatre, Indiana)

Color Plate 25 Patrick Stewart played the title role in an unusual production of *Othello*. Shakespeare wrote Othello as the only black-skinned character in the play, but an adventurous director reversed the races and cast African American actors in all the other roles. Stewart's Othello was the only white-skinned character. (The Shakespeare Theatre, Washington, D.C.)

Color Plate 26 Othello loves his bride, Desdemona, yet he strangles her before the tragedy ends. Othello is a tragic hero who seems happy and successful at the beginning of the play but whose drive to maintain his honor leads him by the end to kill his wife and to commit suicide. (Colorado Shakespeare Festival)

Color Plate 27 Anne Lee Jeffries is shown here playing Blanche DuBois in Tennessee Williams's *A Streetcar Named Desire* at Hartford Stage Company in Connecticut. Not-for-profit resident professional theatre companies regularly revive powerful American dramas that continue to affect audiences half a century after their Broadway premieres.

Color Plate 28 *Kiss Me Kate* is one of Cole Porter's greatest musical comedies. It's based on Shakespeare's *The Taming of the Shrew,* and it's an example of a book musical. It was revived on Broadway in 1999 for the first time in more than thirty years, but it has been on professional and amateur stages regularly. This photo shows Marin Mazzie singing "I Hate Men!"

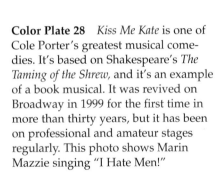

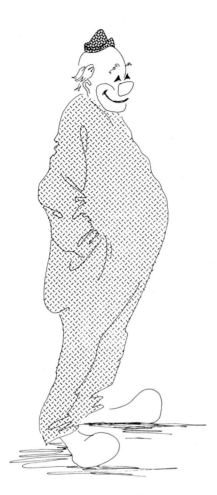

Figure 11.26 The clown's hat is too small and his shoes are too large, and that's why we find him funny. He is disproportionate.

Imbalance is done on rare occasions; the designers of Expressionistic plays know that imbalanced designs are appropriate for the angry tone of those plays. But for the most part, designers arrange mass to create a balanced composition because balance gives us a sense of security and looks the way we want the world to be. We resist the rigidity of symmetrical balance because we find it too artificial; we prefer asymmetrical balance because it provides us with the comforting experience of order without asking us to discard our previous knowledge of what the world truly looks like.

Proportion

The third principle of design describes the relative quantities of color, line, mass, and texture in relation to the whole composition. Proportions change when a part of something becomes bigger or smaller, or when all of something becomes bigger or smaller in relation to something else. Look at the circus clown in Figure 11.26. He wears huge shoes, a baggy clown suit, and a tiny hat. The small hat and big shoes are out of proportion to the clown's body. You sense a lack of proportion immediately.

Experience has taught us to view things in relationship to ourselves. "Man is the measure of all things," wrote the ancient Greek philosopher Protagoras. From infancy, we have observed the relative sizes of things, and we know how they relate to our own essential size. We are frightened by things that are larger than us (skyscrapers, tigers, sharks) and comfortable with things smaller than us (dollhouses, cats, goldfish). When we see images that are distorted out of their correct proportion, we are either amused (Gulliver in Lilliput) or threatened (a mouse named Jerry has nightmares about a huge cat named Tom). The three drawings in Figure 11.27 illustrate how man is the measure of things in this design for *Waiting for Godot.* If the man is unbelievably taller or smaller than the tree, he seems out of proportion and we feel that something is wrong with what we're seeing.

The design for *Waiting for Godot* shown in Color Plate 11 has excellent proportions in the use of all four elements of design. The red-orange ground of the lower half and the blue sky of the upper half are almost equal in proportion, so color is proportionate. Mass is proportionate because the roads seem appropriate to the men who will walk on them and the boulder seems normal in proportion to the men who will sit on it. There is proportion in the straight and curved lines and in the smooth texture of the sky when related to the rough texture of the ground. The proportionate elements of this design give us a feeling of comfort because we recognize what we're looking at.

Rhythm

Rhythm describes the repetition of perceived elements in a design. A designer arranges the four elements of design to achieve an appropriate rhythm.

We derive our sense of rhythm from nature. Day-night, summer-winter, inhale-exhale. Listen to your heart beat: da-DUM, da-DUM, da-DUM. We find the repetition of sights and sounds to be natural and comforting, and we have carried that experience into our expectations of visual composition. We like rhythms that have a perceptible repetition, but we don't like an excessively rigid visual rhythm any more than we like symmetrical balance. We prefer a rhythm that's a bit looser, that doesn't tie us up too tightly. On the other hand, we don't like compositions that have *no* organization through rhythm.

Let's look again at the design for *Waiting for Godot* to recognize how the four elements of color, line, mass, and texture have been arranged to achieve rhythm. The red-orange color is repeated in each rough-textured vertical mass, and it is also organized through the repetition of vertical lines. The tall vertical lines in the foreground and the short lines in the background both divide the space along the horizontal line of the horizon, and that repetition provides a sense of visual rhythm. The composition is not rigid or excessively regular, and it is interrupted by diagonal lines in much the same way that a musical composition might be interrupted by measures of silence. As we sit in the theatre and look at this design, we sense that the principle of rhythm has organized the design in a pleasing fashion.

a.

b.

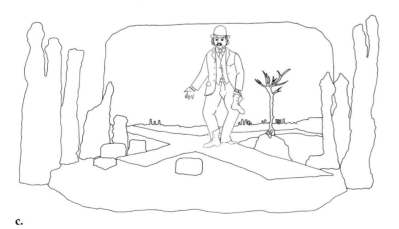

c.

Figure 11.27   a. This man is in proper proportion to the tree, the roads, and the hoodoos. We find this design believable. **b.** This man is too small for his environment and seems unimportant. **c.** This man is too large for his environment and seems unbelievable.

Unity

The fifth and final principle of design is unity. Unity describes the way in which the four elements are organized to create a coherent and aesthetically pleasing composition. When a design is successful, we will have a very difficult time identifying how it has been unified. When a design is unsuccessful, we will quickly identify what doesn't belong, what has made it disjointed, or displeasing, or ugly. Perhaps the quickest way to grasp the concept of unity is to imagine what does *not* belong in the design for *Waiting for Godot*. How about a parade of chorus girls in stiletto heels, green sequin sheaths, and peacock feather headdresses? How about an elevator that comes out of the ground to reveal a television set showing the Super Bowl game? There are rare cases in which jarring and unexpected disruptions of a design's visual unity might be introduced for their shock value, but such disruptions are exceptions.

Here's an analogy to help you grasp the whole concept of the five principles of design. After you have used the four elements of design to make bricks, you use the five principles of design to arrange the bricks into a house. The bricks could be used to make a church or a school; they become a house only when they are arranged according to a particular plan, only when the five principles of design guide you to organize them in a particular way.

IMAGINING DIFFERENT PRESENTATIONS

Many plays written in the last hundred years are so specifically imagined by their authors that there is really only one way to present them on the stage. Other plays, such as *Waiting for Godot,* permit designers great freedom in imagining new ways to present them. We have seen productions of *Waiting for Godot* in which the actors wore mimes' white-face masks, or in which the setting looked like a junkyard, or in which the cast was entirely female. In each instance, an analysis of the design provided us with a way of understanding the production.

None of these variations is inherently "right" or "wrong," any more than three witnesses' differing versions of a traffic accident are inherently correct or false. Each witness strives to tell the truth as he or she saw it. Likewise, theatre artists who interpret and present a play in differing ways are striving to present their understanding of the play and to guide the audience into sharing their emotional and intellectual responses. You cannot disapprove of a version of a play because it is different from what you might have anticipated, though it is entirely proper for you to condemn a production if its interpretation fails to tell the story or if it distorts the play's central idea.

Tom has directed *Waiting for Godot* three times, and it looked different each time. Color Plate 21 shows the scene design for his production at TheatreVirginia in Richmond. He directed that production eight years before he directed the production in Utah that we have been analyzing throughout this chapter. After you've studied Color Plate 21, read his analysis of the design. See how the same artist can interpret a script differently, and see how *your* ability to analyze theatrical design will help you understand your reaction to a performance.

Here is Tom's analysis of the set design for *Waiting for Godot* shown in Color Plate 21. The color is a hue of blue that has been dulled in its intensity by being mixed with its opposite until it is nearly at the middle of the color wheel. The hue has had white added to it so that its value is high. The pale blue panels, which represent an abstracted sky, and the pale green oval at the base of the tree have a similar value and intensity. All three hues convey a cold and calm feeling that suggests an artificial environment that is not a replication of anything found in nature.

The lines are all rigidly straight, and the rectilinear shapes combine with the forced perspective of the lines on the floor to suggest a formal, artificial environment in which humans and nature do not abide. The mass seems very light because the squares of sky appear to float and because the thin tree and small rocks have the appearance of little weight. The mass seems to defy gravity and to make me almost dizzy from its lack of weight. The textures are all extremely hard and smooth, reinforcing the artificial sense of this place. The designer's manipulation of the four elements creates a design that guides me to feel a cold, rigid, artificial, weightless, and hard environment.

The four elements have been organized by the five principles so that the focus is at the back, in the center, and subsequently behind where the characters usually stand. The characters will be seen in relief, against the bold focal point, and because my eye will be guided past them, they might seem diminished in importance.

This composition has a very rigorous balance that is nearly symmetrical. The tree and the rocks are the only items that make this an asymmetrical design. The nearly symmetrical rigidity suggests a world in which humans and nature seem alien, a world in which reason and logic have become maniacal.

The proportion in this design is also artificial and arbitrary. The human figure will seem very large in this set. I can deduce this lack of proportion from the tree, the stump of which suggests the height of a chair. The bottom of the sky panels is lower than the height of the characters.

(Continued)

(*Continued*)

The rhythm in this design is evident in the repetition of regular straight lines, in the repetition of square shapes (the sky panels and the side and back walls), and in the nearly monochromatic hue. This set creates a confining rhythm that any human must strive to disrupt. It looks like a prison cell.

This design is aggressively and almost ostentatiously unified, so much so that it seems an inhuman place for characters to inhabit. My emotional response says this design is distant, intellectual, unfriendly, artificial, and cold.

Exercise   THE EMOTIONAL RESPONSE TO COLOR

1. For each primary color (red, blue, yellow), write two words that describe your emotional association with that color. Compare your answers to those of another student. Did the two of you agree on the emotions that each color stimulates?

2. Write the names of four colors that were evident in the scenery or costuming of a play that you have seen recently. For each color, write four words that you associate with that color. Compare your answers to those of other students who saw the same production. Write a short statement explaining how the other students' color associations are different from yours and how those differences could create dissimilar responses to the same play.

Exercise   ANALYZING COLOR

1. Find an ad that uses the three primary hues exclusively. Explain why the use of primary hues is effective for this ad.

2. Find an ad that uses only primary and secondary hues. Explain why the use of these six hues is effective for this ad.

3. Find a monochromatic ad that is not black and white. Explain how the intensity and the value of the hue have been manipulated. Explain why this monochromatic ad is effective.

4. Find an ad that uses *opposite* hues. Explain why these hues are effective for this ad.

5. Find an ad that uses a large number of hues. Explain why the use of these hues is effective for this ad.

ANALYZING LINE   *Exercise*

1. Take a pen or pencil and three sheets of plain paper on which you can doodle. Select three very different pieces of music—classical, jazz, rap—and let each one play for at least two minutes before you start doodling. That way, the music will establish itself and you will respond directly to it. Then, doodle the lines you feel as you listen to each piece of music.

2. Write a short description of how each piece of music guided you to draw lines. What were your emotional responses to each piece of music?

RESPONSE TO LINE   *Exercise*

Describe your physical and psychological responses to each of the six properties of line in the design for *Waiting for Godot* shown below.

Exercise   ANALYZING TEXTURE

1. Find a picture of a building that illustrates a smooth texture. Explain why this texture is appropriate for this building.

2. Find a picture of a building that illustrates a rough texture. Explain why this texture is appropriate for this building.

3. Find a picture of a building that illustrates rough, smooth, and medium textures. Explain why all three textures are appropriate for the various parts of this building.

12

Scenery, Costume, Lighting, and Sound Design

$\mathcal{D}$esigns influence our experience in the theatre by turning words into pictures and sounds and by helping tell the story of the play.

Playwrights describe the locations, the characters' clothes, and the time of day, and designers turn their words into the objects and pictures we see when we go to the theatre. In *Waiting for Godot,* Beckett wrote, "A country road. A tree. Evening." The scene and lighting designers must turn those six words into pictures that we recognize immediately and that put us in the proper mood for this funny and poignant play. When he wrote, "Estragon is trying to pull off his boot," Beckett gave the costume designer words that must be turned into boots that the actor can pull on and off during the performance. Playwrights tell their story through the words their characters speak, and designers help us understand that story by the visual changes they make as the play progresses. When Beckett has Didi say, "The tree . . . yesterday evening it was all black and bare. And now it's covered with leaves," the scene designer must turn those words into the leaves that tell us time has passed since the end of the previous act. And when Beckett has Didi say, "Yes, now it's night," the lighting designer must turn those words into illumination of the correct color, direction, and intensity to create the illusion of nightfall that we see on the stage.

Theatre communicates visually as well as aurally, and our experience of a play is greatly influenced by the designers' inventions. Because we have very little knowledge of a play before it begins, we are strongly informed and influenced by what we see first. Our experience is then enhanced every time the scenery changes, a new costume appears, or the lights alter the mood. In the previous chapter you learned about the four elements and five principles of design and about how design influences your *feelings.* In this chapter you'll learn how design gives you *information* about the play you are seeing. We are all so accustomed to thinking a play's *words* are the primary way we learn about the story that we overlook the important information we receive non-verbally. Theatrical design has four goals: it tells us about the place, the time, the characters, and the plot of a play; it guides our emotional responses; it helps tell the story; and it teaches us about the underlying values and virtual geography of "the world of the play." Let's take a closer look at how the designers of scenery, costume, lighting, and sound each pursue these four goals in order to influence our theatregoing experience.

The Four Goals of Theatrical Design

1. Providing information
2. Underscoring the emotion of the play
3. Helping to tell the story
4. Revealing the world of the play (the values of the fictional universe)

SCENE DESIGN

Providing Information

Where the Action Is Set   A first glance at the scenery tells us where the action takes place. The location might be a real one that we recognize, such as the Oval Office in the White House (as in the movie *The American President*). It might be a fictional location that we can imagine but that we know has never existed (Amanda Wingfield's parlor in *The Glass Menagerie*). Or we might be looking at the actual stage of the theatre we're sitting in (the stage in *Our Town* or *A Chorus Line*).

What Scene Design Tells Us

- Where the action is set
- When the events take place
- What the story is
- How reality is interpreted

Many movies are filmed in locations we know really exist. In the theatre, a replica of a recognizable location is rarely built on a stage, but when it is, we expect the design to be entirely convincing. We don't want the illusion destroyed by wobbly walls or inaccurate details. A scene designer could build an exact replica of a real location for a production of *Waiting for Godot*, but it would be pointless. Beckett set his play on "a country road" where there's "a tree." The characters don't recognize the place, and the audience shouldn't either.

Most plays are set in a fictional place. In such cases, we expect the design to be convincing. We want to believe that the place could exist, and the design must support our illusion. *Waiting for Godot* is set in a fictional place, and the designer can make it look like any country road and any tree that could exist.

Some plays (or parts of them) are set on the stage that the audience is watching. There's a brief moment in *Waiting for Godot* when Didi and Gogo look into the audience. Beckett wrote the following stage directions and dialogue:

> *(He takes Estragon by the arm and drags him towards front. Gesture towards front.)* There! Not a soul in sight! Off you go! Quick! *(He pushes Estragon towards auditorium. Estragon recoils in horror.)* You won't? *(He contemplates auditorium.)* Well I can understand that.

For that brief moment, the characters have broken through the fourth wall and are in our world. The action has moved from the fictional crossroads to the theatre we're sitting in.

The design tells us if the action is taking place indoors or outdoors, in a cold or warm climate, in a particular nation or city, in a public or private place, in a wealthy or poor place, or in a place associated with a particular character. *Waiting for Godot*, for example, is set outdoors in a climate that is warm by day and chilly by night, in no identifiable country, in a public place where anyone might enter, in a place associated with the character Godot (who never arrives), and in a barren terrain that suggests poverty. If you reflect on all the scene designs you looked at in the last chapter, you'll recognize that each one gives you that same information.

When the Events Take Place   Without using any words, the scene design tells us the era or even the precise year in which the action takes place, the season of the year, and even the time of day. Many designs tell us the era or precise year by the architecture and furniture, though in *Waiting for Godot* that is impossible because the play is set in a timeless natural environment. Many designs tell us the season of the year by the Christmas decorations on the windows or the autumn leaves on the ground. A design for *Waiting for Godot* reveals that the two acts take place on two different days, because there are no leaves on the tree in Act One but there are some signs of spring in the leaves that appear there for Act Two. Many designs tell us the time of day through the use of clocks on the wall or the use of lamps to signify night. Each act of *Waiting for Godot* begins with the sun on high and concludes with the sun having set and the moon having risen.

Each playscript has its unique indicators, and each design will use its own ways to instruct us, but we can expect the design to tell us when the action is taking place.

What the Story Is   The design tells us what is happening as the story develops, because every time the scenery changes, we learn new information that helps us follow the action. Many plays have a sequence of sets that the audience sees, but the changes in *Waiting for Godot* are very simple. Beckett's unusual play is about what happens *while we wait* instead of what happens when something changes. So, when the leaves appear on the tree at the beginning of Act Two, we know time has passed and we may be hopeful that Godot will arrive, but we are in for the same disappointment as the characters because the moon rises at the end of the act, the day has ended, and Godot has not arrived.

How Reality Is Interpreted   The design tells us if the action is set in a familiar world like our own or in a stylized world. In chapter 10 you learned to distinguish between Realism and the other theatrical styles, and the first indicator of style is the scene design. The scene design tells us how reality is interpreted in this play.

Underscoring the Emotion of the Play

The scene design influences our mood through the four basic elements of design: color, line, mass, and texture. If the designer painted the set with a yellow hue that has a high intensity and is tinted to a light value, we are likely to be in for a comedy. Conversely, if the lines of the design are thick and horizontal and if the textures are smooth, we are probably in for a serious drama. A good scene design will shape our mood, and after the performance we can analyze how it guided our experience.

Helping to Tell the Story

A story develops from scene to scene, and the scenery helps us follow the action of the play. If the scenes happen in different locations, the design for each one tells us the where, when, and what of the unfolding plot. We learn this information from the scene design whether it's a full box set providing the illusion of a Realistic location or it's a unit set that only suggests locations that we can imagine. Both acts of *Waiting for Godot* happen in the same place, and the scene design tells us that even if the seasons alter, nothing essential ever changes. That design also shows us a road that led the characters to the place they find themselves, a road that permits Pozzo and Lucky to come and go and that provides a way that Godot might arrive.

Revealing the World of the Play

In addition to providing us with information and shaping our emotional response, the scene design reveals "the world of the play." This phrase is used to describe three things: the geographical arrangement of the place, the basic values that prevail, and the visual metaphor that best expresses the essence of the play (Figure 12.1).

Figure 12.1 The style is Realism, the lines are interrupted, the texture is rough, and the total impression is of, well, a garbage dump. Do you agree that this visual metaphor is appropriate for *Waiting for Godot?*

The scene design tells us the geography of the imagined locations that are out of sight, and if it fails to do this, we can get very confused as we watch the action unfold. The design tells us what's above and below the stage and what lies in the direction of any exit. Any scene design for *Waiting for Godot* tells us where Pozzo and Lucky arrive from and where they leave, and so we sense where to look if *we* were waiting for Godot to come.

"What do the other rooms look like?" asked a very intense student. She had just seen a production of *Dracula,* and she and several other students had remained after the matinee to ask questions of the actors and the director. She wanted to know, "When they go out of the room, what are the other rooms like?" She had believed so completely in the

(Continued)

(Continued)
play that she didn't realize the room she'd been looking at was not part of some larger house. She had to be shown the backstage areas so she could see for herself that when the actor playing Dracula left to go to his coffin, he merely exited the box set and went to his dressing room. The scene designer had successfully created the imaginary geography of the world of the play.

The religious, political, and domestic values that inform the world of the play are less easily discerned, but the designer has to understand them. The Christian imagery in Beckett's dialogue, the political power invested in Pozzo, and the love-hate relationship of the odd couple of Didi and Gogo are values on which the world of the play is based. The designer must create a world in which we believe those values prevail. Though we probably don't think about those values until the performance is over, our understanding and our enjoyment of a play are profoundly shaped by the way in which the scene design has expressed these values.

A successful scene design expresses the world of the play through a bold visual image that distills the essence of the play and conveys it to us sub-liminally. Not every scene design achieves this expression, and not every visual metaphor is bold enough to be perceived by even a sensitized member of the audience, but a good design "speaks" to us subliminally. The visual metaphor for *Waiting for Godot* is specified by Beckett's dialogue: the cross. The tree of life, which is also the hangman's tree, is a symbol for the cross where Christ was crucified. The characters are in torment, hanging between birth and death, like Christ on his cross. The two scene designs discussed in the previous chapter present this visual metaphor in different ways. Color Plate 11 places it center stage in the form of the two roads that cross. Color Plate 21 places it above, with the three sky panels symbolizing the three crosses on Calvary. Although we may not recognize a visual metaphor during a performance, it still shows us the world of the play.

Here is Linda's interpretation of how the scene designs for two very different productions of *Waiting for Godot* both achieve the four goals of theatrical design.

The Realistic design for the first production (Color Plate 11) tells me that the action is set in a fictional location in the canyon lands of America's Southwest. It takes place outdoors, far from civilization. Despite the roads that head toward some unknown destinations, there is nothing to indicate what poor and lonely souls will inhabit this barren wasteland.

The clear sky tells me the action is set in the daytime, and the lack of leaves on the tree tells me the season is not yet spring.

(Continued)

(Continued)

Nothing suggests that the scenery will change, so the only indicators of the story line are the roads that tell me someone may arrive or leave. Perhaps the action will include the interruption of a journey.

The style of the setting is Realistic. I expect this place to be peopled by characters who look and speak and move the way people do in my life.

The world of the play has a geography that places the action in the exact center, but of what? A forbidding wasteland in which no humans dwell? The values that inform this world include the conflict between the humans who built the two roads that cross at center stage and the immense power of nature that surrounds them. The humans seem insignificant by comparison. They live briefly in a world that does not need them. And in the middle of the stage is the Christian cross (slightly askew). It was carved into an unwelcoming and hard natural universe by humans who aspire to the heavens but who are rooted to the ground and who, as the character Pozzo says, "give birth astride of a grave." The action, characters, theme, and the very essence of *Waiting for Godot* are expressed in the visual metaphor of that cross.

The abstract design for the second production (Color Plate 21) tells me that the action is set no place I know or could imagine. I cannot discern if the action takes place indoors or outdoors, since the place is walled in. The design is for Act Two, and it appears to be springtime because the tree is sprouting leaves. It seems to be daytime, since the sky is blue. But I want to say it is "no time," because the hermetically sealed world is alienated from such organic notions as the change of seasons and the rising of the sun.

It is equally difficult to anticipate what the story will be, since there are no entrances for characters to come and go. The design tells me it is *not* an imitation of apparent reality and that whatever happens in the play is likely to be an abstraction of human experience and not a representation of it. The scene design suggests a dream world in which I will encounter the playwright's subjective point of view. The style of this production is Surrealism.

The world of the play has different rules from the world I know. There seems to be no offstage geography, the "sky" floats in defiance of the law of gravity, and there are no socio-political values that I recognize. The visual metaphor that this design presents is a box, a box that humans cannot escape.

The scene designs for both these productions of *Waiting for Godot* lead me to anticipate a theatrical experience that is strange and challenging. The single word that best describes what I feel when I first look at these designs is *"anxiety."*

COSTUME DESIGN

The curtain rises on the barren and motionless setting, and we see an overweight man in a brown tweed coat and brown derby hat struggling to take off his boot (Color Plate 22). Before we know who the character is, his costume tells us information about him, it influences our attitude toward him, and it reveals the world of the play. We obtain this information in the opening moment of a performance and throughout the play. Each time a character enters in a different costume, we learn more about the play and about the character.

Providing Information

What Costume Design Tells Us

- Where the action is set
- When the events take place
- Who the characters are
- What the story is
- How the action is (or is not) like apparent reality

Where the Action Is Set   Costumes tell us if the action takes place indoors or outdoors; the costumes for *Waiting for Godot* indicate that the action is set outdoors because the characters wear their hats throughout. Costumes tell if the climate is warm or cold; *Waiting for Godot* is set in a temperate climate where wool clothing is required, but overcoats are not. Costumes tell if the action is in a public or private place; *Waiting for Godot* is apparently in a public place, since the characters are fully dressed and they greet each other by lifting their hats. Costumes tell if the environment is rich or impoverished; the threadbare costumes of the characters in *Waiting for Godot* reveal their distressed economic condition. Costumes indicate if the action is in a particular country or city; the costumes for *Waiting for Godot* tell us only that the action is set in Europe or someplace where Western European jackets, boots, and bowler hats are worn.

The more you know about clothes, the more they tell you about where the play is set. You can recognize a Texan by his boots, a workman by his hard hat, and an Englishman by his double-vented suit. We once chatted with a hotel manager in Switzerland who could tell what country people came from by the style of their shoes.

When the Events Take Place Costume design tells us the era, the season of the year, and the time of day. Each era of history has developed its own fashions, which are most immediately recognized by the silhouette, that is, the bold outline of the costume.

Take a look at the three silhouettes in Figures 12.2, 12.3, and 12.4. The first shows the fifteenth-century silhouette for a character in Shakespeare's *Henry V*; the second shows the seventeenth-century silhouette for a character in Molière's *The Misanthrope;* and the third shows the twentieth-century silhouette for a character in *Waiting for Godot.*

Figure 12.2 In the fifteenth century, hats were worn indoors and the shoulders were padded to make the silhouette seem extremely manly.

Costumes tell us the season of the year. Overcoats aren't worn in the summer, and linen suits aren't worn in the winter. Certain costumes indicate particular times of year: a football helmet denotes autumn, a Santa Claus suit suggests December, a fancy new straw bonnet tells us it's Easter. The characters in *Waiting for Godot* have no overcoats, so it isn't winter, but they're wearing wool, so it isn't summer. Their costumes tell us it's either spring or fall.

Costumes tell us not only the era and the season but also the time of day. Most of us wear only two sets of clothes each day: what we wear to sleep and what we wear in the daytime. But in earlier eras, people changed clothes many times a day, and many garments still carry the earlier names: a morning suit, a cocktail dress, a dinner jacket, an evening gown, a nightshirt.

Figure 12.3 In the seventeenth century, men wore tall wigs and coats that flared out from the waist.

Who the Characters Are Costumes tell us who the characters are. As Shakespeare says in *Hamlet,* "Apparel oft proclaims the man." Designers can provide us with a lot of information about a character from what they give the actor to wear. Costumes communicate many kinds of information: ethnicity, nationality, vocation, social and marital status, religious affiliation, skills and accomplishments, psychological profile, and state of mind. Here's a discussion of the four most important traits that costumes can reveal: gender and sexuality, age, economic status, and relationship to other characters.

How much can you know about people from the way they're dressed? Look around your classroom. Can you separate the instructor from the students? Can you tell which students are athletes and which study engineering? Which couples are romantically involved? Which students are confident and which are timid? Who is rich? Who is in a cheery mood and who is depressed? Who belongs to a club? Who is a native of a different country or culture? Who is fastidious and who is slovenly? Our clothing tells a lot about us. What can your classmates tell about you?

Figure 12.4 In the twentieth century, men wear short hair and they wear trousers. They wear hats outdoors.

GENDER AND SEXUALITY   In most eras there was a bold distinction between what men and women wore, and the difference in gender is evident in silhouettes. Since the Renaissance, men have worn bifurcated trousers and women have worn skirts. There are glorious exceptions, of course, like the English governor of New York in the eighteenth century who reviewed his troops while dressed as a woman, or movie star Katharine Hepburn, who popularized wearing slacks in the 1930s. Despite the unisex clothing that was popular in the 1960s, most of us can tell the gender of a character (or a real person) from one quick glance. The costumes tell us the characters' genders. The five characters in *Waiting for Godot* are male, even when one of them is played by a female (Figure 12.5). Each character in a play, regardless of gender, has a degree of sexuality. One of the prime reasons we wear clothes is to enhance our sexual attractiveness. As the peacock spreads his colored tail feathers to attract a mate, so we human animals alter our appearance to advertise our sexuality. But we're a lot more subtle about it. The Western European tradition announces female sexuality by revealing parts of the anatomy: the shoulder, the leg, the cleavage, or what ads for today's swimwear describe somewhat coarsely as the "buns." By way of contrast, male sexuality is announced by exaggerating parts of the covered anatomy: adding shoulder pads to coats, stuffing **codpieces,** wearing elevator heels, and sporting colorful neckties that are not very subtle phallic symbols. Although the dialogue of *Waiting for Godot* contains references to sex, none of the characters has any pronounced sexuality, so their costumes do not display it.

In some plays, a character will purposely put on a disguise and change the appearance of gender. In Shakespeare's *As You Like It*, Rosalind dresses in a man's doublet (jacket) and hose (tights) to escape into the Forest of Arden. When she meets her true love, Orlando, she cries out in comic frustration, "Alas the day, what shall I do with my doublet and hose?"

Each era has focused on a different erogenous zone for women. The 1960s miniskirt showed the leg; the 1950s dress revealed the ample bosom; and the late 1990s bared the midriff. What will the zone be in 2020?

AGE   Age can be determined by a quick look at a character's costume. Young people expose their healthy bodies or wear tight-fitting garments, and older people cover their sagging shapes. Typically, the mass of a young character's costume is less than that of an older character's, and young people wear the

Figure 12.5 Costume indicates gender, even when the actor is not the same gender as the character. A female actor plays Didi and a male actor plays Gogo in this production of *Waiting for Godot*. (PlayMakers Repertory Company in North Carolina.)

high-value tints of youth while older people wear the shaded hues of age. Designers of *Waiting for Godot* frequently costume The Boy in short pants, displaying his flesh and establishing his youth.

ECONOMIC STATUS   Economic status is also revealed by what a character wears. A rich character wears gold, silks, and furs to show off wealth. Of course we can be fooled by characters who are in disguise, but as a rule the costume designer *wants* us to know about the character. The threadbare costumes of Didi and Gogo reveal their low economic status.

In the film *Wall Street*, the young hero (Charlie Sheen) explains to his blue-collar father that he must wear expensive, $400 suits in order to look appropriate in his job as a securities trader. He then goes to a power lunch with a high-rolling investor (Michael Douglas) and is told that he has to buy far more expensive suits if he wants to raise his status and enter the corridors of power.

Figure 12.6 The yellow Star of David that the Nazis required all Jews to wear is shown here on the characters in *The Diary of Anne Frank.* Status, religious affiliation, and relationship can be revealed through costume.

RELATIONSHIP TO OTHER CHARACTERS   Costumes tell us how characters are linked to one another by family ties, military allegiances, social affiliation, or romantic attraction. Costume designers frequently use color to link the members of a family so the audience can tell they're related. Stage armies are usually costumed in two very different colors so that we can tell who's on each side. Characters' social affiliations can be seen through both bold and subtle means. The "old school tie" that tells us that an English gentleman went to Eton is a subtle message, and the yellow star that Jews had to wear when the Nazis controlled Europe is a bold statement (Figure 12.6). Romantic attractions are shown usually through color, so if you aren't certain which girl will end up with which boy, look closely at their costumes. The designer will probably have linked the pairs that will end up together. Successful costume designers create costumes that tell us about the individual characters and about their relationships to other characters in the play. Didi and Gogo are dressed somewhat alike, so we know right away that the two are close friends.

 Some costume designers jokingly refer to color linking as "the NFL school of costume design," since their bold choices of color are as immediately distinguishable as the colored jerseys of football players.

What the Story Is   Costume designs help tell the story. Each time a character changes costume, we are told new information that helps us understand what is taking place. When Pozzo and Lucky enter in Act Two, their altered costumes tell us that their status has fallen. They are dirtier, more torn, more disheveled.

How the Action Is (or Is Not) Like Apparent Reality   Costumes tell us the style of the production. One quick glance and we know if the production is Realistic or if it is stylized. *Waiting for Godot* has been interpreted in many ways. The production in Color Plate 22 was Realistic, but the painted costumes in Figure 10.13 tell us that that production was an example of Surrealism.

Underscoring the Emotion of the Play

The costume designer's manipulation of the four elements of design influences our emotional response in profound ways. If the characters in *Waiting for Godot* are dressed in primary hues that have high value, then our response to them will be a happy and cheery one. How different will our response be if the characters are dressed in somber brown or black? If Didi's coat has the formal straight lines of a pinstriped suit, we'll respond differently to him than if he wears a loose-fitting outfit with curved lines. If the mass of Pozzo's costume is weighty, we will take him seriously, whereas if Lucky's seems very light, we may think he's silly. If the textures of Gogo's and Didi's costumes are extremely rough but The Boy's is smooth, the designer is making a statement about their compatibility.

The costume designer's application of the five principles of design influences our experience as profoundly as does the selection of the four elements. Consider how the designer uses the principle of focus. We may believe we have the freedom to look anywhere we wish on a stage, but by manipulating color, line, mass, and texture, the designer will guide our eye to focus on the character that the designer wants us to see. For example, if Pozzo's vest has sparkling gold braid, we might feel he's important and focus on him. If Gogo's silhouette is unbalanced when he has his shoe off, we might feel he's dangerous and focus on him. However, if the designer controls the focus— and the other four principles—then our emotional experience will be what the designer intended.

Helping to Tell the Story

When characters change clothes, we understand that other things are changing as well. Characters are forming new relationships, taking new jobs, going to new places. Each time we see a new costume, we get new information about the unfolding story. At first glance, *Waiting for Godot* appears to be a play about how nothing changes, about how the characters are caught in a fixed condition. Yet even in this apparently static play the costumes help to tell the story.

At the beginning, Gogo is trying to put on his boot, so we infer it had been off earlier. Later in the play, we learn that this action is something he does many times, something he hopes will give him "the impression he exists," as the dialogue says, and we learn that this play is a story about how people repeat themselves. When Pozzo and Lucky reenter in Act Two, their costumes are dirtier and more torn and ragged, which tells us that something has happened to them since we saw them last. Time has passed. Change has happened. We think that maybe something will change for Gogo and Didi too.

Revealing the World of the Play

The world in which the five characters in *Waiting for Godot* live is indicated by their costumes. The temperature gets cold, the road is long and requires boots for the walker, and economic forces exert a strong influence on peoples' lives.

Here's Linda's analysis of Gogo's costume in Color Plate 22.

Gogo is wearing a battered brown derby hat, a badly worn brown herringbone tweed sport coat, and lighter brown wool pants that have a bold checked pattern, are frayed at the cuffs, and are held up by a rope belt. He wears a patterned vest over a dirty dress shirt that has no collar, and he wears long underwear but no socks. His brown workman's boots have no laces.

The action is set outdoors, in a public place where the weather is sometimes cold, and in the late nineteenth or early twentieth century. The character is male and mature with no remarkable sexuality. And he's poor.

The color of Gogo's costume is friendly and warm, the line is curved though frequently irregular, the mass seems heavy (in part because the actor is heavy), and the texture is rough. These four elements combine to show me a character who is sympathetic, casual, and potentially comic. The costume is symmetrically balanced from side to side and asymmetrically balanced from top to bottom—the brown hat and shoes are separated from the brown coat and pants by the expanses of skin at the face and ankle, and the entire figure is divided at the waist by the rope belt. The proportion seems human and normal except for the very large pattern on the pants, which I associate with clowns and comic figures. But the jumble of fabrics cre- ates a very unrhythmic costume: herringbone, solid, and checked fabrics all conflict to convey unpredictability and psychological confusion. The costume does seem to be unified, mostly through the use of color and texture; the designer has manipulated the costume to indicate that the character is potentially chaotic and immature and comedic.

LIGHTING DESIGN

We can't see the actors in the dark. Theatre requires light, whether this illumination comes from the sun, as it did in earlier centuries when theatre was performed outdoors, or from the technologically sophisticated electronic systems used in indoor theatres today.

When plays were performed outside in the sunlight, the illusion of light on the stage was created by the playwright's words. Here's how Juliet tells Romeo that the dawn is breaking and that he has to leave her bedroom before they're found together: "O now be gone, more light and light it grows." This line also told Shakespeare's audience, which was watching the play in the bright afternoon, to imagine that the characters were in a darkened bedroom and that the sun was about to come streaming through the windows. Playwrights also indicated light by what they had the actors do and by the props they had actors carry. An actor shading his eyes tells us the sun is bright; an actor carrying a candle tells us the room is dark.

Here are some interesting historical tidbits about theatre lighting. In 1490, the great artist Leonardo da Vinci used small, reflecting pieces of colored glass to increase and color the light beamed onto the stage from offstage candles. In 1664, a performance in France used 20,000 colored lanterns to provide illumination and atmosphere. In 1803, gas lighting was first installed in a theatre, but the open flame proved dangerous and a number of theatres burned down. In 1879, Thomas Edison developed the incandescent light bulb, and only eleven years later, in 1890, the Savoy Theatre in London introduced electric lighting on the stage. The theatrical lighting we take for granted is only a little more than a hundred years old.

When indoor theatres became the norm, artificial lighting had to be introduced. The first artificial lighting illuminated the stage and the auditorium alike, using candles in big chandeliers. Later, kerosene lamps were used, then gas, then electric lights. Along with electric lighting came sophisticated control of the quantity, the direction, and the color of the light, and that control led to a new theory of lighting design. The English designer Edward Gordon Craig called this theory painting with light. Craig realized that the audience learned information, felt emotions, followed the story, and understood the world of the play as a result of the direction, the color, and the amount of light. It's easy to demonstrate how Craig's theory works. Put a blue cloth over a three-way lamp, set the lamp near the floor, and turn it to its lowest intensity. Next, uncover it, set it near the ceiling, and turn it on high. You've manipulated the color, direction, and quantity of light. How did each arrangement affect your mood?

Edward Gordon Craig's theory is called painting with light. It can be expressed as a formula: color + direction + quantity = mood.

Providing Information

Lighting gives us information both in our real world and in the virtual world on the stage. Light tells us how we are supposed to behave during the performance. When the houselights dim, we're supposed to be quiet, and when they grow bright again, it's intermission or time to go home. In a musical, the lighting tells us to applaud at the end of a song: either the spotlight on the singer is turned off so we know the song has ended, or it "bumps" up in brightness as a way of signaling for applause.

Lighting also creates focus. Remember that focus is achieved by manipulation of the four elements of design. The lighting designer keeps our attention focused on the star who is singing the opening song by (1) shining a white light on her while the rest of the stage is washed in blue; (2) making sure the path of light from the spotlight that follows her points straight lines directly at her; (3) making sure the block of light on her also hits the floor, creating a bold mass; and (4) making sure the light on her is solid while the light on the rest of the stage has a pattern that creates a mottled texture.

Within the virtual world on the stage, lighting tells us the time of day. If the scene takes place outdoors, the light is nearly white in the daytime, rosy pink at dawn or sunset, and steely blue on a moonlit night. Indoors, the light is nearly white in the daytime and yellow at night to create the illusion of table lamps.

Lighting can also tell us about the physical environment in which the action is set. If light streams through a window, we learn what is outside: the sun, the moon, the shadow of the villain. If there's a fire in the fireplace, we understand it is cold outdoors. If the action is set outside, the lighting tells us when night is about to fall (the light dims) or whether there is a large tree offstage (the shadow of leafy branches falls on the floor). *Waiting for Godot* takes place in a barren location and in the daytime until the final sequence of each act, when the lighting tells us that the sun sets and the moon rises.

Underscoring the Emotion of the Play

Lights underscore the emotion of a scene in much the same way that music does. Music is used in films and TV to intensify the mood of a scene; likewise the lighting designer manipulates emotions through colors, direction, and brightness of light—through painting the scene with light.

Lighting designers have the tools and the talents to influence our emotions with color while a performance unfolds. If the stage is bathed in red light, we sense violence or danger. If it's washed in blue light, we become melancholy or depressed.

The direction that the light comes from influences our emotions as well. We are accustomed to having light come from above us. Sunlight comes from above, and so does the artificial illumination that's a substitute for sunlight. But what happens when the designer changes the direction of the light and the shadows go up instead of down? Think how scary the human face looks when a flashlight is held underneath the chin and shines upward. When light comes from a direction other than overhead, our response to it can be extreme.

The sunlight in *Waiting for Godot* shines down on the stage, but when the moon rises, the blue light comes from a lower angle, as though the moon were lower than the sun. This lighting underscores the melancholy mood at the ends of the acts (Color Plate 23).

Each time the lighting changes, the mood changes. A play such as *Waiting for Godot* may have few lighting changes, but a musical such as *Cats* could have well more than a hundred different **cues** during the performance. ("Cue" is the theatrical term used to describe each time the lights change on the stage.) Some cues are obvious to us, as when a character turns on a lamp, but many are done so slowly that our eye doesn't notice.

Helping to Tell the Story

Lighting helps us follow the story in several ways. It helps us understand the passage of time. The dialogue may not tell us that dawn is about to break, but when the horizon begins to glow a rosy pink, we know it. Light can tell us what is going to happen before the characters learn it. A flickering red and yellow light outside the window tells us a building is on fire. Light that suddenly shines from under a door indicates that someone in the adjacent room has turned on a light. Stories can unfold through changes in lighting as well as through characters' actions or dialogue.

Some basic conventions of theatre are achieved through lights. A blackout—when the lights on stage are turned off and then back on—tells us either that time has elapsed or that the action has moved to a new location. In the centuries before lighting could be controlled, a curtain had to be closed or opened to achieve this convention. Sophisticated lighting control has enriched our experience of theatrical performance.

In *Waiting for Godot,* lights tell us the unfolding story only near the end of each act. The stage grows slowly darker as night approaches and then brighter to create the illusion of moonlight.

Revealing the World of the Play

Lighting helps us understand the style of the world in which the action is taking place. If the illumination suggests our own world, we expect the rest of the production to seem familiar as well, to be Realistic. However, if the lighting is different from what we see in our real world, then we know the production is stylized. We may enjoy a happy musical's rosy sunsets and spotlights that follow the singers; or we could be startled by the red light that washes over the stage at the end of an Expressionistic tragedy. In either case the lighting is telling us that the theatrical world we're watching is different from the real world we live in.

SOUND DESIGN

Sound design is a new concept in the theatre—less than half a century old—and it has developed because of the sophisticated technology that is available today. Only in the past few decades has there been a theatre artist whose sole function has been to enhance our experience by "designing" the sounds that we hear, though we know that sound has been an important aspect of performance since the beginning of theatre. The ancient Greeks rolled stones around in huge earthen jars to create a sound that their audiences understood to be thunder. The stagehands at Shakespeare's Globe Theatre shook metal sheets to create the illusion of a thunderstorm. Sound has always been an exciting part of the theatre experience.

Today we hear live sound and we hear recorded sound. A live sound is one that is made during the performance, at the precise moment we hear it in the play. Live sound can be made by an actor shooting a blank pistol or by a member of the backstage crew dropping a box of broken glass. Typical live sounds include telephone rings, door slams, and human screams. Recorded sound is any sound that was made at some earlier time, stored on a tape or digitally mastered minidisc, and then played during the performance. Typical recorded sounds include church bells, car horns, and crickets.

The generic term "sound effects" describes both live and recorded sound, and each effect is called a cue. Some productions have many cues, and others have none. *Waiting for Godot* has only one cue, described shortly.

Designers have two classifications for sound: source and score. Source sound is any sound we recognize and believe we know where it comes from. Typical source sounds include the wind down a chimney, the hoofbeats of a passing horse, and the siren of a police car. The characters in the play hear source sound and react to it because it exists within the reality of their world. Score sound, by way of contrast, is any sound that the characters do not hear because it exists in *our* world, not theirs. Typical score sound is the musical underscoring that intensifies the emotion in a scene.

Providing Information

There's a clear example of a source cue that gives us information in *Waiting for Godot*. That sound is the offstage crash when Lucky and Pozzo fall after their exit in Act Two. That sound, whether it's made live or played back from a recording, is a source cue because we understand where it came from and we imagine that the two characters have fallen amid the stool and basket that Lucky was carrying when the two went out of sight.

Underscoring the Emotion of the Play

Our emotional response to a scene is greatly influenced by the score. The score is designed to guide our emotional response and make the scene more exciting, for example, or more romantic. In a live performance, a recorded score can be played so subtly that we are not aware we hear it and it does not intrude on our willingly suspended disbelief. In such an instance, the theatrical style of the performance is probably Realism. But when we become aware of the score—perhaps because it's played so loudly it startles us—our attention is removed from the world on the stage and we become aware of ourselves hearing the music. In such an instance, the performance may be in one or another of the nonrealistic styles.

Some plays have very elaborate scores composed for them; the composer may be listed on the title page of the playbill or in the bios. Other plays have no score sound. Most productions of *Waiting for Godot* have no cues that could be described as "score" sound, but in Tom's production that was set in America's Southwest, the sound designer recorded the wind blowing through the craggy rocks of a nearby national park and played back that source sound just after Pozzo and Lucky exited in each act so as to intensify the loneliness of the characters. As Gogo and Didi stood in the pool of blue moonlight, the audience heard the gentle whisper of the wind.

Helping to Tell the Story

Source sound helps to tell the story. Like lighting design, sound design can tell us what is happening in ways that the actions and dialogue of the characters cannot. The sound of the police cars screeching to a halt in the final scene of *The Diary of Anne Frank* tells us that Anne and her family are about to be discovered by the Nazis; we learn this sad fact a few moments before the characters realize what is going to happen next. In *Waiting for Godot,* the sound effect of Pozzo and Lucky falling down helps us imagine what happens in the continuing lives of those two characters as they stumble blindly through the night.

Revealing the World of the Play

The world of the play is revealed through source sound. If the world is urban, sound design can provide traffic noises; if the world is a battlefield, the sound of gunfire and cries of battle can make the world seem believable.

The offstage crash in *Waiting for Godot* tells us that Pozzo and Lucky are not very far away, so the sense of the world's space is made apparent. The use of a wind sound tells us that the temperature is dropping as night falls in this natural environment.

Sound Design in Musicals

Musicals are an exciting form of theatre that exposes us to the most complex use of sound. Musicals, for example, offer us a live orchestra. The conductor stands with his or her back turned to the audience, facing the musicians in the orchestra pit and the actors on the stage. Before the curtain goes up, the orchestra plays an overture to put us in the desired mood and to introduce us to the melodies we will be hearing as the show unfolds. Sometimes the orchestra plays music during the performance that underscores the mood in a scene that is acted representationally, in a Realistic style. At other times the orchestra accompanies the singers who perform presentationally, in a Theatricalistic style. At still other times, the orchestra plays music while the scenery changes, another example of Theatricalism. In all these cases, the sound we hear is live; it is score music that originates in our world, not in the world of the play.

But when the actors sing, we hear both source sound and score sound simultaneously. We experience the event on both levels at the same time. The orchestra plays the overture, and the music is definitely in our world: it is score sound. The characters sing to one another, representationally, and the music of their voices is in their world: it is source sound. But the actors also sing to us, presentationally, and this presentation is made very clear at the end of the song, when we are encouraged to applaud the singer, not the character.

This overlay of source sound and score sound is blended through the use of amplification. The singers wear wireless microphones that are turned up when they sing so that we can hear them over the orchestra; this system makes their voices sound electronically amplified, so they don't sound as much a part of the world of the play as they do when they speak dialogue. It is amazing to watch a soundboard operator during a performance as he or she pushes levers to create a balance between the human voices and the orchestra; it is equally amazing how quickly we in the audience grasp the conventions of musical theatre that permit us to disgregard the intrusions on our willingly suspended disbelief so that we can enjoy the emotions of the performance.

Exercise   ANALYZING A DESIGN

Choose a theatrical production that you have recently attended, and provide the title of the play, the date of the performance, and the name of the theatre. Select one aspect of theatrical design (scenery, costume, lighting, sound), and describe how that design provided information, underscored the emotion, helped to tell the story, and revealed the world of the play for the performance you attended.

13

Actors and Characters

When you view theatre, you are watching two actions simultaneously: what the actor does and what the character does. There's a profound difference between the actor and the character, and in this chapter, we describe that difference to you so you can learn to appreciate the actor as much as you enjoy the character. After you grasp this difference, we describe in more detail both how the actor creates the character and the nature of the character being created.

Leonardo DiCaprio is a real person. Romeo was a character that DiCaprio played. Actors use the playwright's words, the designer's costumes,

An actor is a real human being who lives in our world. A character is a fictional being.

Here's a real-life anecdote from Tom's life that illustrates the way people can confuse the actor with the character. I was performing the role of Jerry in Edward Albee's funny and powerful play *Zoo Story*. Jerry is an intense, alienated, and disturbed young man who meets a stuffy businessman on a bench in New York's Central Park. Jerry talks at the businessman for a long time and finally tricks the man into holding a knife so that Jerry can run onto it and commit suicide. The play was quite new when I did it, and the violent ending was considered startling. Some friends joined me in a cab to the theatre, but when we met up after the performance, one of the group held back. She had known me casually before she saw the play and had seen me shortly before the performance began, but apparently the character of Jerry was so unsettling for her that she was frightened to get in a cab with him, er, me. She couldn't separate the actor from the character.

and their own talent and skills to create the characters we see on stage or screen. We *always* see the actors, but we pretend to ourselves that we are seeing the characters. If actors are successful, we *believe* in the characters they play, and the two blend into one. Frequently, we mistake the one for the other. When you describe the movie *Casablanca* to a friend, you may say, "And then Humphrey Bogart shoots the Nazi officer." But Bogart never shot anyone. Bogart fired a blank pistol, and another actor fell down, pretending that his character was dead. Bogart didn't do the shooting, he did the acting. His character shot the other character.

Separating the character from the actor is more difficult when we're talking about movie and television actors. On stage, the character dominates the actor, and after we leave the theatre we remember what the character did. Hamlet died at the end of *Hamlet,* Eliza came back to Henry Higgins at the end of *My Fair Lady,* and Walter Lee told the white man to keep his money in the climactic scene of *A Raisin in the Sun.* On movie and television screens, however, the actor dominates the character, and you remember what the *actor* did. Humphrey Bogart shot the Nazi, Whoopi Goldberg led the choir of nuns, Jimmy Smits solved the crime. There are a couple of reasons why the actor dominates the character in film and television. First, the size of the actors on the screen overpowers you. On the big screen actors' faces are twenty feet tall; they seem more important than you are . . . and more important than their characters. On television, actors' faces in close-up fill the whole screen; they seem more important than the characters. Second, on TV and in the movies, actors look pretty much the same every time you see them, so you grow familiar with them and expect to recognize them from film to film. Larry Fishburne in *Othello* looks pretty much the same as Larry Fishburne in *What's Love Got to do With It?* The cult of personality dominates TV and the movies, and we like to experience film and television through the personalities of familiar actors.

On stage, the actors' faces seem rather small. You see their entire bodies at a distance, and you see them in the context of the scenery and in the company of other actors. Also, stage actors delight in transforming themselves so that they seem like different characters in each role (Figure 13.1). The great actor Laurence Olivier took pride in altering his appearance, his voice, and his posture; in doing so, he astonished audiences with his versatility. Olivier was

Some actors take great delight in fooling an audience. When a male actor wants to remain unknown to the audience, he will list himself in the program under the alias George Spelvin. This practice is widespread. A friend of ours once played two roles in the same play; he used his own name for one role and the name George Spelvin for the other role. He received wonderful reviews as George Spelvin, but was panned in his own name.

Figure 13.1 This actor played Captain Hook in *Peter Pan* in Seattle. Here he is putting on makeup to transform himself into his character. (The Intiman Theatre, Seattle)

able to perform these alterations in film as well as on stage: watch the videos of his performances as the king in *Richard III,* Heathcliff in *Wuthering Heights,* Archie Rice in *The Entertainer,* and the title role in *Othello.*

The distinction between the actor and the character is a hard one to remember. Sometimes we are dominated by the actor and forget the character. Do you remember that James Edward Olmos's character in *Stand and Deliver* was named Jaime Escalante? In this case, the persona of Olmos is what we remember, not the character's name. At other times we are dominated by the character and forget the actor. Do you remember that the character James Bond was played by Sean Connery, Roger Moore, Timothy Dalton, George Lazenby, and Pierce Brosnan? Here the character is what we remember, and we don't pay much attention to the actor. The distinction will become easier once you understand how an actor creates a character.

An actor is a craftsperson who has learned a particular set of skills in much the same way that carpenters and computer programmers have learned their skills. Some actors have learned their skills better than others, and some have more natural aptitude. That's why some actors are better than others.

In practicing the craft, an actor works with the text, the self, and the context. The text is the playwright's written words that comprise the playscript. The self is made up of the actor's voice, body, imagination, and discipline. The context is the circumstances in which the actor works—the time, the space, the other people, the physical circumstances of the setting and costumes, and the audience. Let's look at these raw materials more closely.

The Actor's Raw Materials

- Text
- Self
- Context

TEXT

The text, or playscript, comes from the playwright, and in it the actors find much of the raw material from which they make their performance. The playscript gives clues about the character that the actor must create, and one of the skills that an actor must master is how to analyze a playscript in order to discover the character. A playscript offers four sources of information that the actor must examine.

Four Sources of Character Information

- What the playwright says about the characters in stage directions
- What characters say about themselves
- What characters say about other characters
- What characters do

Stage Directions

The first source of information is what the playwright says about the characters in stage directions that are outside the dialogue. Some playwrights provide lengthy and detailed descriptions of their characters; actors must read these descriptions with great care, taking note of all pertinent information. The English playwright George Bernard Shaw was famous for writing very complete descriptions in which he told the actor what the character looked like and sounded like as well as the character's beliefs and motivations. Few playwrights write as extensively as Shaw, but most provide some information. Some playwrights place their descriptions of a character at the front of their playscripts, some include descriptions at the place in the script where a character first appears, and others sprinkle the information throughout the script, interspersed with the dialogue. The playwright provides stage directions in order to help actors. Actors may trust those directions and must use them to create their characters. Of course, not all playwrights provide descriptions. Indeed, the practice is a relatively recent one, and only in the past 150 years have playwrights included descriptions of the sort that Shaw provided. Shakespeare and other playwrights who wrote in earlier eras expected the actors to extricate information about their characters from the dialogue, and the playwrights expected to be on hand during rehearsals to explain the characters to the actors. Later playwrights, such as Samuel Beckett, wrote almost no stage directions to the actor.

What Characters Say about Themselves

Characters frequently describe themselves in their dialogue and tell others (and you) what they look like, what they sound like, what they believe, and what they know. Much of this information is accurate, but actors have to be careful, because characters can lie. Or they can be wrong. Or they can be deluded. A character may describe himself as very handsome, and he might be. Or he might be lying. Or he might think he's handsome when all the other characters describe him as grotesque. Actors have to be cautious and not take characters' self-descriptions as accurate unless those descriptions are corroborated elsewhere in the playscript. The dialogue does, however, provide some information that actors use in creating their performance.

What Characters Say about Other Characters

A character may say, "Here comes Mary and she looks angry." Or "Mary is the tallest woman I know." Or "Mary can be depended on to tell us the truth; she never lies." The actor preparing the role of Mary must take note of all these descriptions, but she must be cautious about taking them at face value. Is the character who describes Mary's anger saying it honestly or in jest? Is the character who describes Mary as a tall woman telling the truth? Is the character who describes Mary's integrity speaking ironically? The actor must sort out these bits of information and integrate them into her understanding of the character Mary.

Consider the character of Iago in Shakespeare's tragedy *Othello* (Figure 13.2). Iago is one of the greatest villains ever written, and by the end of the play he's described as a "damnèd villain" and a "demi-devil." But early in the play, all the characters like and respect him, and he's described as "a man of honesty and trust." If the actor portrays Iago as the oily villain that the audience knows him to be, the other characters will seem stupid and the play won't make much sense. The information that the actor finds in the dialogue by and about Iago should guide him to create a character who appears to be attractive, modest-spoken, and stalwart.

What Characters Do

The first three sources of information that actors find in the playscript are valuable, but not as important as the fourth: what the characters *do*. Characters are delineated by actions more than by words. Iago, for example, extorts

Figure 13.2 The character of Iago must seem trustworthy and honest in the early scenes of *Othello*. Here, Iago swears an oath to serve Othello faithfully. The split-faced stone mask in the background suggests to the audience that faces can be deceiving and that Othello may be foolish to trust Iago. (Colorado Shakespeare Festival)

money from Roderigo, lies to Othello, beats his wife, Emilia, and stabs Cassio. Despite what Iago says about himself and despite how much the other characters' lines describe Iago as "honest," it is what Iago *does* that makes his character clear to the actor who plays the role.

A good way to discuss this concept of character is by reference to Existentialism, the dominant philosophy of our century. Existentialism was best explained by the French philosopher and playwright Jean-Paul Sartre. Sartre observed that we are the sum total of our actions. Whatever we say we are, and whatever others think we are, we are truly defined by what we *do*. Take this example. Your neighbor is a good family man. He provides well for his wife and children, he goes to church regularly, he pays his taxes, and he maintains his house and yard attractively. He volunteers time to coach the Little League team. He's a careful driver. He is well liked where he works and where he lives. One day he comes home from work and murders his wife and children with a shotgun. No matter how many neighbors and members of his church describe him in terms of the good things he did before that fateful day, the world will forever describe him as a murderer. No matter what justifications and motivations and rationalizations he offers, he is a murderer. He is what he did. He did some good deeds. He killed his wife and children. He is the sum total of his actions.

Man is the sum total of his actions.
— JEAN-PAUL SARTRE

For the first three sources of information about a character, actors write down all the pertinent information and then sort out what is true. They end with a list of physical descriptions, vocal qualities, and personality traits that will help them to create the character. For the fourth source, what the character does, actors have to work harder, but they are helped in this work by the system of character analysis that was developed nearly a century ago by the Russian actor, director, and teacher Constantine Stanislavsky. The **Stanislavsky System** is the dominant system of character analysis used by actors today, and it has a particular vocabulary.

If you understand the basics of the actor's work, you will appreciate how an actor goes about creating a character and you'll be more qualified to judge and describe an actor's performance. Here's a short version of the actor's vocabulary.

Objective: what do I want?
Obstacle: what's in my way?
Action: what do I do to get what I want?

An actor analyzing Oedipus's first scene will determine that Oedipus's objective is "to comfort the citizens of Thebes." His obstacle is the fact that Creon has not yet returned with advice from the Oracle at Delphi. His action is "promising to follow the oracle's advice." Note that the objective is phrased as an infinitive: "to comfort." The obstacle is phrased as a statement: "the fact." The action is phrased as a gerund: "promising." The actor's analysis prepares him for the scene and gives him something very active to do. "Promising" is doing something; it is an action that the character Oedipus might undertake.

 A "role" is the entirety of a character's part in the play. It is called a role because in earlier times actors received their lines written on a roll of parchment paper. (The words "role" and "roll" once meant the same thing.)

A character has one overriding desire in a play: a **super objective.** This super objective answers the question "what do I want?" throughout the character's **role.** A character's complete role is constructed of a large number of units. Each unit begins when the character wants something new, and it continues for the duration of the character's quest for that objective. Units are the building blocks with which a character's total role is built, and the objective for each of the character's units must relate to the super objective. Oedipus's super objective is to find out who killed King Laius. In the unit with the blind prophet, Tiresias, Oedipus's smaller objective is to learn what Tiresias knows because that knowledge may help Oedipus discover the murderer.

A conscientious actor uses the Stanislavsky System to analyze every unit of the role. Actors spend a lot of time at this task before rehearsals begin and continue their work throughout the rehearsal process so that they may perform believably. Actors add what they learn about a character from this rigorous analysis of actions to what they learn about the character's appearance, voice, and behavior from a close reading of the playscript. Actors use all this information to understand the character they are going to create.

Actors trained in the Stanislavsky System use the word "beat" to describe a segment of the role that is even briefer than a unit: a segment with a tiny objective (e.g., to speak to a friend on the phone) and a small obstacle (e.g., the friend hasn't answered yet) that guides the actor to a small action (e.g., listening to the rings). The word "beat" came into use when American students studied with a Russian actress who would talk of a tiny "bit" of action. Her accented English made it sound like "beat," and the word became part of actors' vocabulary.

SELF

Actors' only instruments are their own selves. Actors can grow very jealous of painters who use a brush and of musicians who use a violin, because those artists' instruments are separate from themselves. The better the violin, the better the music it can produce. But the actors' instrument is the self, so there can be no separation between the self and the instrument. Actors must use their own body, their own voice, their own imagination, and their own discipline. Actors apply each of these four aspects of the self to create the character they discovered through their analysis of the text.

The Four Aspects of the Self

- Body
- Voice
- Imagination
- Discipline

Figure 13.3   Actor Kim Pereira was born in India, but he wears the European costume of Lucky in *Waiting for Godot*. (The Laboratory Theatre, Florida)

Body

The actor must look like the character. By analyzing the script, the actor can learn the character's age, size, posture, and carriage. Is the character young or old, tall or heavy, ramrod erect or bent with illness? Does the character move gracefully or with a notable limp? During the performance, we in the audience will hear the same information in the dialogue that the actor reads in the script, and the actor's physical characterization must conform to what we hear. Frequently, the script is not very specific, and the actor's own appearance can represent the character's (Figure 13.3). Many stage actors enjoy developing their characters' unique look and regularly alter their own appearance in the service of their craft. Of course, there are limits to the degree that actors can disguise their own body and appearance, but some amazing physical characterizations can be achieved with the help of costumes and makeup. Figure 13.4 shows how effectively a woman can play the male role of Falstaff in Shakespeare's *The Merry Wives of Windsor*.

A close analysis of the script also guides the actor toward the appearance and mannerisms of the character. Is the character calm or fidgety? Does she wet her lips or comb her hair repeatedly? Is he blond, and must the actor dye his hair or wear a wig? This first and most obvious step in creating a character is achieved by making certain that the actor's body conforms to the dictates of the script. The talented and imaginative actor goes beyond the barest necessities and invents details of the character's physical being that make the character unique and interesting. If her character is confident, the actor may determine that she moves slowly. If the character is timid, the actor may deter-

Figure 13.4 Pat Carroll as Falstaff in Shakespeare's *The Merry Wives of Windsor* at the Shakespeare Theatre in Washington, D.C. The character is male, but the actor is female. The actor has disguised her own body and appearance in order to look like the character.

mine that he rarely looks another character in the eye. Talented actors work to make their characters as individualized and complex as a real person is.

Voice

The actor must sound like the character. Many scripts require a character to have an accent or a regional dialect. If the character's first language is Russian or if the character is from Texas, the actor must be skilled enough to affect the correct speech so as to create a believable character. Similarly, the actor must determine the character's vocal quality. Is the voice high pitched or low? Does the character speak in a nasal whine or with a full-throated and honeyed voice? Does the character have a lisp or a whiskey rattle? Further, the actor must find the character's tempo and rhythm: does the character speak quickly or slowly, evenly or haltingly? Some of this information is found in the script, but much of it will come from the actor's imaginative choices. So long as those choices do not conflict with what the playscript requires, the actor may choose to speak in a way that makes that character unique.

Each person has such a singular manner of speaking that we easily recognize our friends and family on the phone. The actor's job is to create the character's particular way of speaking. If, for example, her character is methodical and well educated, the actor might decide to articulate her consonants very precisely. Or if his character is hard of hearing, the actor might choose to speak just a little too loudly.

Imagination

We all have particular talents, and an actor's talent is merely a different kind of talent from an athlete's or a mathematician's. Actors have a talent for feeling themselves into their characters by using their imagination. Actors, poets, and other artists often have an ability to feel more broadly and deeply than the average person. They also have a talent for communicating this feeling to others. This talent is called "empathy," which is different from sympathy. When we sympathize with someone's sadness, we have an intellectual understanding of it, but we remain apart from it. We "share" their sadness, says our dictionary. However, when we empathize with that sadness, we feel it in our bodies. We "participate" in it.

This talent for empathizing with someone else is essential because actors must convince the audience to suspend its disbelief and pretend that the actors' characters are real. But actors must have more than native talent. Actors must achieve an empathetic identification with their character in *every performance,* so they can't depend on inspiration alone. They must also have a technique for reproducing the emotion *on demand.* Stanislavsky discovered a way for actors to reproduce emotion; he called this process **emotional recall.** Stanislavsky taught actors to recall moments from their own life experience in which they had felt an emotion very similar to the one that the character experiences, and to use their own emotion as a substitute for the character's. Here's an example from Shakespeare's *Henry V.* The script says that the Princess of France is in love with King Henry of England, so the actress has to experience the emotion of love at the moment she sees the actor playing Henry. To do that, the actor needs to recall that emotion from her own life by concentrating very hard on remembering the physical sensations that existed when she felt an exhilarating love—what she saw at that time, what she heard, what she smelled, tasted, touched, and felt. Through this concentrated act of remembrance, the actor can reexperience her own true emotion. After she has repeated this exercise frequently, she can recall the emotion of love quite readily. Then, during rehearsals, she can recall the emotion every time she speaks the character's lines. After many repetitions of this dual effort, a sort of magical transference brings about a fusion of the character's lines and the actor's emotion. The result of all this hard work is a truthful performance that the audience believes.

In the process of creating their character, actors must use their skill at imagining with as concentrated a rigor as they use their skill at imitating physical and vocal behavior. An actor's ability to imagine emotion can be increased through training and through experience, but a natural talent for empathy is essential. A long role requires an actor to create a large number of the character's emotions, and much self-discipline is needed to create the truthful emotions that an audience will find believable throughout a performance.

One result of the technique of emotional recall is that the audience is regularly tricked into believing that the actor has turned into the character. An actor acquaintance told us that he went to see a film starring Marlon Brando, and he went with the great actor's sister. Brando is celebrated as one of the finest modern actors because of his extraordinary ability to use emotional recall to create believable emotions for his characters. As they sat in the darkened theatre, our friend told us, Jocelyn Brando kept up a running commentary on Marlon's performance with observations like: "That's Marlon being mad at Dad," "Now he's using the time he got a puppy," "That's when he got a bad report card." The character's emotions were persuasive, and the actor's substitutions were invisible to everyone but his sister.

Discipline

The fourth aspect of the actor's self that must be applied in the preparation of a performance is discipline. In order to do the careful analysis of the text, the rigorous physical and vocal delineation of the character, and the imaginative creation of the character's emotions, the actor must be as disciplined as a research chemist, a concert pianist, or a professional athlete. Acting is hard work, and the actor's willpower must be used to ensure that the necessary discipline is observed.

In preparing the role of Othello, Laurence Olivier worked on his voice for six months before rehearsals began, and he managed to lower his speaking range from a light baritone to a bass-baritone. He also pumped iron to build up his body so that he would look more like the mighty warrior Othello is described as (Figure 13.5). One of the reasons Olivier was a great actor was because he disciplined himself rigorously in the practice of his craft.

CONTEXT

Acting is not a solitary art, and the fellow artists and the physical circumstances in which the actor works contribute to the context in which a performance is created. Context includes the amount of time in which the work must be done, the space in which the production is rehearsed, the other people the actor works with, the particular circumstances of the production (the setting and costumes that will be used), and the audience.

Time is part of the actor's context. You've just read about the extensive work actors do in preparing a role, and you may wonder when they do it.

Figure 13.5 Laurence Olivier played the role of Othello only after he had spent months building up his body through rigorous physical exercises and lowering the pitch of his speaking voice through rigorous vocal exercises.

Typically, actors are hired only a few weeks before the first rehearsal. They have a very short time in which to analyze the script and begin recalling true emotions that they can substitute for their characters' feelings during the rehearsal period. When rehearsals begin, actors work an eight-hour day six days a week. In addition, they spend whatever time they can at home, learning lines, continuing their analysis, and recalling their own emotions. Conscientious actors spend forty-eight hours a week in rehearsal and another twenty-four hours a week working on their role at home. A typical rehearsal period in American theatres today is less than four weeks, so time is an important part of the actor's context.

The space the actor works in is another part of the actor's context. Most plays in America are rehearsed in empty rooms that are inadequate and inappropriate. Rehearsal halls are rarely as large as the stage is; many have obstructing pillars, flickering fluorescent lights, or dirty bathrooms. Unfortunately, the actor's typical work space is not conducive to the pursuit of excellence.

People are the third part of an actor's context. Actors work very closely with other actors, not all of whom they like or respect. Yet actors must collaborate with one another so that their characters' objectives can meld together smoothly and so that the performance can be a safe and effective one (Figure 13.6). Actors also must work with a director, choreographers, musical directors, fight directors, musicians, costume designers, and stage managers. An actor's performance is shaped to a very significant degree by the work of the other people involved in the production.

Figure 13.6 When Macbeth and Macduff fight, the two actors must collaborate to ensure that they don't get hurt and that the audience can suspend its disbelief. The actors' rehearsals for this fight involved the director, the fight choreographer, the costume designer, the scene designer, the property master, the lighting designer, and the stage manager. An important part of the actor's context is other people.

It is common for a production to be designed before rehearsals begin, so actors must accommodate their work to the stage setting and the costumes that have been planned by others. Design is another part of the actor's context.

Finally, of course, is the audience. Each performance of a play is different because each audience is different. Sometimes the theatre is filled with enthusiastic people who laugh and applaud; sometimes the theatre is half empty and the audience rattles candy wrappers and talks out loud. The audience influences the actors' work significantly and forms a part of the context in which they work.

Exercise CHARACTER ANALYSIS

Select a production that you have seen recently. List the title of the play, the playwright, the name of a specific character, and the actor who played that character. Answer the following questions about that actor's physical characterization.

1. Describe an aspect of the character's appearance that was required by the playscript.

2. Describe an aspect of the character's appearance that seemed to be the actor's invention.

3. Describe a trait of the character's physical behavior that was required by the playscript.

4. Describe a trait of the character's physical behavior that seemed to be the actor's invention.

5. Describe a trait of the character's physical behavior that seemed to be the actor's own behavior.

6. What particular physical skills did the character require of the actor that might have been learned in formal training?

Answer the following questions about that actor's vocal characterization.

7. Describe a trait of the vocal characterization that was required by the playscript.

8. Describe a trait of the vocal characterization that seemed to be the actor's invention.

9. Describe a trait of the vocal characterization that seemed to be the actor's own voice.

10. What particular vocal skills did the character require of the actor that might have been learned in formal training.

Answer the following questions about that actor's character interpretation.

11. What was the character's super objective?

12. Describe a moment in the actor's performance that seemed to be based on emotional recall.

14

The Director's Impact

The director has the artistic responsibility for the entire production. The director interprets how the playwright's script will be presented, coordinates the work of the designers and actors, and shapes the performance that the audience experiences. The director makes such decisions as where the actors stand when they say their lines, through which doors they enter and exit, what movements they make, what the characters look like, what the scenery looks like, and where the spotlights should focus. The best summary of a director's duties came from our friend's nine-year-old son. "My dad's a director," he said. "In a theatre, he's the one who tells everybody where to go and what to do and what to say and how to say it."

Directors, of course, give directions. The word "direction" describes at least four different functions: *guidance,* or telling how to get someplace (e.g., guiding the actors to proper entrances and exits); *instruction,* or showing how to do something (e.g., instructing the actors in how to bow to a king); *explanation,* or telling what something means (e.g., explaining to the actor the meaning of a particular line); and *inspiration,* or telling why something is important (e.g., inspiring the actors to prepare for opening night). A good director performs all four of these functions with skill, imagination, and taste.

EVOLUTION OF THE DIRECTOR

The job of the director is a relatively new one in the theatre; for centuries the theatre got along satisfactorily without a director. Let's look at how directors came into being and how directors' tasks were accomplished before theatre had directors.

The earliest theatrical era for which we have recorded information is called the Golden Age of ancient Athens, from about 450 B.C.E. to 350 B.C.E. Sophocles (SOF-oh-kleez) and other playwrights of ancient Athens supervised rehearsals of their own plays and performed many of the functions of the director. The Athenian theatre was very sophisticated in its organization, and the government assigned a rich person to finance the production of a playwright's script. This financier was called a *choregus* (ko-RAY-gus). If the playwright was not available to oversee rehearsals or was not skilled at some of the tasks of the director—such as coaching the actors or staging the chorus's dances—the choregus would engage a specialist called a *didaskolos* (die-DAS-ko-lus). The first part of the word "didaskolos" comes from the same stem as the word "didactic" and suggests our word "teacher." With the help of the didaskolos the playwright gave direction to the performance, because the playwright knew what the lines meant, why the characters did what they did, and what the audience should feel. The ancient Greeks began a theatrical practice that was to last for centuries.

Two thousand years later, the playwright was still the director; Shakespeare supervised the staging of his own plays. Shakespeare was an actor as well as an author and a partner in the business, so he could tell the other actors how to perform his plays. In *Hamlet* he has the young prince give instructions to a troupe of actors, and these famous lines are probably the sort of direction Shakespeare gave to his fellow actors:

HAMLET   Speak the speech, I pray you, as I pronounced it to you, trippingly
     on the tongue: but if you mouth it, as many of your players do, I had as
     lief the towncrier spoke my lines. Nor do not saw the air too much
     with your hand, thus, but use all gently . . . suit the action to the word,
     the word to the action.

TRANSLATION   Say the words, I beg you, just the way I said them, and articu-
     late them clearly: because if you mumble, as some of you actors do,
     then I'd just as soon have the public announcer say them. And don't
     flap your hands around, like this, but be selective in your gestures . . .
     match your actions to what the words tell you to do, and say the words
     so they make sense with what you're doing.

Some playwrights even today direct their own plays, although it doesn't happen very often. Playwright David Mamet directed his hit *Oleanna,* and Martin Charnin wrote and directed the musical hit *Annie.*

The function of director moved out of the playwright's hands when theatre became a profitable business and when decisions on how to do a play started being made on the basis of what would sell tickets rather than on what would serve the playwright's intentions. This change began in Shakespeare's time, but it didn't become standard practice until the eighteenth century. People who made a living in the theatre learned that audiences would pay to see stars, so the leading actors grew in importance until they had the power to say how things should be done. Over the years, the function of director shifted from the playwright to the actor. For two hundred years, theatre was directed by persons we call actor-managers. These stars ran the business and were its main attraction. For two centuries, actor-managers told the actors where to go and what to do and what to say and how to say it. Actor-managers directed the productions to suit their own egos, and plays were edited so theirs was the starring role. This practice led to financial rewards, though it created artistic distortions.

One of the greatest American actor-managers was Edwin Booth, brother of the infamous John Wilkes Booth, the man who assassinated Abraham Lincoln. A current actor-manager is Tony Randall, best known for the role of Felix on the TV series *The Odd Couple*. Randall founded the National Actors Theatre, which produces plays on Broadway.

 The last great actor-manager of the English stage was Donald Wolfit, whose career ended in the 1950s. A wonderful play called *The Dresser* is about Wolfit, and it was made into a film starring Albert Finney and Tom Courtenay.

Toward the end of the nineteenth century, another major change took place. The actor-manager was supplanted by a new worker in the theatre who was neither a playwright nor an actor; this new position, the director, gave shape to the performance. Most theatre historians identify the first director as George, Duke of Saxe-Meiningen, and most date the beginning of modern directing from the year 1874. Saxe-Meiningen was a small duchy in Germany. As the ruler, Duke George made the laws, collected the taxes, and ran his duchy to suit himself. He also loved theatre, so he used his tax revenues to make theatre, and he hired his citizens to work in his theatre. He alone decided how the plays would be done. He interpreted the scripts, oversaw the designs, and told the actors where to go and what to do and what to say and how to say it. He was meticulous in his concern for detail, and everything about his productions was done for the purpose of making a single, clear, artistic work. He did not write the scripts, and he did not act in the productions. Instead, he stood in front of the stage and shaped all aspects of the production so that they had an artistic coherence. In short, he directed.

George, Duke of Saxe-Meiningen, is credited with being the first director in the modern sense of that word.

In 1874, Saxe-Meiningen took his theatrical troupe on tour. In each of the capitals of Europe, the artful and carefully rehearsed productions of the Saxe-Meiningen players amazed audiences and excited theatre artists. No one had seen productions in which everything was arranged to support one theatre artist's point of view. No one had seen productions in which the leading actor stood where that character needed to be in order to tell the story, instead of at center stage; in which each minor actor was a believable character who helped tell the story; in which the designs helped tell the story instead of making the star seem more attractive. Quickly, other directors imitated Saxe-Meiningen's way of presenting plays, and two of the most influential were the Frenchman André Antoine and the Russian Constantine Stanislavsky.

Antoine founded a small theatre in Paris called the Théâtre Libre (tay-AH-tra LEE-bra). The name "Free Theatre" did not mean that admission was free, but that the artists were freed from governmental supervision and artistic traditions. The Théâtre Libre became the prototype for small theatre companies across Europe and America, and it presented artfully rehearsed plays that were carefully directed.

Stanislavsky founded the Moscow Art Theatre, which is still in operation today. Here Stanislavsky introduced the acting system explained in the previous chapter. The books he wrote describing his work as a director were mightily influential, and our sense of what a director does can be traced from Saxe-Meiningen to Stanislavsky to Americans such as Elia Kazan, who directed Tennessee Williams's *A Streetcar Named Desire.*

Why did the concept of the director develop when it did and not earlier? We believe the process was a logical outgrowth of Determinism, the same philosophy that led to the theatrical style of Realism. The playwrights who wrote realistic plays accepted Determinism as the truth of human experience, and directors realized that humans can be best understood if they are studied in a context that reveals how they are determined. To do that, one single person had to shape the production, to direct it. The audience who looks at a theatrical production through a proscenium arch is like the scientist who looks at a subject under a microscope. An objective eye was needed to put actions and behavior into perspective and arrange a coherent world that the audience could study. And that's what the director provided.

DUTIES OF THE DIRECTOR

The director's job is a complicated one, and each director does it a bit differently. The duties that a director performs, however, can be summarized into a list of seven aspects. Let's look at each of these in detail.

Seven Aspects of a Director's Work

1. Selecting the script
2. Choosing the key collaborators
3. Conceptualizing the production
4. Realizing the conception in sight and sound
5. Casting the roles
6. Rehearsing the production
7. Being the spiritual leader

Selecting the Script

In American theatre today, directors rarely get to choose the plays they direct. Back when playwrights were their own directors and later when actor-managers chose the plays, scripts were selected by the people who would oversee the production. But when the director evolved as someone different from the producer, who finances and controls the business, the director became an employee. In America's commercial theatre, the producer hires the director; in not-for-profit theatres, the artistic director selects the scripts and hires the directors. In most cases, the director selects the script only indirectly, by deciding whether or not to accept the job that has been offered.

Directors accept a job offer based on the same criteria that we all use when making a career choice: to pay the rent, to advance a career, to maintain the health insurance that goes with a union contract. Directors would *like* to consider such questions as: Is the script theatrically vital, and is it emotionally and intellectually moving? Will it say something to an audience that the director believes is important? Does the script reveal some truths about human experience that will help to make this world a better one? Unfortunately, directors rarely make their choices on these bases.

Choosing the Key Collaborators

The director is accountable for all artistic facets of a production. Because few directors are equally skilled in the other crafts of the theatre, directors need a team of collaborators who will design the scenery, costumes, lighting, and sound; who will conduct the musicians and coach the singers; who will choreograph the dances and stage the fights; and who will provide research and analytical materials for the artistic team to use. Because the director will guide their work a compatible team must be chosen that has a common vision and a common way of working. The better the collaborators, of course, the more hope there is for a vital and successful production. One of the sad realities of American theatre today is that directors rarely get to choose their collaborators. Commercial producers hire the designers they want, and so do artistic directors of not-for-profit theatres. The optimal creative team is rarely assembled.

 A professional football coach resigned, explaining that his employers interfered with his work and wouldn't let him hire the players he wanted. "If they want me to cook the dinner," he said, "they've got to let me shop for the ingredients." Theatre directors have the same lament.

Figure 14.1 In this production conference, a scene designer and a director explore the ideas that the designer has presented in a three-dimensional model and a two-dimensional painted sketch. (Georgia Shakespeare Festival)

Conceptualizing the Production

Conceptualizing the production is an intellectual and creative process through which the director and the key collaborators determine how the script is to be interpreted and how that interpretation is to be realized on the stage. The director is the single person whose vision gives shape to the work of all the collaborators so that the production has a unity, a focus, and a purpose. The director provides a unique image and gives a central organizing authority to the production. The director keeps things moving toward a single goal.

The production is conceptualized through a sequence of conferences in which each of the key collaborators presents the work-in-progress (Figure 14.1). The director uses these conferences to guide creative efforts toward a common vision. At the first of these conferences, the director presents a clear description of what the production will be like. This presentation usually includes a visual metaphor that will stimulate the creative processes of the designers and an aural metaphor that will do the same for the composer and sound designer. In order to create these metaphors, the director will have researched the biography of the playwright and analyzed the structure, characters, theme, style, and genre of the play before talking with the key collaborators. Most directors have had extensive formal education and training in such research and analysis.

A visual metaphor is a unique image made by juxtaposing visual elements that communicate a feeling for the play that cannot be expressed in any other form. Here's the visual metaphor Tom provided his designers at the first conference for his production of Sophocles' *Oedipus the*
(Continued)

> (*Continued*)
> *King:* "A torn and blood-stained cloth of gold that is draped on a glis-teningly white, broken, and scarred Ionic column that stands alone in the center of a large circle of dusty brown earth and is lit by streaks of golden sunlight at early dusk." Tom's aural metaphor for that produc-tion was: "A man's voice imitating the cry of a bird as its wing is slowly torn off."

The second conference permits the designers and other key collabora-tors to bring to the table the work they are developing. Presentations include pencil sketches of designs, snatches of melody lines, and choreographic rou-tines. The director approves or rejects what the collaborators have developed, and suggests revisions. At subsequent conferences, the early drawings are fol-lowed by color renderings of the revised designs, completed compositions, and finished ideas for the choreography. At some point in the process, the director gives the go-ahead to the collaborators, and they begin to turn their ideas into scenery, costumes, light, sound, and dance.

Realizing the Conception in Sight and Sound

Even after directors begin to rehearse the actors, they must make periodic checks to ensure that the scenery, costumes, lighting, sound, and choreogra-phy are all progressing toward the image of the production that was described at the first conference.

Casting the Roles

If the audience doesn't believe in the characters, the whole show fails no mat-ter how beautifully it's designed or how well it's written. The audience expe-riences the play through the characters, so the director had better have a talent for casting. Directors say that casting is 80 percent of directing. A little luck doesn't hurt, either.

Particular qualities and skills are needed for each role, and the director must find actors who possess them. The actor playing the title role in Shake-speare's *Henry V* must speak long speeches in a way that makes their mean-ing clear, and he needs to be trained in stage combat as well. The actor who plays Walter Lee Younger in *A Raisin in the Sun* must be convincing in his rage and frustration. The actor who plays Kim, the female lead in the musical *Miss Saigon*, must be Asian, beautiful, and young and must have a gorgeous soprano singing voice (Figure 14.2). In short, the actors must meet the audi-ence's expectations of the character. That's why typecasting is so common in the theatre. Some plays, fortunately, have characters who can be cast from any age group, any gender, and any ethnic background. Some adventurous direc-tors interpret a play nontraditionally, thereby opening up roles for actors who might otherwise not be considered (Color Plate 24).

Figure 14.2 Lea Salonga originated the role of Kim in *Miss Saigon*. The role demands that the actress be young, beautiful, and Asian and have a gorgeous soprano voice.

Casting is also difficult because the director must choose from available actors. The director may want Denzel Washington to play Walter Lee Younger, but if Washington is busy making a film or can't come to terms on the salary, then the director must choose another actor. Like politics, theatre is the art of the possible. It is one compromise after another.

Rehearsing the Play

Rehearsing is what most people think of when they picture a director at work. They conjure up an image of a person yelling, pleading, and communing with actors who are carrying their scripts around in a dingy rehearsal hall that has lines drawn on the floor marking out what the setting will be like. This image is not far from the truth, though we have already learned that much of a director's work is done before the first rehearsal ever begins. Nevertheless, the rehearsal hall is where the production comes to life. A director performs five kinds of work in rehearsals.

The Director's Rehearsal Work

1. Staging
2. Coaching
3. Structuring the dynamics
4. Standing in for the audience
5. Orchestrating the final rehearsals

Staging   Staging is usually done in a rehearsal hall. Lines are drawn on the floor to indicate where the walls of the set will be, and the director begins the process of arranging the actors' movements, known as **blocking.** The actors' movements are blocked out, and the director places the actors with an eye to how various "pictures" help to tell the story. Directors follow fundamental practices of visual composition when they block out the staging, and you ought to be able to follow the story just by looking at a sequence of still pictures of a production.

Some blocking is very formal—the choreography of a musical like *Miss Saigon*, for example. Some blocking results from a playwright's specific instructions in the script—Jack's attempts to snatch his cigarette case back from Algernon in the opening scene of *The Importance of Being Earnest*, for example. And some blocking is invented by the director in order to tell the story visually.

When Tom directed Shakespeare's *Much Ado about Nothing*, he invented staging for the moment when the wedding of Claudio and Hero is disrupted by the evil Don John, who confirms Claudio's accusations and says, "these things are true." He staged a group of monks so that the candles they were carrying formed a Christian cross. It added sparkle and religious symbolism to the stage picture. When Don John announced that the bride was a whore, he strode through the monks, scattering the cross into streaking lights of chaos. The story was told visually at both a literal and symbolic level.

Coaching   Coaching the actors to perform their roles requires directors to work closely with the cast (Figure 14.3). Since each actor works in a unique way and since directors must work with many actors on each production, directors must have flexible working methods. One actor responds best to coaxing, another to demonstration, another to intimidation, another to discussion, and yet another to improvisation. Directors must do whatever brings results. Actors need to understand why their characters do things—they must understand the character's motivation—and to be helpful, directors must understand the actor's process and the vocabulary that derives from the

Figure 14.3 Coaching the actors is one of a director's most important jobs. Note the scripts in the actors' hands and the lines taped on the floor of the rehearsal hall to help the actors learn what the set will be like. (Merrimack Repertory Theatre, Massachusetts)

teachings of Stanislavsky. In addition to being good at conceptualizing a production and in addition to understanding how to tell a story visually, a director needs to be skilled at coaching actors.

Here's an old theatre joke. A veteran director tells a young actor to move to the window and look out while he says his line. The actor starts to do it, but stops and asks the director, "What's my motivation?" The impatient director snarls back, "How about your paycheck?"

Structuring the Dynamics The director must structure the dynamics of the performance in very much the same way that the conductor of an orchestra structures the dynamics of the symphony during rehearsals. The director must decide when the dialogue should be loud or soft, when the actors should speak fast or slow, when their movements should be hurried or deliberate, and when the stage picture should be large or small. While there are some guidelines for this craft (at moments of excitement, for example, the performance should get louder and there should be a lot of movement), much of this work is subjective and reflects the director's own sensibilities.

Standing in for the Audience Directors try to imagine how the audience will see and hear the production. The director is the audience's stand-in. Directors must make countless judgments that will anticipate the audience's response. In structuring the dynamics, coaching the actors, and staging the action, directors must make thousands of decisions on the assumption that the

Figure 14.4   The director from the Peterborough Players in New Hampshire orchestrates the final rehearsals that bring all the elements of the production together. Here, a director gives instructions to a stage manager who relays them over a headset to the stagehands.

There's an old saying that applies here: "A hit play is well acted, and a flop is badly directed."

audience will like what the director likes. One measure of a director's quality is the degree to which the director's tastes are shared by the audience. If the audience finds the pace of the action too slow, or if the audience doesn't believe in an actor's performance, or if the audience gets confused by the staging, then the director has failed.

Orchestrating the Final Rehearsals   The final phase of the director's work includes the technical and dress rehearsals that take place in the theatre after the weeks of work in the rehearsal hall. The technical and dress rehearsals are when the actors first go onto the set and when they first wear their costumes, when the lights are focused and all the light cues are rehearsed, when all the production elements that the collaborators have been refining are added to what the actors have been rehearsing. The director's job is to ensure that all the parts and pieces are true to the original vision and that the various elements of the production are coordinated by the stage manager so that they contribute to the total effect (Figure 14.4). The fit of the costumes, the speed of the scene shift, the volume of the actors, the color of the lights, the tempo of the musicians—these aspects and more must be orchestrated toward a coherent production that expresses the director's vision.

The final element that is added is the audience, and the final rehearsals are called **previews,** or preview performances. At a preview, the director watches both the performance *and* the reaction of the audience, so as to see what should be changed at the next day's rehearsal. The preview audience's responses help the director to shape the performance.

Being the Spiritual Leader

Leading a large group of temperamental artists and craftspersons is the director's charge throughout all this work, from the first conference with the key collaborators to the opening night.

 A director's work ends with the first performance. Theatre directors are not like athletic coaches and symphony conductors, who attend each game or concert. After opening night, the stage manager takes over the responsibility for supervising performances, and the director's job is done.

The playwright, actors, designers, stagehands, box office treasurer—all have placed their confidence in the director. They all need the director to show them the way and provide all the answers. In some instances the director must be the stern parental figure who says, "Do it *now,* and do it *right!*" In other instances the director must be the nurturing parental figure who says, "You're doing wonderfully, and they're going to love you."

Good directors are a mixture of skills, experience, talent, and knowledge with a gift for organization and a sensitivity for the audience. In addition, good directors have so much charisma that people will accept their leadership, listen to their advice, and believe in their direction.

IMPORTANCE OF THE DIRECTOR

In the century since George, Duke of Saxe-Meiningen, showed his carefully directed productions to the artists of Europe and changed forever the way we make theatre, there has grown an interesting debate about the nature of the director's work. Is the director an interpretive artist or a creative artist? That is, does a director merely interpret the creative work of the playwright and put it on a stage, or does a director create a piece of theatre from many raw materials, only one of which is the writer's script?

The interpretive argument is that the director is dependent on the playwright who has created the story and characters. Theatre got along fine without directors for more than 2,000 years; all the director does is facilitate the work of the actors and designers.

The creative argument is that the director is the primary creative force, the singular artist who imagines the production. The director manipulates the actors, supervises the design, and brings the literary script to theatrical life. The script is only a blueprint for a production, whereas the performance is the creation of the director.

There's good evidence and logic on both sides of this argument, and it's unlikely that either view will prevail. Whichever side of this argument you are on—and you're likely to change sides depending on the production you're using as an example—one thing is true. Since 1874, the director is the person in the theatre who "tells everybody where to go and what to do and what to say and how to say it."

Exercise ASSESSING HOW A PLAY WAS DIRECTED

Select a play that you have attended recently. List the title of the play, the playwright, the director, and the name of the theatre where the play was performed. Answer the following questions about this production.

1. Why do you think the director chose to direct this play?

2. Based on the information in the playbill (or any other source available to you), do you think that the director had the choice or did not have the choice to collaborate with one or more of the designers? Explain your answer.

3. Describe how the music or sound supported or obscured the director's concept.

4. Which actors do you think the director cast well? Why?

5. Which actors do you think the director cast poorly? Why?

6. Describe a moment in the staging that you believe was required by the script.

7. Describe a moment in the staging that you believe was invented by the director.

8. Describe why you believe the director did (or did not) structure the dynamics well.

9. Judging from the response of the audience, do you think the director was a good stand-in for the audience during the rehearsals?

10. Do you feel that the director of this play was an interpretive artist or a creative artist? Explain your answer.

15

The Playwright's Story

The very earliest study of theatre was *The Poetics*, written by the ancient Greek philosopher Aristotle (AIR-iz-tot-ul). After more than two thousand years, *The Poetics* is still read and respected, and in it Aristotle describes a play as "an imitation of an action." In playwriting terms, the word "action" describes any event that changes the status quo. If a door is open and somebody closes it, that's a physical action. The status quo has been changed. If a character has a change of mind, that's an intellectual action that changes the status quo as completely as a physical action does.

A play imitates many small actions as it unfolds. A playwright uses the raw materials of dialogue, description, character, and action to make a scene, which is the small segment of an entire play in which one conflict is introduced and resolved. A scene is the building block for making a play. It is one brick that, when placed with many other bricks, goes to make up the whole building. A scene imitates a small action, and the totality of all the scenes makes a play. A play imitates one major action. That major action is the **plot,** the story that is told, that takes you on a journey from the status quo at the beginning to the changed circumstances at the end. Aristotle explains that the plot is "the life and soul of the drama," because he knew that the plot is the most important element in a play. It's the story that keeps us interested.

The correct name for someone who creates a playscript is playwright. A playwright "wrights" (constructs) a play in much the same way that a shipwright "wrights" (constructs) a ship. The activity of writing a playscript is called playwriting. The word "playwrite" does not exist.

THE PLAYWRIGHT'S TOOLS

A playwright is an author who tells a story in which the status quo gets changed. The tools that the playwright uses to tell this story are dialogue, stage directions, characters, and actions.

The Playwright's Tools

- Dialogue
- Stage directions
- Characters
- Actions

Dialogue

Dialogue describes the speeches that the characters say, and it's the playwright's primary material. Most of the words a playwright writes are dialogue, and the dialogue is the entirety of the words that the audience hears spoken from the stage. Here's a sample bit of dialogue:

HE   I want to leave the room.

SHE   If you do, I won't sleep with you.

HE   I'll be back in three minutes.

SHE   If you leave, that's it.

HE   The five thousand dollars out there is very important to me.

SHE   You don't want me.

HE   I want the five thousand dollars more.

SHE   Come back in here.

Without any of the additional tools that the playwright uses, it is very difficult to know how this dialogue would be spoken or by whom, or what the dialogue means. As you read this sample conversation, you probably formed an initial sense of the meaning. Hold on to that impression while we discuss how the playwright's other tools inflect the dialogue.

Stage Directions

Some of a character's actions are *implicit* in the dialogue. In the eight lines of sample dialogue, the actor playing HE must exit in order for SHE's last line to make any sense. But playwrights often include *explicit* descriptions in their stage directions as well. These descriptions tell the actors what their characters do or feel at particular moments. Although the audience never hears these descriptions, these stage directions are used by the playwright to shape what the audience experiences in performance. Let's add some stage directions to these same eight lines just the way a playwright might.

HE   I want to leave the room.

SHE   *(crying)* If you do, I won't sleep with you.

HE   *(disgusted)* I'll be back in three minutes.

SHE   If you leave, that's it.

HE   *(getting up)* The five thousand dollars out there is very important to me.

SHE   You don't want me.

HE   I want the five thousand dollars *more.*

    (HE exits)

SHE   Come back in here.

Now the meaning of the dialogue is much less ambiguous. By including these stage directions, the playwright has ensured that the actors will perform the roles in a particular manner and that the audience will not only hear the dialogue but will hear it spoken in a particular way and will see the characters do particular things. Has your first understanding of the dialogue remained the same, or has it changed? Let's see what happens if the final stage direction is altered.

HE   I want the five thousand dollars *more.*

    (HE starts to leave. SHE pours a drink over his head. HE hits her with a pillow, they roll about on the bed, and they kiss. HE exits and she calls after him, laughing.)

SHE   Come back in here.

Now the dialogue ends happily instead of angrily. By altering only this one stage direction, the playwright has changed the meaning of the dialogue and more precisely defined the nature of the characters. Stage directions added to dialogue go a long way toward making a play come alive.

> Some plays have no dialogue at all and are made up entirely of descriptions and stage directions. Samuel Beckett's *Act Without Words* is an excellent example of this unusual kind of play. The entirety of the audience's experience is formed from watching the actors doing the actions described by playwright Beckett.

Characters

Aristotle defines a character as "the agent for the action." Without a character, there'd be no way for the audience to hear the dialogue or see an action happen, so the character is the agent that speaks the dialogue and enacts the stage directions. Characters give body and coherence to the dialogue and the descriptions.

Let's return to our eight lines of dialogue. Did you imagine that the characters were your age? If so, the meaning of the action is quite clear: it's a lovers' quarrel. But what if the characters are a young mother and her five-year-old son? Read the initial dialogue again, without the stage directions, and imagine it being spoken by these two new characters.

This time, HE wants to continue playing his game, and SHE wants him to take a nap. The line "I won't sleep with you" is no longer a euphemism, but is now a simple declarative sentence. And the references to five thousand dollars lose their reality and their urgency, don't they? Indeed, you can probably imagine the lilting melody in the mother's voice that conveys a gentle warning as SHE says the last line, "Come back in here."

By using the raw materials of dialogue and description, the playwright reveals the characters' actions, but until you know who the characters are, you can't understand what's going on. You learned in chapter 13 that actors get information about their characters from four sources in the playscript: what the playwright says about the characters in stage directions, what characters say about themselves, what characters say about other characters, and what characters do. In these same four ways, the playwright shapes the characters. The playwright writes the descriptions in which particular emotional attitudes are described and specific activities are defined; the playwright writes the characters' own dialogue, in which they describe themselves; the playwright writes the other characters' dialogue, in which they describe each other; and most important, the playwright creates the characters' actions—both the physical actions and the intellectual choices that define each character. The playwright uses these four devices to create the characters who make it possible for the story to be told.

Actions

You learned a simple definition for action at the beginning of this chapter: an action is any event that changes the status quo. Here's a more complex definition: an action is the product of the energy of a goal against an obstacle. For example, your goal is to leave the room; the obstacle is the locked door; you overcome the obstacle by unlocking the door—you have produced a result, exerted an energy, changed the status quo, completed an action. Here's an example from *Oedipus the King* (Figure 15.1). Oedipus wants to learn who killed the previous king, Laius; that's his goal. His obstacle is that no one will step forward with any information. Oedipus overcomes his obstacle by decreeing that anyone who withholds information is as guilty as the person who committed the murder. Oedipus completes his action—changes the status quo, produces a result—with his decree because he obtains from Tiresias an answer, albeit a cryptic one, to his question, "Who killed Laius?"

Figure 15.1 Oedipus interrogates an old servant as he seeks the answer to the question, "Who killed King Laius?" This ancient Greek tragedy retains its emotional power and its intellectual relevance for today's audiences because, just like Oedipus, we are all seeking to learn our true identities. (Classic Greek Theatre Festival, tour of New Mexico)

THE PLAYWRIGHT'S METHODOLOGY

How does a play get written? First, the playwright imagines the action to be imitated and the plot that will embody that action. The playwright next determines which scenes to include and in what order. Finally, the playwright writes the dialogue and stage directions for those scenes. Sounds simple and orderly, right? DON'T BELIEVE IT! If writing plays were that easy, any of us could be another Shakespeare. We've teased you by presenting a very orderly and rational description of what playwrights do, but playwrights are creative humans, and the creative mind doesn't work in an orderly and sequential fashion. Quite the contrary, creative endeavors are usually far more chaotic. Because playwrights are creative, not analytic, they tend to work associatively, not sequentially. (For a fuller explanation of associative logic and sequential logic, refer back to the discussion of Surrealism in chapter 10).

Where do playwrights work? In their heads. On a piece of paper. At a computer screen. There's no special place where playwrights imagine their characters and stories, and no special time of day when they invent the dialogue. One playwright we know talks out loud while driving on the freeway; another only gets going when she's staring at her computer screen. The English playwright Noel Coward wrote *Private Lives* in forty-eight hours while sitting on a hotel bed in Shanghai. Other playwrights spend years on a play.

Playwrights frequently begin their work with an image that appears to them out of nowhere and that fits somewhere in the middle of the play. Tennessee Williams said that before he began writing *A Streetcar Named Desire*, all he knew was an image that came to him of a woman wearing a slip, sitting at a table, beneath a bare lightbulb (Figure 15.2). Williams started with a visual

Figure 15.2 The character of Blanche DuBois in Tennessee Williams's *A Streetcar Named Desire* has an emotional breakdown near the end of the play. This picture from the 1998 revival shows how the lighting designer helped the audience understand her mental state.

image; other playwrights begin with words. A writer imagines snatches of dialogue, impressions of characters, and feelings of outrage in no particular order and forges them into a coherent pattern.

At some stage of the writing, the associative process gives over to the sequential and the playwright's work becomes a coolly rational act. This aspect of the playwright's work *can* be described. We'll explain how the playwright imposes order on creativity, and we'll start with the story of an English prince that Shakespeare used as the basis for one of his greatest plays.

Once upon a time there was a young Prince of England named Henry who lived a riotous and drunken life as a young man. He frequented taverns and brothels and kept company with criminals. When he was crowned king, he changed his behavior and was determined to become a good king. To achieve this goal, he decided to reconquer the territories in France that had belonged to England in earlier years. Henry sought legal sanction, financial support, and religious endorsement to start a war; he put down a small rebellious plot at home; he invaded France and fought several battles against fierce odds, conquered the walled town of Harfleur, and won a huge victory at Agincourt. He then signed a peace treaty that included his marrying the Princess of France. It appeared that all would end happily, but Henry died soon after, at an early age, and his successors squabbled among themselves and permitted France to reconquer the territories he had won.

One rational decision that the playwright has to make is when in the story to begin the plot and when to end it. Shakespeare wanted his audience to feel patriotic about Henry's military conquests, so he began *Henry V* after Henry has been crowned and he ended it with Henry's marriage to the Princess of France. Another playwright might have wanted to show the audience how Henry's drunken adolescence hurt the kingdom and might have chosen a different beginning and ending.

After deciding where to begin and end the play, the playwright must decide what parts of the story to include and what characters are needed for those scenes. Shakespeare chose to exclude the scene in which Falstaff, Henry's closest boyhood friend, dies, but he included the scene in which Falstaff's friends lament his dying. Like any playwright, Shakespeare made hundreds of choices about what scenes and what characters to include and exclude.

The Playscript's Structure

The playwright must next determine the order of the scenes; the plot must be given a structure. The word "structure" is defined as "the order of the incidents," and playwrights can arrange the order of the scenes in their plots in whatever way best tells the story and conveys the meaning they intend. Stories have a beginning, a middle, and an end, but playwrights can structure the events of their plot in a variety of ways. We are going to discuss three structures that you should be able to recognize.

Three Common Structures for a Playscript

1. Linear
2. Cinematic
3. Contextual

Linear   The most common structure for a playscript is a linear one, so it's the one you will encounter most often. The incidents of the plot are arranged in a sequential line, hence the adjective "linear" (LIN-ee-er). The incidents are arranged chronologically, along the line of time, and the first scene happens near the beginning of the story. *Henry V* is arranged chronologically, and so is *Oedipus the King*.

The linear structure has some variations that you will observe in the plays you'll see. A bold difference between the two examples we're using is that *Henry V* jumps from one year to another and excludes events that happen between scenes, whereas *Oedipus the King* goes straight through from start to finish with no gaps in its timeline. Both are linear, but *Henry V* is episodic and *Oedipus the King* is continuous.

A second difference between these two examples is that *Oedipus the King* has only one simple plot, while *Henry V* has a complex plot that interweaves three stories. One story is about King Henry, a second involves his tavern friends, and the third is about the French. Sometimes these stories overlap and intersect, but each remains coherent.

No qualitative distinction can be made between a simple and a complex plot, or between a continuous and an episodic linear structure. No play is better than another because of its structure, but some stories lend themselves to one or another of these structures.

Cinematic   Ever since movies introduced the idea that a story can be told in **flashback,** some playwrights have chosen to arrange the incidents in their plots in a nonchronological order. The structure of the plot is not the same as the order of events in the story. Imagine *Oedipus the King* with a cinematic structure:

> Once upon a time blind Oedipus wanders away from the city of Thebes. He walks past Mount Cithaeron (ki-TIE-ron), past the spot where he was abandoned as a baby, and he remembers (and we see in a flashback) how the Shepherd rescued him and gave him to the Corinthian Shepherd. Oedipus staggers on his way, and in the next scene he is a youth in Corinth, thinking he's the prince of that land. The next scene flashes forward to Oedipus in Thebes, listening as the Corinthian Shepherd reveals that Oedipus is the son of the Theban royal family.

The order of the incidents in this version is jumbled and out of chronological sequence. A playwright might choose this structure if the story of Oedipus's coming to terms with the knowledge of his true birth is more important than the story of Oedipus's discovery of that truth.

Another cinematic plot structure allows the playwright to introduce scenes that are on a different level of reality. In Arthur Miller's *Death of a Salesman,* several scenes are presented not as they happen in objective reality but as the title character, Willy, imagines them. The audience encounters the subjective reality inside Willy's head. The clearest example is the scene in which Willy is playing cards with his neighbor Charley, and he imagines his dead brother Ben is in the room with them. Charley can't see or hear Ben, but Willy and the audience can. More than one level of reality is going on.

Contextual   The contextual structure is rather rare. One example is *The Private Life of the Master Race,* written by the twentieth-century German playwright Bertolt Brecht. This play is made up of twenty-seven different short scenes: some are twenty minutes long and some are only two minutes long. Each scene is independent of the others in the sense that it has its own characters and a complete plot. Each can stand on its own as a complete work, however short it might be. No cause-and-effect logic leads from one scene to the next; the play has no traditional plot with a beginning, middle, and end. Instead, the play is a collection of short playlets, similar to a bound collection of short stories. Productions of *The Private Life of the Master Race* usually include only nine to twelve of the scenes. The director selects which scenes to include and determines the order in which they are to be presented. As a result, the content of any two productions might be significantly different.

So what gives this play its artistic coherence? All the scenes are variations on the same subject. Each scene shows how depressing it was to live in Germany in the 1930s when the Nazi regime was in power. Each of the scenes relates to the others because they share a common subject, and each scene takes its importance and its meaning from the context in which it is placed, from its relationship to the totality of scenes.

A more common example of a contextual structure is a musical review such as *Side by Side by Sondheim* or *Oh Coward!* These entertaining theatrical events are sometimes called anthologies and are comprised of songs and comic sketches drawn from a wide variety of sources, but all are by the same composer. The composer gives this production its context, and each song belongs in the play only because it was written by that composer.

Contextually structured plays can be difficult for the average theatregoer to enjoy because most of us have a very strong habit of plays with a linear structure. We like a story with a beginning, middle, and end; we are often confused by plays that do not have a clearly understood episodic or cinematic structure.

A novel with a contextual structure was published in 1969. *The Unfortunates,* by B. S. Johnson, has twenty-seven chapters that are not bound into a traditional book; instead they are held in a box. Readers are instructed to begin by reading the chapter titled *First* and to conclude by reading the chapter titled *Last.* The other twenty-five chapters can be read in whatever order the reader chooses. *The Unfortunates* tells the story of a Saturday afternoon in one man's life, and it includes memories of earlier times and descriptions of events on that afternoon. The story takes on different meanings depending on the order in which the chapters are read.

The Playscript's Theme

Playwrights organize the structure of their plot to communicate a central idea. A play may serve up many ideas that stimulate thought—many teachers and critics use the word "theme" to describe an idea that might be discussed—but the playwright's *major* concern is the idea that is expressed through the plot of the play. That idea is its theme.

There is a simple way that you can figure out the theme of a play, and it works whether the play is profound, like *Oedipus the King,* or frivolous, like a TV situation comedy. First, tell yourself the plot of the play. Next, condense the plot down to one simple sentence. Your sentence should begin, "This is the story of . . ." Last, make a generalization from that sentence, something that applies universally.

Here's an example, using Sophocles' *Oedipus the King:* "This is the story of Oedipus, who tries to escape the fate that the oracle of Apollo tells him but who discovers to his horror that he has fulfilled it by killing his father and marrying his mother." The generalization based on that synopsis might suggest that the theme of this play is "People are the victims of their fate."

Exercise   ANALYZING A PLAYWRIGHT'S PLAYSCRIPT

Select a play that you have attended recently. List the title of the play and the playwright. Answer the following questions about this production.

1. Tell the story of the play in a simple sentence that begins "This is the story of . . ."

2. State the theme of the play, the generalization about human experience that you can extrapolate from your description of the story.

3. Describe a moment in the play when the story is advanced by an action that is *not* expressed in dialogue.

4. Describe a moment in the play when the story is advanced by an action that *is* expressed in dialogue.

5. Describe the structure that the playwright used for this play.

16

Should Your Friends Go?

*W*hen you walk out of the theatre, somebody's bound to ask you if you liked the play, and sooner or later some friends are going to ask you if they should go. Even though you have learned a fair amount about how theatre is produced and how designs communicate nonverbally, and even though you may have thought hard about the function that theatre serves in our society, you may not yet be certain how to organize your thoughts and feelings so that you can express them in a helpful way. We can help.

GOETHE'S THREE QUESTIONS

Nearly two hundred years ago, a German named Goethe (GER-ta), who was an important novelist, playwright, poet, and critic, wrote an essay in which he described three questions that you can use to organize your thoughts and feelings about a play.

Goethe's Three Questions

1. What was the artist trying to do?
2. Did the artist succeed in doing it?
3. Was it worth the doing?

To see how Goethe's three questions work, let's apply them to the actor. The first question is, "What is the artist trying to do?" When we substitute "the actor" for "the artist," this question turns into, "What is the actor trying to do?" Here's a chance to apply what you learned in chapter 13 about how an actor creates a character. Begin by thinking through the play and deciding what the character is like. What did the playwright's dialogue say that the character looked like, sounded like, behaved like? Now ask yourself if the character that the actor created was the same as the character that the playwright defined in the text. If not, was the actor trying to create a character different from the one the playwright described? Goethe's first question might help you analyze the actor's work better if you phrased it like this: "What character was the actor trying to create?"

Goethe's second question is, "Did the artist succeed in doing it?" When you apply this question to the actor, it turns into, "Did the actor create the appearance, voice, and emotional complexity of the character, and did you believe in the character?" For example, ask yourself if the actor creating the character of Iago succeeded to the extent that the other characters could believe he was an honest man. Did *you* believe in Iago? By answering Goethe's second question, you are making a reasoned and informed judgment about the actor's performance. If the actor succeeded in what he or she was doing, you probably liked the performance and you may have liked the entire play. If the actor failed, you probably disliked the performance, which may have influenced how you felt about the entire play. After you have asked these first two questions about several of the actors, you will be able to understand your attitude toward the play in great detail and you will be better able to explain to your friends whether they should go.

Goethe's third question, "Was it worth the doing?" requires you to decide if the actor's effort was justified. If the actor succeeded in creating the character differently from the way the playwright described that character, you can decide if you think the actor's effort helped or hindered your enjoyment. If it helped, then what the actor did was worth the doing. If it hindered, then what the actor did was not worth the doing. If, on the other hand, the actor succeeded in creating the character as described by the playwright, then you can decide if that *character* was worth creating. Here's an example. Was the actor's successful creation of Iago a useful tool for showing you how easily people are fooled by a villain who has the outward appearance and manner of an honest man? And did that demonstration help to make the theme of the play clear, even though the character of Iago is morally offensive? Goethe's third question requires you to take a stance as to what you believe is good and bad, what you think should or should not be presented on a stage. When you share that opinion with your friends, they will know what you're talking about.

Let's do this exercise a second time to analyze the work of a scene designer. "What was the artist trying to do?" turns into "What kind of reality was the scene designer trying to create, and what is the location, time, and value system of the fictional world?" Use the information that you learned in chapter 10 about theatrical styles to answer the first part of this question. You can tell your friends, for example, if the production presents the Surrealism of a subjective reality or the Classicism of an idealized reality. The analysis of scene design that you learned how to do in chapter 12 will help you answer the second part of the question; you will understand how the scene design communicates information, how it underscores the emotion of the play, how it helps to tell the story, and how it defines the world of the play. When you have analyzed the scene design so that you know what the designer was trying to do, you can consider whether the designer was successful or not. If the designer was striving to create a Realistic interior but the walls wobbled, the designer failed. If the designer was trying to create an Expressionistic exterior and you felt that the characters were oppressed, the designer succeeded. Once you have determined whether the scene designer succeeded, you can turn to Goethe's third question. This question requires you to judge if the designer's interpretation was appropriate for the play. Not all designs are appropriate, and you must ask yourself if the scene design was a valuable way to communicate the theme and mood of the play. In short, was it worth the doing?

When your friends ask if they should go to the play, they often want to know two things: what was the play about and what was your opinion of the playwright's work. As a third and final exercise in judging a play, let's apply Goethe's three questions to the playwright. "What was the artist trying to do?" turns into "What was the playwright trying to say with this play; what was he or she trying to make you feel?" At the end of the previous chapter, you learned how to state the theme of a play by forming a single sentence that tells the plot and by drawing a universal statement from that sentence. Use the same method to answer the first part of this question. Answering the second part requires you to learn another way of analyzing a play. You need to learn the vocabulary for describing how a play makes you feel.

GENRES

Plays are categorized into **genres** (ZHON-ras). Each genre has different traits and evokes a different emotional response. When you know which genre the play belongs in, you will have the vocabulary you need to describe to your friends how the play made you feel.

Scholars have a whole slate of names to define the emotional reactions that various kinds of plays evoke. We are going to look at the six most common genres. When you recognize the traits of each genre, you will be able to identify the emotions and feelings that correspond to that genre.

Six Common Genres

- Comedy
- Farce
- Drama
- Tragedy
- Melodrama
- Tragicomedy

Figure 16.1   The twinkle in Falstaff's eye tells the audience that *The Merry Wives of Windsor* is an example of the genre of comedy. (Colorado Shakespeare Festival)

Comedy

If the play made you laugh a lot and made you feel good because the story ended the way you wanted it to, with all the right people paired up and the world restored to order, then the play was a comedy (Figure 16.1). Comedy is the genre of play that makes you laugh, that has plots that end happily, and that reaffirms the values you hold to be important. Some people like to distinguish between "high comedy," "domestic comedy," and "low comedy." A high comedy is filled with elegant and rich characters who are very concerned for how they behave; this kind of play is sometimes called a "comedy of manners." It gets most of its laughs from the clever things the characters *say*. A domestic comedy is usually about middle-class people, and much of the laughter results from the awkward and embarrassing situations that the characters are put in by the crafty playwright. The situation comedies you see on TV, from *Cheers* to *Seinfeld* to *Friends*, fall into this category. A low comedy is about stupid characters, and we laugh at them because of what they *do* more than what they say. A good example is the movie *Dumb and Dumber*. High comedy, domestic comedy, and low comedy are three variations on the genre of comedy because all three make you laugh, have plots that end happily, and reaffirm values you hold to be important.

Farce

A play that makes you laugh a lot and lets you feel liberated by the entirely consistent but wildly anarchic and unbelievable things that happen is called a farce. If you've seen a Road Runner cartoon, you've had this experience. Farces are peopled with eccentric and/or stupid characters who speak in a very simple dialogue (Color Plate 25). There's a very fast tempo in farce, with characters running in and out of doors so that they meet the very characters they shouldn't. You may see a fair amount of violence in a farce but it doesn't have any serious impact. The characters get hit on the head, but their skulls don't crack open. A farce is similar to a low comedy, but there's a good way to tell them apart. In a farce, the improbable happens, and when we see it, we feel joyously liberated because the constraints we all live with are abandoned, and mayhem prevails. We all want to escape the limits of our real world, and farce lets us do so for a brief time in the imaginary world of theatre.

Drama

When you leave a performance of a serious play that makes you feel sad because the characters have been defeated, you have encountered a drama. (Some critics and scholars use interchangeably such terms as "drame," "serious drama," and "drama." The last of these terms is the one heard most often, so it's the one we use.) The central character in a drama struggles for something you believe is worth wanting, and you root for that character to get it. When he or she doesn't, it's almost the same as your not getting it, and that makes you sad. The character's defeat reminds you that the world is not the way you wish it were; it reminds you that the good die young, the sick don't recover, the boy doesn't get the girl, and nobody lives happily ever after (Figure 16.2). You are reminded of some truths that you know but have managed to ignore. But here's a strange fact: audiences *enjoy* dramas. We tell ourselves that we only want to watch comedies that make us happy and cheerful and take us away from our everyday problems. But a drama gives us a different sort of pleasure. It lets us feel our deep emotions without getting personally involved. We know that the outcome of the play will not directly affect our own lives.

Tragedy

"Tragedy" is the most misused term you'll come upon in discussions of theatre, and one reason for that misuse is that most of us have never experienced a tragedy—not in the theatre, not in our lives. People regularly apply the term "tragedy" to anything sad. But a play that tries to make you feel sad is called a drama, not a tragedy. A tragedy is a serious play that tries to make you feel exhilarated because the hero's experience has taught you some profound truth about *your* life. Far from making you sad, a tragedy guides you to feel a sort of calm affirmation that your worst expectations about life are true, and you feel wiser for knowing this certainty. Unlike a drama, a tragedy touches you *directly*. You feel awe for the central character who, in spite of knowing

Figure 16.2   Henrik Ibsen's *Ghosts* tells the story of a mother whose son is dying from an inherited disease. This sad play is an example of the genre of drama. (Virginia Museum Theatre)

that the goal can be attained only at the cost of his or her own destruction, brings ruin down on all concerned by continuing to seek the goal because there is no other way to be true to his or her self. A tragedy makes you feel proud that there are such characters, but at the same time you feel pity for what happens to them. You admire characters like Othello who defend their integrity even when it requires them to kill their loved ones and themselves (Color Plate 26). You come away from a tragedy knowing something more about yourself; you know how to live your life differently, and that knowledge exhilarates you.

Melodrama

The plays you encounter most and respond to most enthusiastically are the plays that touch you least profoundly (Figure 16.3). They are called melodramas; these plays provide entertainment that has the appearance of being serious but that you know is not. You know that the plot and characters in an episode of the TV show *Law and Order* are not serious, though they seem

Figure 16.3   The noble-hearted labor organizer Joe Hill waits in a prison cell for the executioner's squad while his close friend mourns for him. Barrie Stavis's melodrama, *The Man Who Never Died*, was produced by the National Theatre of Cyprus.

to be so. Melodramas focus more on their complicated plots than on their two-dimensional characters. A melodrama provides a story with many exciting twists that are intensified by the thrilling music that underscores the action (that's where the term "melodrama" comes from; drama that uses melody to enrich its emotional impact). Melodramas teach a very simple moral—usually that good conquers evil—and you don't take melodramas seriously because you know they don't reflect the truth of life. Instead, they reflect the way you wish life were. You wish the cops would catch the pushers, but you know that rarely happens. Melodrama reinforces the view of life you wish were true, and it does so with a terrifically exciting story and with characters who are not psychologically complex but who respond to events beyond their own making. Melodrama provides you with a diversion from life's real problems. While it may be true that tragedy is more sublime because it affects the way we truly live, melodrama gives us great pleasure of a different sort.

Tragicomedy

If you leave the theatre agitated, frustrated, and anxious, you have seen a tragicomedy. The composite word "tragicomedy" gives you some clue that these plays are made up partly of the serious subject matter of tragedy and partly of the laugh-inducing stuff of comedy. You laugh at serious things, you cry at funny ones, and you feel disoriented and discombobulated. This genre developed in the twentieth century, in an era that philosophers call "The Age of Anxiety." The human condition seems more uncertain than ever. The bomb could drop at any moment. Our control over our world is slipping, and the old comforts of religion and political authority don't hold as much assurance for us as they once did. Tragicomedies reflect this truth of the human condition and try to make us feel anxious (see Color Plate 23).

Now that you are familiar with the six most common genres and understand what kind of emotional response each genre tries to evoke, you can figure out if the playwright succeeded in making you feel that way. For example, you might be tempted to say "I didn't like it," when what you really mean is "It made me feel uncomfortable." Now that you know that discomfort is precisely the emotion that a tragicomedy is supposed to elicit, you can tell your friends what the playwright was trying to do. You will have answered Goethe's first question.

Let's ask the second of Goethe's questions. "Did the artist succeed in doing it?" translates into "Was the theme of the play clear?" and "Did I feel the emotions that are appropriate for that genre?" You might discover that the playwright wrote a comedy to make you laugh, but you didn't laugh. After you tell your friends what the playwright was trying to do, you can tell them if he or she succeeded in doing it.

The third of Goethe's questions requires you to make a judgment that reveals as much about you as it does about the artist's work. "Was it worth the doing?" translates into "Was that idea important for me to think about?" and "Are those feelings appropriate in this situation?" What do *you* believe is worth the doing? Is it worth the doing for a playwright to give an audience two hours of joyous laughter when the play's theme is that women should be starved and beaten and psychologically abused until they learn to obey their husbands? Be careful how you answer, because we've just described the theme of Shakespeare's *The Taming of the Shrew,* and millions of people believe that play is worth the doing, even in our current age of political correctness, because the joy they get from laughing is more important to them than Shakespeare's troublesome message. What about a play that encourages teenagers to lie to their parents, to blaspheme and curse, to marry without their parent's consent, to kill in revenge, and to commit suicide? Is *Romeo and Juliet* worth the doing? These questions aren't just trick questions. They should challenge you to analyze what a play is trying to say and what it is trying to make you feel, so that you can decide if you think those results are worth the doing (Figure 16.4). *Romeo and Juliet* is trying to say that when society oppresses young people and supports a value system of brutal competition between neighbors, ruin comes upon everyone. *Romeo and Juliet* has a theme that ought to be heard, and when you balance its valuable theme against its less attractive elements, you will probably decide that *Romeo and Juliet* is, indeed, worth the doing. Each of us holds particular values, each of us has unique beliefs, and each of us will approve or condemn different plays.

Figure 16.4   The theme of *Romeo and Juliet* is so important that it out-weighs complaints against the play for its depiction of teenagers who lie to their parents, marry without their par-ent's consent, and com-mit murder and suicide. The play's message speaks to us whether the costumes suggest the Italian Renaissance or, as in this photo, today's world, as in this recent production at a Califor-nia summer festival.

JUDGING A PLAY

Exercise

Select a play that you have attended recently. List the title of the play and the name of the theatre where the play was performed.

1. Using Goethe's three questions to organize your thoughts about an actor in this play, write a one-page essay telling a friend why he or she should or should not go to see the actor's performance.

2. Using Goethe's three questions to organize your thoughts about the play-wright, write a one-page essay telling a friend why he or she should or should not go to this play.

17

Aristotle's Guide to Pleasure

$\mathcal{M}$odern guidebooks tell you where to find pleasure. You use a guidebook to locate good restaurants, nightclubs, and beaches. Whatever kind of pleasure you seek, your guidebook points you in the right direction. Guidebooks are nothing new, of course, and when Aristotle wrote the first guidebook about theatre, he understood that people seek pleasure, so *The Poetics* not only describes theatre, it tells you how and why theatre gives you pleasure.

Aristotle was an ancient Greek philosopher who was born in Athens in 384 B.C.E. and who died in 322 B.C.E. at the age of sixty-two. He was a student of the equally famous Greek philosopher Plato, and he wrote essays on so many subjects that modern scholars call him "the greatest thinker of antiquity." Aristotle's works were lost to Europe when the Roman Empire collapsed, and from approximately 400 C.E. to about 1000 C.E. his wisdom was kept alive by Arab scholars in Syria and Spain. When Europeans climbed out of the dark ages and rediscovered Aristotle, the Renaissance began, and the great poet Dante called him "the master of those who know." Aristotle wrote about astronomy, physics, rhetoric, ethics, politics, metaphysics, biology, botany, and poetics (the study of literary expression).

Aristotle's *Poetics* is an important essay that is still taught and studied today because it explains the primary purpose of theatre, because it provides us with a methodology for analyzing the form of theatre, and because it defines the six elements out of which theatre is made.

Aristotle believed that the primary purpose of all human activities is to provide pleasure. However, Aristotle wasn't talking about the "pleasure principle." He didn't write about back rubs and aromatherapy. On the contrary, he believed that nothing gives us more pleasure than learning the *truth.* He knew that we humans love to learn about ourselves, and he recognized that theatre provides us with an exceptional way to study human behavior and to learn the truth about human nature. He recognized that while we're watching the characters in a drama, we're observing case studies of human behavior and that we can learn from them. He knew that theatre—at its optimum—is a vitally important experience that can help us understand the truth, and he believed that a knowledge of the truth gives us pleasure.

Aristotle believed that the primary purpose of theatre is to provide pleasure and that the greatest pleasure comes from learning the greatest truth.

Aristotle studied the Greek dramas he knew, and he used as his primary example of excellence, Sophocles' *Oedipus the King.* This great play remains important today, in part, because Aristotle held it up as a paradigm.

THE THREE UNITIES OF THEATRE

Aristotle's study led him to believe that plays give an audience the greatest pleasure when their form observes three organizing traits that we have come to call the three unities: the unity of action, the unity of time, and the unity of place. Aristotle provided us with a methodology for learning about a play by analyzing its formal organization.

The Three Unities

1. The unity of action
2. The unity of time
3. The unity of place

The Unity of Action

A play should have only one simple plot, Aristotle argued, so that the audience can learn from its clear example and not be confused by secondary plots. That's why he praised *Oedipus the King,* which has a single, direct story to tell. Aristotle discerned that the plot of a play has "a beginning, a middle, and an end," and he argued that the most pleasing plays have plots that occur in that order. Playwrights have invented new forms of plots in the centuries since Aristotle, and today we also enjoy plays in which the ending of the story is at the beginning of the play, with the rest of the plot presented as a flashback. Further, we like Shakespeare's plays *because* they have multiple and complex plots. Still, many of the finest plays written today have a single plot that presents its beginning, middle, and end in that order.

The Unity of Time

Aristotle believed that we get the greatest pleasure from plays in which the action occurs in one passage of consecutive time. He praised *Oedipus the King,* in which the action takes place in one single day. But how long is a day? Over the centuries, critics have interpreted Aristotle's notion of the unity of time to mean one twenty-four-hour day, or one twelve-hour day from dawn to sunset, or even that the duration of the virtual action on stage should exactly equate to the real time the audience lives through—if the story unfolds over the course of two hours, then the play that is telling that story should take two hours to perform. Today, we have a more tolerant attitude toward the playwright's use of time than Aristotle did, and yet many fine modern plays have a plot that takes place in one day.

The Unity of Place

Aristotle believed that we get the greatest pleasure from plays that set their action in one place, the way Sophocles' *Oedipus the King* is set entirely in the public square in front of the palace in Thebes. Today, with the popularity of dramatic structures that have the flexibility of movie scripts, we like plays that jump about from one place to another. Yet some of the greatest modern plays are set in a single location and have a unity of place.

THE SIX ELEMENTS OF THEATRE

Aristotle's analysis of theatre led him to another profound discovery. He concluded that theatre is made up of six elements. Even today, two thousand years later, no one has added a seventh element. That he was able to sum up theatre in a way that no one else has been able to add to is amazing, considering that in Aristotle's time, scientists believed that the physical universe comprised only four elements whereas today the periodic table contains 109 elements. In the twenty-five hundred years since Aristotle wrote *The Poetics,* no one has ever identified a seventh element of theatre, and that is one of the many reasons his seminal essay has remained a major influence.

The Six Elements of Theatre

1. Plot
2. Character
3. Thought
4. Diction
5. Music
6. Spectacle

Plot

Aristotle described plot as "the life and soul of the drama." He meant that plot was the most important of the six elements, the one without which the drama could not exist. Until a plot unfolds, there is no play. When you tell people a story to entertain them, to provide an example, or to make a point in an argument, you tell the events that happen. In a drama, those events comprise the plot.

Plots can be organized in many different ways. In chapter 15 we discussed the three structures that a playwright might use: linear, cinematic, and contextual. Aristotle only knew about linear plots, and he elaborated on his definition by saying plot is "the arrangement of the incidents." That is, the plot is the totality of the incidents in the story that the playwright has selected to include in the play, and those incidents are arranged in a particular sequence. The drama that Aristotle studied in preparation for writing *The Poetics* was not as varied as the drama you see in the theatre today, but except for a few modern plays that have a contextual structure, a play has a plot that gives it a life and a soul.

Character

Aristotle described character as "the agent for the action." Character is the element that makes the action possible. When you attend the theatre, you watch what the characters do, and when you try to describe a play, you describe what the characters did. The play unfolds when the characters enact the incidents of the plot. The characters cannot exist independent of what they do, for they achieve their being through the actions they perform, and the all-important plot can't unfold without the characters who do the actions. The two are inextricably bound together. Aristotle recognized character as the second most important element of theatre.

Thought

Thought is the meaning of the play, sometimes called the message or the theme. The plot tells the audience a particular story, and the theme is the generalization, the universal idea that the audience draws from it.

Some scholars use the Greek word "dianoia" (dee-a-NOY-a) for this element. That's the word Aristotle wrote in *The Poetics*. The dictionary defines "dianoia" as "the process of thought." Erudite scholars like to use the Greek word, but "thought" is a very satisfactory description of this third element.

As you learned in chapter 15, a play's theme can be stated by distilling the plot down to a single sentence and then extrapolating a generalization from it, a universal truth. The theme, or thought, of a play is important, of course, but it can only be communicated through the plot. And the plot can only be presented through its agents, the characters. Aristotle teaches us that the six elements are interconnected and that they have an order of importance in which the element of thought comes third.

Diction

Aristotle's fourth element is diction, and the term describes both the vocabulary the playwright uses and the order in which the words are placed. No two people speak the same way. You might leave for class and say, "Peace be with you," as you go out the door, while your friend might call out, "Have a good one." The meaning of both phrases is the same, but the vocabulary is different and so is the order the words come in. The diction is different. By creating a character's diction, the playwright makes that character unique. Imagine this exchange:

A   I wonder, my compatriot, if thou and I art kindred after all?

B   Shucks, I don't know, no how.

The diction of the first character uses a large vocabulary ("kindred") and a complicated word order that is grammatically correct. The second character's diction has a smaller vocabulary and the uncomplicated and ungrammatical word order of an uneducated person.

We regularly misuse the word "diction" as a synonym for "articulation." Articulation describes the muscular activity through which we separate consonants from vowels so that we can shape sounds into recognizable words. A person with lazy or sloppy speech is guilty of poor articulation. Diction, by way of contrast, describes the playwright's vocabulary and the sequence in which the words are arranged.

Just as each character's diction can be unique, so can each playwright's. Shakespeare's diction is different from Henrik Ibsen's. Each playwright's diction establishes the level of the play's seriousness and its level of realism. A serious play such as *A Doll's House* has a different diction from that of a comedy such as *The Odd Couple*. A realistic play such as *A Raisin in the Sun* uses slang and everyday language that imitates real life, very different from the unreal diction of Shakespeare's lofty verse. No real person ever spoke like the characters in *Henry V*, and the diction helps us understand that the play is not trying to imitate real life.

Aristotle formed his judgment of a play's diction from studying the ancient verse tragedies of Sophocles. Aristotle believed that the diction of the best plays has the proper amount of ornamentation and elegance. He valued highly plays that were written in verse and that used elaborate images because he believed their diction gave an audience the greatest pleasure. To demonstrate this idea, compare this diction with Shakespeare's. Here's Tom's clumsy version of some lines from *A Midsummer Night's Dream*:

> And as quickly as an author's imagination gives birth to
> Things that have never existed, that's how quickly his pen
> Describes them. And he gives these wispy fantasies
> A place to exist, and he names them.

Aristotle would argue that Shakespeare's lines are more beautiful and therefore give greater pleasure:

> And as imagination bodies forth
> The forms of things unknown, the poet's pen
> Turns them to shapes, and gives to aery nothing
> A local habitation and a name.

Millions of people would agree with Aristotle. Shakespeare's a better poet than Tom is.

One of the things that makes Shakespeare difficult for us to read today is his diction. Shakespeare uses a larger vocabulary than we do, and the order in which he arranges words is frequently quite different from the order we're familiar with. People who grow skilled at reading Shakespeare find they admire his diction and prefer his plays to those of many modern writers.

Music

For Aristotle, the element of music included everything we hear in a performance, such as the sound effects, the musical accompaniment, and the sounds of the actors' voices when they speak, chant, and sing their lines. Aristotle believed that the more the actors used their voices to embellish the playwright's words, the more the audience would feel the characters' emotions. He recognized that the playwright's poetry can't be expressed by flat, dull speech, so he was particularly attentive to the variety of sounds the human voice can make. He admired the actors' ability to manipulate the volume, tempo, and pitch of their speech, for he recognized that they could express emotion through the music of their voices. That's why actors performing Greek plays—and those by Shakespeare, Molière, and other playwrights who wrote in a "heightened" or "elevated" diction—sometimes speak differently from the way we speak every day. Those actors are providing pleasure through the sounds of their voices as well as through the intellectual content of their speeches. Just as priests chant to give added emotion to a religious service and just as characters in a musical comedy burst into song when they're happy, so actors in classical plays sometimes speak their lines in a musical manner.

In today's theatre, an audience hears the performance in ways Aristotle never imagined. We have electronic music, amplified human speech, and pre-recorded sound effects. Even though technology has increased the kinds of music we have in today's theatre, Aristotle's original analysis of the elements of theatre remains essentially unchanged. Music remains a less important element than plot, character, thought, and diction because it is not essential to the plot. Music enriches our experience, but it does not help us learn the truth, and the knowledge of the truth is what gives us pleasure.

Spectacle

Aristotle's analysis of theatre led him to believe that what the audience sees is the least important of the six elements. Indeed, he might well have believed that a blind person could satisfactorily experience theatre.

Radio drama is a form of theatrical performance in which the entirety of the experience is communicated aurally. There is no spectacle. In the 1930s and 1940s, weekly radio dramas such as *The Shadow* and *The Mercury Theatre of the Air* were as popular as television programs such as *Seinfeld* and *Touched by an Angel* are today. Drama can be experienced without Aristotle's sixth element.

The tragedies and comedies of ancient Greece presented much less visual stimulation than there is in contemporary theatre. Unlike our Broadway musicals in which the scenery is almost constantly in motion, the scenery in ancient Greek theatres was stationary. The principal actors didn't move about much, and they wore masks so their facial expressions never changed. Moreover, in Aristotle's time there were never more than three major characters on the stage at any time. Compare that to Shakespeare's *Henry V* in which large armies cross the stage. The theatre that Aristotle analyzed was far more dependent on what the audience heard than on what it saw, and so he argued that spectacle was the sixth and least important element of the theatre.

There are examples of theatre today in which there is spectacle but no music. Samuel Beckett wrote a short play titled *Act Without Words.* The play has no dialogue, and the actors do not make any sounds. There is no music played, and there are no sound effects. Watching it is a little like watching a silent movie. And yet the play is highly entertaining. Audiences laugh at funny bits of stage business and are profoundly moved by the plot.

Today theatre communicates to us visually so much more than it ever did in the past that many theatre artists think Aristotle was wrong and that the element of spectacle should be ranked higher than sixth. Theatre has become visually very complex because theatre audiences' ability to absorb visual information has been shaped by television, a medium in which visual change is a vital device for telling the story.

To realize how habituated you are to visual stimulation, try this exercise. Sit in front of your TV set, turn on any dramatic program you like, and mark on a piece of blank paper every time the image changes. Every time the camera cuts to a different angle or the scene changes to another location, make a mark with your pencil. You will discover that the image changes every few seconds and that you see hundreds of different pictures in a short time. If this exercise engages you, do it for a commercial and then for a music video. You may be astounded by how many changes your eye is habituated to seeing. Think how different such visual complication is from what you see in the live theatre.

ARISTOTELIAN ANALYSIS   *Exercise*

Select a play that you have attended recently. List the title of the play and the playwright. Answer the following questions about this production.

1. Which of the three unities did the play observe?

2. State the plot in a single sentence.

3. State the thought, or theme, in a single sentence.

4. Which one or two characters did you feel were the principal agents for the action? Support your choice with a description of how these characters embodied the plot.

5. Did you find music or spectacle to be the more important element? Why?

Epilogue
The Theatrical Experience

*T*ake a look at the definition of theatre you wrote in the exercise for chapter 1. You've learned so much since you wrote it that you may want to revise it, and if so, you can use the exercise at the end of this chapter. Before you do, we want to expand your thinking one last time. Here's *our* definition of theatre:

> Theatre is an experience that results from witnessing an imitation of human actions that entertains an audience while it conveys a symbolic meaning that the audience values.

We want to expand on each of the seven key ideas mentioned in our definition.

The Seven Ideas in Our Definition

- Experience
- Imitation
- Human actions
- Entertainment
- A form of communication
- Symbolic meaning
- Value

Experience Theatre is an experience that happens to you while you're witnessing a live performance.

Imitation   Theatre is made by people. It does not exist in nature. Things that exist in nature are authentic. Things that are made by people are imitations. A tree built out of papier-mâché is not authentic; it's an imitation of a tree. And theatre is an imitation of human actions.

Human Actions   Human actions can be physical actions, intellectual actions, and spiritual actions. Physical actions include such simple things as closing a door, kissing, fighting, and dying. Intellectual actions include arguing a political point, deciding a question of law, or solving a riddle. Spiritual actions include seeking a truth, forgiving an enemy, or reconciling one's dreams with reality. In most plays, all of these human actions are imitated, but we tend to value most highly those plays that focus on spiritual action.

Entertainment   Whatever else it does, theatre entertains us. Today, we equate the verb "to entertain" with "to amuse," but the earlier and proper meaning of "to entertain" is "to keep, hold, or maintain in the mind." Theatre must hold our attention.

You can recognize a "good" play, says a friend of ours, because the audience leans forward in their seats, intent on what's taking place on the stage. You can recognize a "bad" play if you see the audience sitting back in their seats, bored. And a "really bad" play is one that drives them out of their seats and back to their homes. Our friend has found a simple way to acknowledge that theatre must be, along with everything else, "entertainment." It must keep, hold, or maintain itself in your mind. It must amuse you, yes, but it must also address ideas that engage your mind.

A Form of Communication   Theatre "conveys a symbolic meaning," we wrote. The word "conveys" implies that theatre sends messages from the stage to the audience. Theatre is a form of communication in the same way that painting and writing and speech are forms of communication.

Symbolic Meaning   The words, characters, and actions that are conveyed from stage to audience *stand for something else.* They symbolize someone or something different from what they are. The actors portraying Gogo and Didi in *Waiting for Godot* are symbols; they stand for all of us. Because audiences understand their symbolism, audiences understand what the action of the play stands for. The meaning of the human action that is imitated is something that we can grasp.

Value   The meaning has value because the symbolic action addresses our pressing concerns. As the English director Peter Brook says, "Theatre . . . is a clear, pitiless, accurate mirror which shows life as it is." We value plays that help us look into the mirror and see the truth about ourselves, our society, and our spiritual universe.

Exercise SECOND DEFINITION OF THEATRE

Write as complete and clear a definition of theatre as you can.

Appendix
To Learn More: Plays,
Books, and Videotapes

Plays

Act Without Words. Samuel Beckett. A short play by the author of *Waiting for Godot* that has no spoken dialogue.

The Adding Machine. Elmer Rice. An American play from the 1920s that is an example of Expressionism. Mr. Zero, a bookkeeper who is oppressed by his job and his wife, goes mad, kills his boss, and has strange experiences in the afterlife.

Annie. Martin Charnin. A Broadway musical based on a comic strip character. The song "Tomorrow" comes from it.

As You Like It. William Shakespeare. One of Shakespeare's most beloved comedies; an example of an episodic and complex linear dramatic structure. It is the story of Rosalind's love for Orlando, and it includes the famous "Seven Ages of Man" speech.

The Bear and the Cub. William Darby. The first play written in America. It was presented in a tavern in Virginia in 1665, and the playwright and two other men were charged with the crime of "presenting a play." The English magistrate found them "not guilty of fault." Today, only theatre historians read this short play that has more historical importance than theatrical value. For our purposes, the court proceeding is an illustration of the struggles in early America between the idea of theatre as a profit-making venture and the belief that theatre is an immoral activity.

The Beggar's Opera. John Gay. An English ballad opera written in 1728 that enjoyed the first long run in theatrical history.

The Black Crook. Charles M. Barras. A melodramatic play that was produced in New York in 1866 and ran for 475 straight performances. Historians describe it as the first American musical comedy because it included songs and dances.

Breakfast at Tiffany's. Edward Albee, Abe Burrows, Nunnally Johnson, and Bob Merrill. A Broadway musical starring Richard Chamberlain and Mary Tyler Moore that closed during previews. It was based on the novel of the same title by Truman Capote and the popular film that starred Audrey Hepburn. This flop is an example of how the finest theatre artists can fail to create a successful production.

Brigadoon. Alan Jay Lerner and Frederick Loewe. A musical about a mysterious village in Scotland that appears only one day each hundred years; an example of American musical at its best.

Cabaret. John Kander and Fred Ebb. Musical that is an example of how short stories can be the source for the plot of a musical. The stories were written by Christopher Isherwood and set in Berlin in the early 1930s.

Camelot. Alan Jay Lerner and Frederick Loewe. Musical about King Arthur that is an example of the best work of the writing team of Alan Jay Lerner and Frederick Loewe.

Carrie. Michael Gore, Dean Pitchford, and Lawrence D. Cohen. A musical based on the popular novel (and the movie) of the same title by Stephen King. It was a celebrated failure that lost all the Broadway investors' money. *Carrie* is an example of how risky the business of theatre can be.

Cats. Trevor Nunn and Andrew Lloyd Webber. A musical based on poems by T. S. Eliot that is among the most popular musicals ever produced. The song "Memories" comes from it. *Cats* has no narrative; rather, it is an example of contextual dramatic structure.

Chicago. John Kander and Fred Ebb. A musical based on a 1920s play of the same title. It is about two women who become celebrities because they are criminals and is an example of a show directed and choreographed by the same man: Bob Fosse.

A Chorus Line. Michael Bennett. Long-running Broadway musical about dancers that is an example of an ensemble musical that has no starring role.

Crazy for You. George Gershwin and Ken Ludwig. A Broadway musical of the 1980s that reworked a hit musical of the 1930s named *Girl Crazy*. *Crazy for You* is a bright-spirited musical filled with song and dance that appeals to large audiences. It is also an example of how musicals are based on other materials, in this case, on an earlier musical.

Cyrano de Bergerac. Edmond Rostand. A late-nineteenth-century French play in verse that is an example of Romanticism. It is set in the seventeenth century and tells the story of Cyrano, whose extraordinarily large nose makes him too shy to profess his love for Roxanne. Steve Martin's film *Roxanne* is based on this play.

Death of a Salesman. Arthur Miller. A powerful American drama about a character named Willy Loman; an example of a serious drama that has a complex, cinematic structure.

The Diary of Anne Frank. Albert Hackett and Frances Goodrich. Based on *The Diary of a Young Girl,* the popular autobiography by a Jewish girl of thirteen who hid from the Nazis during World War II. The play is an example of a simple, episodic, linear dramatic structure, of Realism, and of the genre of serious drama.

Dionysus in '69. Richard Schechner. An avant-garde play of the late 1960s that demonstrates the traits of environmental theatre. Based on an ancient Greek tragedy by Euripides, it includes nudity, ritualized actions, and audience interaction.

A Doll's House. Henrik Ibsen. An example of the genre of serious drama by the Norwegian playwright known as "the father of modern drama."

Dracula. Bram Stoker. A melodramatic novel by the nineteenth-century English writer Bram Stoker that has been the source for many plays and movies. The title character is a vampire.

The Dresser. Ronald Harwood. This English play about a great English actor illustrates what an actor-manager was like.

Driving Miss Daisy. Alfred Uhry. An award-winning play about the relationship between a wealthy Jewish widow in Atlanta, Georgia, and her black chauffeur. It is an example of the kind of serious play that is more commonly produced Off Broadway than on.

En Gggarrrde! René Daumal. An example of Surrealism. This French play is a curiosity that is not performed today. (We're not certain it was ever performed.)

The Entertainer. John Osborne. An English play from the 1950s that demonstrates how social conflicts can be the subject of serious plays. It also shows how English music hall entertainment was a close parallel to American vaudeville.

Fiddler on the Roof. Jerry Bock and Sheldon Harnick. A musical about Jewish life in a peasant village in Russia at the end of the nineteenth century. *Fiddler* ran for more than 3,000 performances; it starred Zero Mostel on stage and is an example of a book musical.

A Funny Thing Happened on the Way to the Forum. Burt Shevelove, Larry Gelbart, and Stephen Sondheim. A popular Broadway musical based on an ancient Roman comedy. *Forum* originally starred Zero Mostel and was revived on Broadway in the 1990s with Nathan Lane and later Whoopi Goldberg in the leading role. This book musical gives a good sense of what American vaudeville was like.

Gandhi. Gurney Campbell. An unpublished biographical play about Mohandas Gandhi, the Hindu nationalist leader and martyr, that flopped on Broadway in 1970. It has been blessedly forgotten by everyone except us, and we remember it only because Tom acted in it. It is an example of failure in the commercial theatre.

Ghosts. Henrik Ibsen. Important drama by "the father of modern drama" and an example of Realism.

Girl Crazy. George and Ira Gershwin. One of the finest examples of American musical comedy. It included such hit songs as "Embraceable You" and "I Got Rhythm." A revised version titled *Crazy for You* was a Broadway hit in the 1980s.

The Glass Menagerie. Tennessee Williams. A classic American play by one of our greatest playwrights. *The Glass Menagerie* tells the semiautobiographical story of Tom Wingfield's affection for his emotionally challenged sister and his struggles with his domineering mother that end with his leaving home to become a writer. The play is an example of Theatricalism and of simple, episodic linear structure.

Good News. Lew Brown, B. G. DaSylva, and Ray Henderson. An example of a musical comedy. The action is set on a college campus in the 1920s.

The Great Passion Play. Tom Jones, revised by Don Berrigan. An example of the many outdoor religious plays performed annually. This one is presented in Eureka Springs, Arkansas, to audiences of thousands, and it tells the story of Jesus's last days on earth.

Guys and Dolls. Abe Burrows, Frank Loesser, and Jo Swerling. A classic American musical about sentimental gangsters in New York City. It is an example of a book musical and of a musical based on short stories (these, by Damon Runyon).

Gypsy. Stephen Sondheim and Jule Styne. A musical based on the autobiography of striptease artiste Gypsy Rose Lee. It starred Ethel Merman on stage and Rosalind Russell on film, and is an example of a book musical.

Hair. Galt McDermott, James Rado, and Gerome Ragni. The first important musical to have a rock score, to be entirely sung-through, and to be an ensemble musical. It was a sensation on Broadway because of its subject matter (the youth revolution of the 1960s) and because it presented total nudity. The song "The Age of Aquarius" has become a pop standard.

Hamlet. William Shakespeare. One of Shakespeare's greatest plays and an example of the genre of tragedy.

Hedda Gabler. Henrik Ibsen. Important drama by "the father of modern drama" and an example of Realism.

Henry V. William Shakespeare. An example of the genre called history play.

The Hill Cumorah Pageant. Orson Scott Card. A religious pageant performed outdoors annually in upstate New York. It tells the beginnings of the religion of the Church of Jesus Christ of Latter-day Saints. This pageant is an example of the outdoor religious dramas that are popular all across America.

HMS Pinafore. W. S. Gilbert and Arthur Sullivan. An example of the English operetta and one of the finest of this team's creations.

The Iceman Cometh. Eugene O'Neill. A four-and-a-half-hour-long play by one of America's greatest playwrights. It has had three major revivals in New York starring (in chronological order) Jason Robards, James Earl Jones, and Kevin Spacey. It is an example of great serious drama.

The Importance of Being Earnest. Oscar Wilde. A comedy of manners written in 1895 and thought by many to be the greatest example of high comedy written in English.

Jesus Christ Superstar. Tim Rice and Andrew Lloyd Webber. An example of a sung-through rock musical; based on the story of Jesus.

Joe Egg. Peter Nichols. An example of the genre of tragicomedy; written in England in the 1960s.

Joseph and the Amazing Technicolor Dream Coat. Tim Rice and Andrew Lloyd Webber. A rock musical based on the Old Testament story of Joseph; the first collaboration of this team. It has become a popular musical for school groups to produce and is an example of a musical based on biblical stories.

Kaspar. Peter Handke. Avant-garde play by an Austrian playwright; an example of the kind of highly intellectual and convention-breaking plays that are successful Off Broadway but that mainstream audiences do not like.

The King and I. Richard Rodgers and Oscar Hammerstein II. A book musical based on a play *(Anna and the King of Siam)*. It starred Yul Brynner on stage and on film.

La Cage aux Folles. Jerry Herman and Harvey Fierstein. An example of a traditional book musical; based on a French play that had been made into a French movie. The American film *The Birdcage,* starring Gene Hackman, Nathan Lane, and Robin Williams, is based on the French film but not on the American musical.

Leave It to Jane. Guy Bolton, P. G. Wodehouse, and Jerome Kern. An example of the book musical, which this writing team brought to its maturity in the early decades of the twentieth century.

Les Miserables. Claude-Michel Schönberg and Alain Boublil. A hugely popular Broadway musical that is an example of a sung-through musical that has no spoken dialogue. It is based on the classic French novel by Victor Hugo.

The Lion in Winter. James Goldman. An entertaining play about the family struggles of Henry II of England, his wife, Eleanor of Aquitaine, and their three sons; an example of the popularity of melodrama. It was revived on Broadway in 1999 with Laurence Fishburne and Stockard Channing.

The Lion King. Roger Allers, Irene Mecchi, Elton John, Tim Rice, Lebo M, Julie Taymor, Mark Mancina, and Hans Zimmer. Director Julie Taymor used actors and puppets to turn the Disney movie into a hit Broadway musical in the late 1990s.

A Little Night Music. Stephen Sondheim. Sondheim's most popular musical; an example of a musical based on a film (Bergman's *Smiles of a Summer Night*). It includes the song "Send in the Clowns."

The Lost Colony. Paul Green. One of America's oldest and most celebrated outdoor dramas. It tells the story of the English settlement on Roanoke Island, North Carolina. Paul Green sought to create an indigenous American folk drama, and *The Lost Colony* is an example of the historical plays that attract large audiences each summer.

Macbeth. William Shakespeare. One of the greatest tragedies ever written. This exciting play ends with a great sword fight.

The Man of La Mancha. Mitch Leigh, Joe Darion, and Dale Wasserman. A Broadway musical based on Cervantes's classic Spanish novel *Don Quixote*. It includes the popular song "The Impossible Dream" and is an example of Romanticism.

The Man Who Never Died. Barrie Stavis. A melodrama about Joe Hill, a labor organizer and song writer who was arrested and executed by a firing squad in Salt Lake City, Utah, in 1915. Hill was a martyr to the labor movement and is the subject of songs, movies, books, and plays.

Marvin's Room. Scott McPherson. An example of the kind of bittersweet Off Broadway play that is rarely produced on Broadway but that reaches a large audience anyway.

Mercury Theatre of the Air. An example of radio drama. This program was a weekly broadcast of a play or a dramatization of a novel and starred Orson Welles. The broadcast in 1938 of a dramatization of H. G. Wells's *The War of the Worlds* created a panic among listeners who actually believed Martians had attacked New Jersey. The radio broadcast exists on audiocassette, and there are many books describing the event.

The Merry Wives of Windsor. William Shakespeare. A comedy featuring the character Falstaff.

A Midsummer Night's Dream. William Shakespeare. One of his greatest comedies. It has been made into movies on many occasions, most recently starring Michelle Pfeiffer and Kevin Kline. It is an example of Romanticism.

The Mikado. W. S. Gilbert and Arthur Sullivan. An example of an English operetta; set in nineteenth-century Japan.

The Misanthrope. Molière. An example of seventeenth-century French comedy of manners. Alceste, who cannot make the small compromises that people must in order to live in society, loves Célimène, a coquette who is the opposite of everything Alceste believes in. It is an example of Classic theatre in which excessive behavior is exposed as undesirable.

Miss Saigon. Claude-Michel Schönberg and Alain Boublil. A musical about the American military forces in Vietnam in the 1970s. This musical featured many Asian-American performers and the audience-pleasing spectacle of the simulation of a helicopter landing on stage. It is an example of the power of spectacle in American musicals and of the movement toward racial diversity in casting.

Much Ado About Nothing. William Shakespeare. One of Shakespeare's funniest comedies. *Much Ado* was made into a popular movie in the 1990s directed by and starring Kenneth Branagh. It is an example of high comedy.

My Fair Lady. Alan Jay Lerner and Frederick Loewe. A musical based on George Bernard Shaw's comedy *Pygmalion.* It tells the story of the flower girl Eliza Doolittle, who is taught upper-class English speech by Henry Higgins and becomes a lady. On Broadway it starred Rex Harrison and Julie Andrews. *My Fair Lady* is an example of American musical theatre at its best and is also an example of a book musical.

Nicholas Nickleby. David Edgar. Charles Dickens's nineteenth-century novel adapted into an eight-hour, two-part play by England's Royal Shakespeare Company. It is an example of Theatricalism.

Not about Nightingales. Tennessee Williams. An early play by the great American playwright that was discovered in a library long after his death and produced in London and then New York in 1999. It is set in a prison and reveals that even before he wrote *The Glass Menagerie* in 1944, Williams's writing was excellent. This is an example of serious drama and of Realism.

The Odd Couple. Neil Simon. Perhaps the greatest comedy by the most successful commercial playwright of all time. The play was a hit on Broadway in the 1950s, then a movie, then a TV series, then rewritten for a Broadway revival with two female stars. This example of Realistic domestic comedy is about the relationship of two divorced men, Felix and Oscar, who are mismatched.

Oedipus The King. Sophocles. Greek tragedy used as an example in Aristotle's essay *The Poetics.* It is an example of Classicism.

Oh Coward! Ned Sherrin. A musical review of songs, poems, and autobiographical passages by the great English playwright, songwriter, and entertainer Noel Coward. *Oh Coward!* is an example of a review and of a play with a contextual dramatic structure.

Oklahoma! Richard Rodgers and Oscar Hammerstein II. The first fully integrated American musical in which songs and dances are organic to the story telling; an example of Romanticism and of a book musical. It premiered in 1943 and is based on Lynn Rigg's American play *Green Grow the Lilacs.* It is set in the Oklahoma territory at the time of statehood and tells the love story of Curly and Laurie. Many of the songs are American popular classics, including the title song and the opening number "Oh, What a Beautiful Mornin'."

Oleanna. David Mamet. An example of late-twentieth-century American Realism. This Off Broadway play about a professor and a student demonstrates episodic linear structure.

Once on This Island. Lynn Ahrens and Stephen Flaherty. An example of the use of Caribbean music for the score of a musical.

Orlando Furioso. Luca Ronconi and Edoardo Sanguinetti. An Italian play from the 1970s that was based on a Renaissance poem and was performed in a large tent in New York City. It was an example of environmental theatre.

Othello. William Shakespeare. One of Shakespeare's greatest plays; an example of tragedy. It tells the story of the tragic love of the black general Othello for the white Venetian woman Desdemona. They are the victims of the archvillian Iago.

Other Peoples' Money. Jerry Sterner. An Off Broadway play that was made into a movie starring Danny DeVito. It is representative of the kind of serious drama that is more frequently produced Off Broadway than on.

Our Town. Thornton Wilder. A classic American play and an example of the style of Theatricalism. Though conceived for the stage and though most effective in live performance, an adaptation was made for television starring Hal Holbrook as The Stage Manager.

Pacific Overtures. Stephen Sondheim. A musical based on Admiral Dewey's military "opening up" of Japan to the Western powers in the mid-nineteenth century. It's an example of how Asian art has influenced theatre design. Though very imaginative musically and visually, this was one of Sondheim's least successful shows commercially.

Pal Joey. Richard Rodgers and Lorenz Hart. An example of the best of musical comedy and has some of the most clever lyrics written for Broadway.

Parade. Jason Robert Brown and Alfred Uhry. An example of a musical based on a real historical event, in this case the trial and lynching of a Jewish man in Atlanta in the early twentieth century; conceived and directed by Harold Prince. Though *Parade* won several critics' awards, it was not a commercial success.

The Passion Play. An outdoor pageant play that is performed by the citizens of the small town of Oberammergau, Germany, one summer each decade. This major tourist attraction is an example of outdoor religious drama. It tells the story of Jesus, and it has been performed for centuries. It also uses mansion, or simultaneous, staging of the kind popular in the Middle Ages.

The Phantom of the Opera. Andrew Lloyd Webber, Charles Hart, and Richard Stilgoe. Based on the popular novel by Gaston Leroux that has been made into several movies. This musical is an example of Romanticism and of the immense money-making potential of commercial theatre.

Picasso at the Lapin Agile. Steve Martin. Written in the 1990s by American comic, movie actor, and writer Steve Martin. This, his first stage play, was a hit Off Broadway and plans to make it into a movie were announced. It tells of the fictional meeting of the painter Pablo Picasso and the physicist Alfred Einstein in a Paris cabaret in 1904. It is an example of the kind of quirky comedy that can succeed Off Broadway, but not on.

Pippin. Stephen Schwartz and Roger O. Hirson. A hit musical of the 1970s that starred the African-American performer Ben Vereen and is an example of the practice of casting racially diverse actors. It was also the first musical to use television advertising as a major marketing tool.

The Pirates of Penzance. W. S. Gilbert and Arthur Sullivan. An example of English operetta that is frequently revived because of its comic story and songs.

The Prisoner of Second Avenue. Neil Simon. A domestic comedy about a middle-aged man who loses his job and fights with his wife. The action is set in a New York City apartment and is best performed in a box set.

The Private Life of the Master Race. Bertolt Brecht. This play contains up to twenty-seven short playlets depicting life in Nazi Germany during the 1930s. It has no central story to tell and is an example of theatre with a contextual structure.

Private Lives. Noel Coward. A brilliant comedy of manners.

Quilters. Molly Newman and Barbara Damashek. A musical about the lives of women in rural nineteenth-century America. It is an example of contextual structure, as it has no narrative story; its structure is assembled from songs and speeches in the same way a quilt is sewn together from small scraps of cloth.

A Raisin in the Sun. Lorraine Hansberry. An example of Realism by an African-American playwright.

Rent. Jonathan Larson. A musical about young people living in poverty in New York City's East Village area. It is loosely based on the opera *La Boheme. Rent* is an example of a musical that moved from Off Broadway to Broadway, and it is also an example of a musical that uses the popular music idiom of the 1990s.

Richard III. William Shakespeare. Popular because of the villainous title character and exciting plot. It is sometimes called a history play.

Romeo and Juliet. William Shakespeare. One of Shakespeare's most popular plays and an example of the genre of tragedy.

The Shadow. A weekly radio series that was broadcast in the 1930s and 1940s, starring Orson Welles. The title character used mental telepathy to make the villains believe he was invisible. It is an excellent example of how drama may be effective using only sound to communicate its story. Many episodes are available on audiocassette.

Show Boat. Jerome Kern and Oscar Hammerstein II. The most respected show from the heyday of musical comedy in the 1920s. Its serious subject (interracial marriage) and its wonderful songs, such as "Old Man River," have made it an enduring hit that is revived often.

Side by Side by Sondheim. Stephen Sondheim. An anthology of songs from Sondheim's many Broadway musicals that is performed by a narrator, three singers, and one pianist; an example of the review format and of contextual dramatic structure.

The Sound of Music. Richard Rodgers and Oscar Hammerstein II. The last show written by this team. This example of a book musical was revived on Broadway in the 1990s.

South Pacific. Richard Rodgers and Oscar Hammerstein II. Based on James A. Michener's *Tales of the South Pacific.* This was one of Rodgers and Hammerstein's biggest hits; it includes several of their most popular songs, such as "Some Enchanted Evening," and is an example of how commercial theatre can produce enduring art.

Spartacus, the Gladiator. Robert Montgomery Bird. A very popular nineteenth-century American play about the ancient Roman who led a slave revolt. It is better known today for the movie starring Kirk Douglas that shortened the title to *Spartacus.*

Speed the Plow. David Mamet. A play that starred Madonna on Broadway; an example of Realism and of late-twentieth-century American playwriting.

A Streetcar Named Desire. Tennessee Williams. One of America's greatest plays, later made into a movie starring Marlon Brando and Vivien Leigh. It is an example of the blend of lyricism with Realism.

Summer and Smoke. Tennessee Williams. Another of Williams's plays that was made into a movie. The original Broadway production was only moderately successful, but the Off Broadway revival was a hit that is often called the beginning of the Off Broadway movement. This play is an example of the kind of serious drama that thrives Off Broadway.

Sunday in the Park with George. Stephen Sondheim and James Lapine. One of Sondheim's most respected musicals. It uses the nineteenth-century French painter Georges Seurat as its central character. The subject of the musical is the difficulty of making a piece of art, and it is an example of a sung-through musical that does not have any book or dialogue scenes.

The Sunshine Boys. Neil Simon. A very funny farce about two old vaudeville comics who have a love-hate relationship and who are asked to come out of retirement to perform one of their famous sketches for a television broadcast. A film was made starring Walter Matthau and George Burns.

Sweeney Todd. Stephen Sondheim. A musical about a mass murderer in nineteenth-century London. This example of a sung-through musical is among Sondheim's most respected creations.

The Taming of the Shrew. William Shakespeare. One of his most popular comedies.

TEXAS. Paul Green. A play by the premiere playwright of outdoor historical drama that includes songs and dances. It is performed in Texas in the summer months and is an example of the outdoor historical pageants that are enjoyed by tens of thousands of people each summer all across America.

La Traviata. Giuseppe Verdi. An opera based on the nineteenth-century play *The Lady of the Camellias,* by the French author Alexandre Dumas, *fils.* It is an example of Romanticism.

Treemonisha. Scott Joplin. A sung-through musical for an entirely African-American cast that was written by the African-American composer who popularized the musical form called ragtime.

Very Good Eddie. Guy Bolton, P. G. Wodehouse, and Jerome Kern. An example of the best of the early-twentieth-century musical comedies by the trio that brought the form of book musicals to maturity.

Victor/Victoria. Leslie Bricusse and Henry Mancini. An example of a book musical that is based on a popular film of the same title. It starred Julie Andrews, repeating her film role as a nightclub entertainer in Paris.

Waiting for Godot. Samuel Beckett. An example of a tragicomedy that many say is the greatest play of the twentieth century.

West Side Story. Arthur Laurents, Stephen Sondheim, and Leonard Bernstein. A musical that updates the story of Romeo and Juliet to New York City in the 1950s; an example of America's finest musical theatre.

The Wizard of Oz. Elizabeth Fuller Chapman. A dramatization of the children's novel by Frank L. Baum that was made into the classic movie starring Judy Garland. This play is an example of theatre for children.

Zoo Story. Edward Albee. A one-act American play from the 1950s that is an example of tragicomedy and was Albee's first major play.

Zoot Suit. Luis Valdez. An example of Theatricalism. This play with songs is about the struggles of the Mexican-American population of Los Angeles in the 1940s. Loosely based on real events, it starred James Edward Olmos on stage in Los Angeles and New York.

Books

De Architectura. Vitruvius. A book about theatre architecture written by an ancient Roman. It was rediscovered by scholars in Renaissance Italy and has had a profound influence on the way theatres have been built ever since.

The Empty Space. Peter Brook. A theoretical book about the nature and purpose of theatre by a prominent English director. It has influenced almost everyone in the theatre since its publication.

Life the Movie. Neal Gabler. A popular sociological study of the way in which real-life behavior is shaped by the self-conscious perception of life as a performance; an example of the theory underlying Postmodernism as a theatrical style.

The Naked Ape. Desmond Morris. A best-selling book from the field of popular anthropology that described the similarities of human behavior and that of other primates.

The Odyssey. Homer, translated by Robert Fagles. An epic poem about the ten-year wanderings of Odysseus after the conquest of Troy. This is a written basis for much of our knowledge of Greek mythology.

The Picture of Dorian Gray. Oscar Wilde. A late-nineteenth-century novel that was later made into a movie. It explores the difference between a person's outward appearance and inner reality, and it is an influential study of the dark side of human psychology.

The Poetics. Aristotle. The earliest written analysis of drama. It has been the measure for all thinking about theatre for more than two thousand years.

"Six Axioms of Environmental Theatre." Richard Schechner. Essay that appears in *Public Domain,* a collection of Schechner's theoretical writings. The essay describes and defines environmental theatre.

Tom Jones. Henry Fielding. An eighteenth-century comic English novel that was made into a popular film starring Albert Finney; demonstrates presentational style.

Wuthering Heights. Emily Brontë. A best-selling Romantic English novel from the nineteenth century that was made into a popular film starring Laurence Olivier.

Videotapes

Alice in Wonderland (1999). Dir: Nick Willing. Cast: Whoopie Goldberg, Ben Kingsley, Christopher Lloyd, Tine Majorino. Although there are lots of other film versions of Lewis Carroll's fantasy, the modern technology employed in this version provides an excellent example of the style of Surrealism.

Alien (1979). Dir: Ridley Scott. Cast: Sigourney Weaver, Tom Skerritt. The crew of a futuristic cargo ship has a monster on board that eats human beings and continually changes shape. This science fiction/horror film provides an example of the design element of mass. An unfamiliar mass, the alien, is composed of human, animal, and reptile parts that evokes a fearful response in the viewer.

The American President (1995). Dir: Rob Reiner. Cast: Michael Douglas, Annette Bening. The President of the United States, a widower, falls in love with a perky environmental lobbyist. Much of the action of this film takes place in the White House. By creating a replica of a real location that we recognize, the Realistic scene design provides us with information about where the action is set.

Annie (1982). Dir: John Huston. Cast: Albert Finney, Carol Burnett, Aileen Quinn. This $40 million movie version of the Broadway musical *Annie* was based on the comic strip *Little Orphan Annie*. It's an example of a book musical.

As You Like It (1936, B&W). Dir: Paul Czinner. Cast: Laurence Olivier, Elisabeth Bergner. In this early film version of Shakespeare's comedy of the same title, Rosalind dresses up like a man to escape into the Forest of Arden where she meets her true love, Orlando. Of course Orlando thinks she's just one of the guys because of the information about gender that her costume communicates.

———— (1978). Dir: Basil Coleman. Cast: Helen Mirren, Richard Pasco. This BBC Television production is an example of a Romantic comedy with an episodic structure.

———— (1986). Dir: John Hirsch. Cast: Roberta Maxwell, Andrew Gillies. This film of the 1983 production by Canada's Stratford Festival is an example of how a stage performance can be recorded on film for future viewing.

Baywatch (TV situation melodrama). This show was the most watched TV series of the 1990s, and it continues to appeal to large audiences through reruns and syndication. It is an example of how even the most banal stories convey a theme.

The Beggar's Opera (1983). Dir: Jonathan Miller. Cast: Roger Daltrey. This BBC Television production is an example of the English ballad opera.

The Blob (1958). Dir: Irvin S. Yeaworth Jr. Cast: Steve McQueen, Aneta Corseaut, Olin Howlin. This movie was Steve McQueen's first starring role. He is a teenager battling both parents and a hungry hunk of gelatinous ooze from outer space. Today's high-tech special effects make this early science fiction film look pretty primitive, so our psychological response to the design element called mass may include a few more giggles than it did for the viewers in 1958. But as the shape of that unfamiliar or amorphous mass grows or shrinks in volume, our response adjusts accordingly.

———— (1988). Dir: Charles Russell. Cast: Kevin Dillon, Shawnee Smith. This remake of the 1958 original provides another example of the impact of the design element of mass.

Breakfast at Tiffany's (1961). Dir: Blake Edwards. Cast: Audrey Hepburn, George Peppard. Hepburn plays the character of Holly Golightly in this offbeat love story of a New York writer and a party girl. One of the celebrated examples of a commercial theatrical flop was the Broadway musical based on this hugely popular movie. The stage version was a demonstration of how very talented folks can fail.

Brigadoon (1954). Dir: Vincente Minnelli. Cast: Gene Kelly, Van Johnson. Two Americans discover Brigadoon, a Scottish village with a life span of only one day every hundred years. This film version of a classic American book musical is an example of how a stage play can be altered for the different demands of the medium of film.

Cabaret (1972). Dir: Bob Fosse. Cast: Liza Minnelli, Joel Gray. The Nazi party in 1931 has not yet assumed control of Germany. The local cabaret is the setting for a story that shows how political events impact young lovers and the country. Bob Fosse directed both the original Broadway musical and the film with a cynical tone. This is a fine example of a book musical.

The Cabinet of Dr. Caligari (1919, Silent, B&W). Dir: Robert Weine. Cast: Werner Krauss, Conrad Veidt, Lil Dagover. This early German classic film is an excellent example of the style of Expressionism.

Camelot (1967). Dir: Joshua Logan. Cast: Richard Harris, Vanessa Redgrave. The legend of King Arthur and the knights of the Round Table is the subject of this American book musical.

Carrie (1976). Dir: Brian de Palma. Cast: Sissy Spacek, John Travolta. Carrie White, a high school student, is severely humiliated by her classmates and stifled by the conservative beliefs of her mother. In this film, she takes her revenge on everyone who ever rejected or ridiculed her. Seems like an unlikely subject for a Broadway musical, so no wonder it opened and closed in one night and created another example of Broadway's legendary flops.

Casablanca (1942, B&W). Dir: Michael Curtiz. Cast: Humphrey Bogart, Ingrid Bergman. This tale of romance set during World War II in Casablanca, Morocco, provides a classic example of how the actor dominates the character on film. Humphrey Bogart the actor completely dominates Rick Blaine, the character he plays. We are always aware that we're watching Bogart—and enjoying every moment of it.

Casino Royale (1967). Dir: John Huston, Ken Hughs, Robert Parrish, Joseph McGrath, Val Guest. Cast: Peter Sellers, Ursula Andress, David Niven. Originally intended as a spoof of the popular James Bond (Secret Agent 007) films, this film is much sillier than the original Ian Fleming novel it was based on. When Mata Hari's daughter (Ursula Andress) goes to Germany, she walks into a scene design done in the style of Expressionism. Watch *The Cabinet of Dr. Caligari* first and then you'll recognize the style of the scene design used in this sequence.

Cats (1998). Dir: David Mallet. Cast: Elaine Page, Sir John Mills. Video version of the longest-running musical in London's West End theatre history, it features original cast members and is an example of contextual dramatic structure and of an ensemble musical.

Cheers (TV situation comedy). Cast: Ted Danson. An example of domestic comedy, this show is about middle-class people, and much of the laughter results from the awkward and embarrassing situations the characters who frequent a bar in Boston find themselves in.

A Chorus Line (1985). Dir: Richard Attenborough. Cast: Michael Douglas, Alyson Reed. The screen version of Michael Bennett's hit musical that ran for fifteen years on Broadway is an example of an ensemble musical.

Cyrano de Bergerac (1950, B&W). Dir: Michael Gordon. Cast: José Ferrer, Mala Powers. The film version of the play of the same name is a glorious example of the style of Romanticism. The greatest professions of love must be those Cyrano speaks to Roxanne.

———— (1974). Dir: William Ball, Bruce Franchini. Cast: Marsha Mason, Peter Donat. This American Conservatory Theatre stage production was originally broadcast on the PBS television series Theatre in America and is an example of Romanticism.

———— (1984). Dir: Terry Hands, Michael Simpson. Cast: Derek Jacobi, Sinead Cusack. The Royal Shakespeare Company's video version of their stage production of Rostand's play is an example of Romanticism.

———— (1990, in French, with subtitles). Dir: Jean-Paul Rappeneau. Cast: Gérard Depardieu, Anne Brochet. This is the most recent, big-budget movie version of this great Romantic play.

Death of a Salesman (1966). Dir: Alex Segal. Cast: Lee J. Cobb, Mildred Dunnock. This made-for-TV version of Arthur Miller's play starring the actor who originated the role in 1949 is an example of how the television medium accommodates the cinematic dramatic structure.

———— (1985). Dir: Volker Schlondörf. Cast: Dustin Hoffman, John Malkovich, Kate Reid. This impressive television version of the Arthur Miller play is an example of the genre of serious drama.

The Diary of Anne Frank (1959, B&W). Dir: George Stevens. Cast: Millie Perkins, Joseph Schildkraut. This film adaptation of the Broadway play of the same name about a Jewish girl of thirteen who hid from the Nazis during World War II contains an excellent example of source sound—the police cars screeching to a halt in the final scene tell you that Anne and her family are about to be discovered by the Nazis.

———— (1967). Dir: Alex Segal. Cast: Max Von Sydow, Lilli Palmer, Diana Davila. ABC's Sunday Night at the Theatre television production of the Broadway play demonstrates how television's intimacy supports the style of Realism.

A Doll's House (1973). Dir: Joseph Losey. Cast: Jane Fonda, David Warner. This screen version of Henrik Ibsen's play about a liberated woman in the nineteenth century and her struggle to achieve her freedom is an example of Realism.

———— (1989). Dir: Patrick Garland. Cast: Claire Bloom, Anthony Hopkins. The television production was based on a stage production and is an example of the power of the actor over the character in the electronic media.

———— (1983, B&W). Dir: George Schaeffer. Cast: Julie Harris, Christopher Plummer, Jason Robards Jr. Originally broadcast live on television on November 15, 1959, this is an example of the difference between the vitality and energy of live TV and the dullness of much of the recorded TV that has become the norm in recent years.

Dracula (1979). Dir: John Badham. Cast: Frank Langella, Laurence Olivier. Frank Langella's career was launched when he starred in the Broadway production of *Dracula.* Either on stage or on film, the scene designer's castle must create the geography of the world of the play. When Dracula exits the room, we need to understand where he is going.

The Dresser (1983). Dir: Peter Yates. Cast: Albert Finney, Tom Courtenay. This film version of the play of the same title about Donald Wolfit, the last great actor-manager of the English stage, is a demonstration of what actor-managers were like.

Driving Miss Daisy (1989). Dir: Bruce Beresford. Cast: Morgan Freeman, Jessica Tandy. This is an example of the kind of Off Broadway play that is later made into a successful film. It tells the story of the twenty-five-year relationship between Miss Daisy and her wise chauffeur, Hoke.

Dumb and Dumber (1994). Dir: Peter Farrelly. Cast: Jim Carrey, Jeff Daniels. A good example of the genre of low comedy, this is the story of two dim bulbs who unwittingly become involved in a high-stakes kidnapping scheme.

EDtv (1999). Dir: Ron Howard. Cast: Matthew McConaughey, Jenna Elfman. A story about instant fame, overnight success, and sharing your life with a few million of your closest friends, this film is a demonstration of the self-consciously "performed" life that is at the theoretical base of the style of Postmodernism.

The Entertainer (1960). Dir: Tony Richardson. Cast: Laurence Olivier, Brenda de Banzie. Laurence Olivier took pride in altering his appearance, his voice, and his posture, and in astonishing the audience with his versatility. If you've seen him in Romantic roles such as Heathcliff in *Wuthering Heights* or in tragic roles such as Shakespeare's *Othello* or *Richard III,* see if you can recognize him as Archie Rice, the self-deceiving, low-moraled, small-talent vaudeville song-and-dance man in the film version of John Osborne's play of the same title.

Fiddler on the Roof (1971). Dir: Norman Jewison. Cast: Topol, Norman Crane. Based on a fine example of an American book musical, this film tells the story of Tevye, the proud but put-upon father clinging desperately to the old way of life he knows best.

42nd Street (1933, B&W). Dir: Lloyd Bacon. Cast: Dick Powell, Ruby Keeler. This popular movie about the making of a Broadway musical shows us a stereotypical director at work. This is an example of how a movie can be the source for a Broadway musical—in this case a stage hit that Gower Champion directed in 1980.

A Funny Thing Happened on the Way to the Forum (1966). Dir: Richard Lester. Cast: Zero Mostel, Phil Silvers. An example of the great American musical brought to life again on film. Zero Mostel, the original star, is involved in a never-ending sequence of zany plots and comic routines derived from vaudeville to gain his freedom and help his young master get the girl of his dreams.

Girl Crazy (1943, B&W). Dir: Busby Berkeley. Cast: Mickey Rooney, Judy Garland. Hollywood turns a great American musical comedy into a spectacle-filled film. Mickey Rooney is sent to a small college in the Southwest in the hopes that he will get over being "girl crazy." No such luck. He meets Judy Garland and they decide to put on a show.

The Glass Menagerie (1966). Dir: Michael Elliott. Cast: Shirley Booth, Hal Holbrook. A CBS Television production of Tennessee Williams's play is an example of both Theatricalism and episodic dramatic structure.

——— (1987). Dir: Paul Newman. Cast: Joanne Woodward, John Malkovich. Scene design creates Amanda Wingfield's parlor, a fictional location that you can imagine but that you know has never existed. In this version of Tennessee Williams's play, Amanda Wingfield is a faded southern belle whose strong opinions drive her son out of the house and her shy daughter deeper within herself.

Good News (1948). Dir: Charles Walters. Cast: June Allyson, Peter Lawford. In this film version of the American musical comedy of college life (as it used to be), the football hero resists temptation, wins the big game, and gets the girl, and everybody sings and dances.

Guys and Dolls (1955). Dir: Joseph L. Mankiewicz. Cast: Marlon Brando, Jean Simmons, Frank Sinatra. This is a film version of one of the best book musicals in Broadway history.

Gypsy (1962). Dir: Mervyn Leroy. Cast: Natalie Wood, Rosalind Russell. This film version of the book musical is based on the life of stripper Gypsy Rose Lee and her relationship with her mother.

——— (1993). Dir: Emile Ardolina. Cast: Bette Midler, Cynthia Gibb. When you compare this made-for-television version of the classic Broadway musical to the film or to a stage production, you discover the differences between the three media.

Hair (1979). Dir: Milos Forman. Cast: Treat Williams, John Savage. This is the film version of the 1960s American musical that introduced rock music into the staid world of the Broadway musical. An uptight Midwesterner pals up with a group of hippies celebrating the Age of Aquarius.

Hamlet (1948, B&W). Dir: Laurence Olivier. Cast: Laurence Olivier, Basil Sydney. Costumes tell you who the characters are. Listen for Polonius to say, "Apparel oft proclaims the man." Olivier won the 1948 Oscar for best actor and (as producer) for best picture.

——— (1969). Dir: Tony Richardson. Cast: Nicol Williamson, Gordon Jackson. Prince Hamlet must face the challenge of avenging his father's murder in this example of a tragedy.

——— (1980). Dir: Rodney Bennett. Cast: Derek Jacobi, Claire Bloom. The

BBC Television production of the tragedy includes the full text of Shakespeare's play, as distinct from the many film versions that edit the script extensively.

———— (1990). Dir: Franco Zeffirelli. Cast: Mel Gibson, Glenn Close. This opulent film version of the Shakespearean tragedy demonstrates how spectacle influences our experience of a play.

———— (1990). Cast: Kevin Kline, Dana Ivey. This PBS Television Great Performances production demonstrates how American actors can perform Shakespeare as well as English actors can.

———— (1993, animated). Dir: Dave Edwards. This thirty-minute animated version of Shakespeare's story demonstrates how the concept of character can be revealed through drawings as successfully as when it is embodied by a live actor.

———— (1997). Dir: Kenneth Branagh. Cast: Kenneth Branagh, Julie Christie. This film of Shakespeare's tragedy demonstrates the power of spectacle competing for our attention with the power of the spoken word.

Hedda (1975). Dir: Trevor Nunn. Cast: Glenda Jackson, Patrick Stewart. This is an adaptation of Henrik Ibsen's *Hedda Gabler* with cast members of the Royal Shakespeare Company. This film is produced as an example of the style of Realism, with a box set representing a sitting room in Norway in 1890 and with the characters wearing the appropriate clothes of the period, speaking in everyday language, and behaving in a normal way.

Hedda Gabler (1963, B&W). Dir: Alex Segal. Cast: Ingrid Bergman, Michael Redgrave, Ralph Richardson. This CBS Television production illustrates how this Realistic play can be effectively made for the small screen.

Henry V (1944). Dir: Laurence Olivier. Cast: Laurence Olivier, Robert Newton. The "virtual time" of Shakespeare's story about young King Henry's war against France arcs over many years, and all of it happens in the fifteenth century, yet we continue living in our real time in the twenty-first century. We emphathize with characters who live in the "virtual place" we call England while we sit in our own hometown. This version also provides us with a vibrant illustration of what going to the theatre was like in Shakespeare's time.

———— (1987). Dir: David Giles. Cast: David Gwillim, Rob Edwards. This BBC Television production includes the entirety of Shakespeare's text, whereas the films by Olivier and Branagh edit the script. This is an example of a history play.

———— (1989). Dir: Kenneth Branagh. Cast: Kenneth Branagh, Derek Jacobi. This interpretation of Shakespeare's history play seems to reflect our own era in its antiwar sensibility. If you compare it to the film by Olivier, you will see an example of how one director may interpret a script differently from another director.

The Iceman Cometh (1960, B&W). Dir: Sidney Lumet. Cast: Jason Robards, Robert Redford. This is a television production of Eugene O'Neill's play that made Jason Robards an overnight star. This is an example of the genre of serious drama.

The Importance of Being Earnest (1952). Dir: Anthony Asquith. Cast: Michael Redgrave, Edith Evans. Jack's attempt to snatch his cigarette case back from Algernon in the opening scene is an example of blocking, which results from a playwright's specific instructions in the script. The play is an example of high comedy, or comedy of manners.

Jesus Christ Superstar (1973). Dir: Norman Jewison. Cast: Ted Neeley, Carl Anderson. The plot illustrates segments of Christ's later life in this example of a completely sung-through musical. There is no book and no spoken dialogue.

The King and I (1956). Dir: Walter Lang. Cast: Yul Brynner, Deborah Kerr. A widowed teacher falls in love with the King of Siam in the film version of this American musical by Rodgers and Hammerstein. Yul Brynner shaved his head to create the character of the king and has been associated with the role ever since.

La Traviata (1982). Dir: Franco Zeffirelli. Cast: Teresa Stratas, Placido Domingo. This film version of Verdi's opera appeals to the general audience as well as opera fans, so it is an example of an opera for all of you who have never experienced one before. This is the story of a courtesan who finally finds love but dies of tuberculosis.

The Last Emperor (1987). Dir: Bernardo Bertolucci. Cast: John Lone, Peter O'Toole. This Realistic film dramatizes the life of Pu Yi, China's last emperor, and much of it was shot on location in Beijing, where the real emperor lived.

Law and Order (TV situation melodrama). An example of the genre of melodrama. This popular TV series about lawyers and police officers focuses more on complicated plots than on complex characters. It provides stories with many surprising twists that are underscored with exciting music, and it teaches a very simple moral that good usually conquers evil.

Les Misérables (1995). Dir: John Caird. Cast: Colm Wilkinson, Philip Quast. This concert version of the hit musical brings together a company of more than 250 performers, featuring many of the stars who have appeared in the musical worldwide. It is an example of a sung-through musical.

The Life and Adventures of Nicholas Nickleby (1994). Dir: John Caird and Trevor Nunn. Cast: Roger Rees and the Royal Shakespeare Company. Shot on stage at the Old Vic Theatre in London, this is an adaptation of the original eight-hour stage production. It is an example of Theatricalism.

A Little Night Music (1978). Dir: Harold Prince. Cast: Elizabeth Taylor, Diana Rigg. This film version of the book musical that gave us the song "Send in the Clowns" is an example of why musicals are better on stage than on film. The Theatricalism of the original performance does not lend itself to the Realism of cinema.

The Lion in Winter (1968). Dir: Anthony Harvey. Cast: Katharine Hepburn, Anthony Hopkins, Peter O'Toole. An example of the style of Realism, this historical drama imitates the world of an earlier time. It tells the story of the clash of wits between England's King Henry II and his wife, Eleanor of Aquitaine.

The Man of La Mancha (1972). Dir: Arthur Hiller. Cast: Peter O'Toole, Sophia Loren. This adaptation of the hit Broadway musical is an example of the style of Romanticism. The pinnacle of Romanticism may be when Don Quixote sings "The Impossible Dream."

Marvin's Room (1996). Dir: Jerry Zaks. Cast: Meryl Streep, Diane Keaton, Leonardo DiCaprio. This is an example of the kind of gritty Off Broadway play that is frequently turned into a movie. A woman who has spent twenty years caring for family members discovers she has leukemia. This forces a reunion with her estranged sister and wayward nephew.

The Merry Wives of Windsor (1970). Dir: Jack Manning. Cast: Leon Charles, Gloria Grahame. This filmed stage production of Shakespeare's play with the colorful Sir John Falstaff out to seduce two married women is an example of the genre of comedy. No fish in this version.

―――― (1987). Dir: David Jones. Cast: Richard Griffiths, Judy Davis, Ben Kingsley. This BBC television production is an example of the genre of comedy.

A Midsummer Night's Dream (1935, B&W). Dir: Max Reinhardt. Cast: James Cagney, Olivia de Haviland, Mickey Rooney. In this comedy about love, Shakespeare's diction includes a larger-than-usual vocabulary, and the order in which he arranges words is frequently quite different from the one we're familiar with. Once you get used to it, you may find that you admire his diction and prefer his plays to those of modern writers.

―――― (1981). Dir: Elijah Moshinsky. Cast: Helen Mirren, Peter McEnery. This BBC Television production is an example of the style of Romanticism.

―――― (1992, animated). Dir: Robert Saakiants. This animated version of the story in which an enchanted wood is the setting for a hilarious night of confusion as the four young lovers try to resolve their passions despite some meddling from the mischievous forest spirits demonstrates that character can be represented by drawings and that the difference between the actor and the character is total.

―――― (1993). Dir: Peter Hall. Cast: Diana Rigg, David Warner. Originally released in 1968, this version is by the Royal Shakespeare Company. It was shot in an actual wood and is an example of how a fantasy can nearly be translated into an example of Realism.

―――― (1999). Dir: Michael Hoffman. Cast: Michelle Pfeiffer, Kevin Kline. This newest film version demonstrates the enduring popularity of Shakespeare's comedy.

The Mighty Aphrodite (1995). Dir: Woody Allen. Cast: Woody Allen, Helena Bonham Carter. Shot on location in Sicily in the ruins of an ancient theatre, this comedy in which Woody Allen's character becomes obsessed with discovering the identity of his adopted son's mother mocks ancient Greek tragedy at the same time that it illustrates the convention of the chorus.

Mikado (1939). Dir: Victor Schertzinger. Cast: Kenny Baker, Martyn Green. Members of the D'Oyly Carte Opera Company provide an excellent example of Gilbert and Sullivan's operetta.

———— (1987). Dir: John Michael Phillips. Cast: Eric Idle, Bonaventura Bottone. This version of the Gilbert and Sullivan operetta features Monty Python personality Eric Idle as the Lord High Executioner in the town in Titipu. It demonstrates how a director may reinterpret a play from its original version.

The Misanthrope (1986, in French, with subtitles). Dir: Pierre Dax. Cast: Jacques Charon, Jean Rochefort. Molière's comedy is performed in the traditional manner, demonstrating seventeenth-century costumes, manners, and theatrical conventions. Although we know these people are actors who live today, we willingly suspend our disbelief and understand the convention that allows us to accept their "virtual time" and "virtual place" as that of seventeenth-century France.

Much Ado about Nothing (1992). Dir: Stuart Burge. Cast: Cheri Lunghi, Robert Lindsay. This BBC Television production is an example of the genre of high comedy.

———— (1993). Dir: Kenneth Branagh. Cast: Kenneth Branagh, Michael Keaton. The director's inventive blocking serves to tell the story visually. In this example of comedy of manners, a confirmed bachelor, Benedick, trades witty remarks with Beatrice while unwillingly falling in love with her.

My Fair Lady (1964). Dir: George Cukor. Cast: Rex Harrison, Audrey Hepburn. This film based on the Broadway musical illustrates how character dominates actor, so we remember that Eliza came back to Henry Higgins at the end of the show instead of how Audrey Hepburn returned to Rex Harrison.

The Odd Couple (1968). Dir: Gene Saks. Cast: Walter Matthau, Jack Lemmon. The diction in this comedy reflects the different personalities of the two divorced men who try living together. Felix is "Mr. Clean" with precise diction, and Oscar is a total slob with sloppy diction. Together, their dialogue provides an example of how a playwright manipulates diction to reveal character.

———— (TV situation comedy). Cast: Tony Randall, Jack Klugman. You might run into this popular TV series that was a spin-off from the Broadway play on a TV channel that shows a lot of reruns. This is an example of the genre of domestic comedy.

Oedipus the King (1957). Dir: Sir Tyrone Guthrie. Cast: Douglas Campbell, William Shatner. This is an example of Greek tragedy, performed in a style that approximates the rituals of ancient Greek theatre. It was filmed in a thrust theatre.

———— (1967). Dir: Philip Saville. Cast: Christopher Plummer, Donald Sutherland. Filmed on location in an ancient Greek theatre, this demonstrates how a ritualistic drama can be altered to be a Realistic drama.

———— (1987). Dir: Don Taylor. Cast: Michael Pennington, Sir John Gielgud. Part of Sophocles' trilogy, *The Theban Plays,* as produced for English television, this includes scene and costume designs that are an example of the style of Postmodernism.

Oklahoma! (1956). Dir: Fred Zinnemann. Cast: Shirley Jones, Gordon MacRae. This movie adaptation of Rodgers and Hammerstein's Broadway musical is about a country girl, Laurie, who is courted by Curly, a cowboy. The villainous Jud, who also pursues Laurie, and the dream ballet that advances the plot in choreography instead of dialogue are innovations that made *Oklahoma!* a landmark in the American musical theatre.

Oleanna (1994). Dir: David Mamet. Cast: William H. Macy, Debra Eisenstadt. David Mamet directed his stage production for the screen. A university professor is accused of sexual harassment by a female student in this example of Realism.

Othello (1952). Dir: Orson Welles. Cast: Orson Welles, Suzanne Cloutier. This example of the genre of tragedy is also an exciting illustrating of how a play may be adapted for film.

———— (1965). Dir: Laurence Olivier. Cast: Laurence Olivier, Frank Finlay, Maggie Smith. The original cast of the 1964 production by the National Theatre of Great Britain recreates a celebrated stage production.

———— (1982). Dir: Frank Melton. Cast: William Marshall, Ron Moody. This film of a stage production is an example of an African-American actor playing a role that was traditionally played by a Caucasian actor.

———— (1982). Dir: Jonathan Miller. Cast: Anthony Hopkins, Anthony Redley, Bob Hoskins. This BBC Television production demonstrates how actors can offer interpretations of famous roles that differ from any others. Hopkins and Hoskins make the roles of Othello and Iago "their own."

———— (1995). Dir: Trevor Nunn. Cast: Willard White, Ian McKellan. This television production records a Royal Shakespeare Company hit production, and Ian McKellan's performance as Iago demonstrates how presentational acting, which is usually seen only on the stage, can be effective on television.

———— (1995). Dir: Oliver Parker. Cast: Laurence Fishburne, Kenneth Branagh. This film version demonstrates the enduring appeal of a four-hundred-year-old play.

Other People's Money (1991). Dir: Norman Jewison. Cast: Danny DeVito, Gregory Peck. In this example of the kind of Off Broadway play that makes for an exciting movie, a ruthless corporate raider connives to take over another man's business while romancing his daughter.

Our Town (1940, B&W). Dir: Sam Wood. Cast: Frank Craven, William Holden. The play tells the simple story of day-to-day life in Grover's Corners, New Hampshire. On stage, this play is an example of the style of Theatricalism. A character named "The Stage Manager" talks directly to the audience and tells them who the characters are and where the action is taking place. The audience sees the objective reality of an empty stage, but is asked to imagine the kitchens and drugstore that The Stage Manager describes in words while the actors walk about on stage, miming doors, newspapers, and ice cream sodas. The objective reality is a theatre, and the performance imitates the way theatre imitates life. This film version ignores the Theatricalism that made the play important and tries to turn the story into an example of Realism.

———— (1980). Dir: George Schaeffer. Cast: Ned Beatty, Hal Holbrook, Sada Thompson. This version of Thornton Wilder's play is an excellent example of the style of Theatricalism.

Pal Joey (1957). Dir: George Sidney. Cast: Frank Sinatra, Rita Hayworth. This film version of the Rodgers and Hart musical comedy about a hip guy who hopes to open a slick nightclub in San Francisco includes some of the finest songs ever written for Broadway.

The Picture of Dorian Gray (1945). Dir: Albert Lewin. Cast: George Sanders, Hurd Hatfield. The difference between objective and subjective realities is the subject of this film version of the story by Oscar Wilde. Dorian Gray is a young man whose portrait ages while he remains eternally youthful.

Pippin (1981). Dir: Bob Fosse. Cast: Ben Vereen, Chita Rivera. Pippin doesn't like the university, or politics, or war, or love, so for Charlemagne's son and heir, life becomes a quest for fulfillment. This television recording of a live stage production demonstrates the style of Theatricalism.

The Pirates of Penzance (1983). Dir: Wilford Leach. Cast: Angela Lansbury, Kevin Kline, Linda Ronstadt, Rex Smith. This film version of Gilbert and Sullivan's operetta demonstrates how a director can update a play. When you hear the lyrics of the songs, you'll understand why operettas are also called comic operas.

Private Lives (1931, B&W). Dir: Sidney Franklin. Cast: Norma Shearer, Robert Montgomery. This film version of the English playwright Noel Coward's hit play about a divorced couple who meet by accident while on their second honeymoons illustrates the kind of witty dialogue that is a trademark of the genre of high comedy.

A Raisin in the Sun (1961, B&W). Dir: Daniel Petrie. Cast: Sidney Poitier, Claudia McNeil. A black family tries to make a better life for itself by moving from a crowded apartment into a house that happens to be in an all-white neighborhood. This is an example of the style of Realism and of the genre of melodrama.

———— (1988). Dir: Bill Duke. Cast: Danny Glover, Esther Rolle. This TV remake of the 1961 movie is in color and includes dialogue that was cut from the original play and film.

Richard III (1955). Dir: Laurence Olivier. Cast: Laurence Olivier, Ralph Richardson, John Gielgud. This is a film version of Shakespeare's popular play about the villainous King Richard III of England. Laurence Olivier took great pride in altering his appearance, his voice, and his posture for his portrayal of the title role. It is an example of how the character can be more memorable than the actor, even when the actor is one of the century's greatest.

———— (1987). Dir: Jane Howell. Cast: Martin Shaw, Brian Protheroe. The BBC Television production includes all of Shakespeare's script, as opposed to the movie versions, which edit the script severely. This is an example of the genre of history play.

——— (1995). Dir: Richard Loncraine. Cast: Ian McKellan, Annette Bening. Shakespeare's history play is moved from the fifteenth-century Wars of the Roses to the 1930s. Ian McKellan alters his appearance in a much different way than Olivier chose to do in his portrayal of Richard. This film also demonstrates how a director can interpret a script in a unique way.

Romeo and Juliet (1936, B&W). Dir: George Cukor. Cast: Norma Shearer, Leslie Howard. Costume design helps us tell the difference between the two families, Capulet and Montague, in Shakespeare's tragedy about a pair of young lovers who are destroyed by the hatred of their rival families. Shakespeare's tale is perhaps the greatest tragic love story of all time.

——— (1955). Dir: Renato Castellani. Cast: Laurence Harvey, Susan Shentall, Flora Robson. This film, when compared to other versions of *Romeo and Juliet,* demonstrates how casting influences the tone of a production.

——— (1968). Dir: Franco Zeffirelli. Cast: Olivia Hussey, Leonard Whiting. This film version provides an example of how costumes can add to the audience's understanding of character, place, and time. This is the most Romantic of the many films based on Shakespeare's tragedy.

——— (1983). Dir: William Woodman. Cast: Esther Rolle, Dan Hamilton. Esther Rolle is wonderful in the role of Juliet's nurse in this production, which is an example of how casting actors from varied ethnicities can enrich a play.

——— (1987). Dir: Alvin Rakoff. Cast: Patrick Ryecart, Rebecca Saire, Michael Hordern, John Gielgud. This BBC Television production uses the entirety of Shakespeare's script and is an example of a complex and episodic linear dramatic structure.

——— (1988). Dir: Joan Kemp-Welch. Cast: Christopher Neame, Ann Hasson. Made for British television, this version illustrates how a classic play may be altered for the tastes of another era and yet retain its power.

——— (1993, animated). This short animated version of Shakespeare's tale demonstrates that character exists independent of an actor.

——— (1996). Dir: Baz Luhrman. Cast: Claire Danes, Leonardo DiCaprio. This modern adaptation of the classic love story is moved to the futuristic urban backdrop of Verona Beach, Florida. It is an example of how a director may influence the production of a play.

Roxanne (1987). Dir: Fred Schepisi. Cast: Steve Martin, Darryl Hannah. This updated version of *Cyrano de Bergerac* is an illustration of Romanticism in a contemporary American setting.

Seinfeld (TV situation comedy). The stock characters and familiar setting make this plot-driven domestic comedy very popular.

The Shadow (1994). Dir: Russell Mulcahy. Cast: Alec Baldwin, John Lone. This film brings to sight the hero of the 1930s weekly radio drama *The Shadow.* His famous line is "Who knows what evil lurks in the hearts of men? The Shadow knows." In his adventures, our hero tries to thwart the evil plans of Shiwan Kahn and save the world from danger. The commercial failure of this film demonstrates why certain conventions of storytelling work better in one medium than another. Radio listeners can enjoy the imaginary appearance and actions of the character of Lamont Cranston better than a movie audience, which has the real appearance of the actor on the screen.

Shakespeare in Love (1999). Dir: John Madden. Cast: Joseph Fiennes, Gwyneth Paltrow. This delightful romp lets us experience what going to the theatre was like in Shakespeare's time. It provides examples of the Elizabethan stage and audience.

Show Boat (1936). Dir: James Whale. Cast: Irene Dunne, Paul Robeson. This is the first film version of the great American musical comedy depicting the lives and loves on a Mississippi show boat in the early 1900s. Paul Robeson sings "Old Man River" the way it is supposed to be sung.

———— (1951). Dir: George Sidney. Cast: Kathryn Grayson, Howard Keel. This film version of the Jerome Kern and Oscar Hammerstein show is the most enduring and provides an excellent example of a musical comedy.

The Sound of Music (1965). Dir: Robert Wise. Cast: Julie Andrews, Christopher Plummer. This film version of the musical about a girl who leaves her convent to care for a widower's children is an example of a book musical and of the style of Romanticism.

South Pacific (1958). Dir: Joshua Logan. Cast: Mitzi Gaynor, Rossano Brazzi. This film adaptation of the American musical about life and love in Polynesia during World War II demonstrates the effectiveness of a book musical.

Spartacus (1960). Dir: Stanley Kubrick. Cast: Kirk Douglas, Jean Simmons. This is the fictional story of an actual slave revolt against the Roman Empire in which Spartacus took part. As portrayed by Kirk Douglas, he embodies the Romantic hero who lived and died for the bold cause of freeing the slaves.

Spellbound (1945, B&W). Dir: Alfred Hitchcock. Cast: Ingrid Bergman, Gregory Peck. A psychiatrist tries to help a patient suffering from amnesia. The dream sequences, designed by Salvador Dali, are fine examples of the style of Surrealism.

Stand and Deliver (1988). Dir: Ramon Menendez. Cast: Edward James Olmos, Lou Diamond Phillips. The film is an example of how we remember the names of movie actors more than the characters they play. Edward James Olmos stars as Jaime Escalante, a high school math teacher who motivates his students to excel.

Star Wars (1977). Dir: George Lucas. Cast: Mark Hamill, Harrison Ford. This science fiction adventure movie is an example of Romanticism.

A Streetcar Named Desire (1951, B&W). Dir: Elia Kazan. Cast: Vivien Leigh, Marlon Brando. This film version of Tennessee Williams's play of the same title had the same director and star as on Broadway. It is an example of episodic linear structure.

———— (1983). Dir: John Erman. Cast: Ann-Margaret, Treat Williams. This version was made for television and demonstrates the style of Realism.

Summer and Smoke (1961). Dir: Peter Glenville. Cast: Geraldine Page, Laurence Harvey. This is the film version of Tennessee Williams's play that was revived at a Greenwich Village theatre and that launched Off Broadway theatre as the vital "engine room" for serious American plays.

Sunday in the Park with George (1986). Dir: James Lapine. Cast: Mandy Patinkin, Bernadette Peters. This is a taped version of a performance of Stephen Sondheim's musical of the same title. Watch for the two songs "Putting It Together" and "Color and Light" in this sung-through musical.

Sweeney Todd (1982). Dir: Harold Prince. Cast: Angela Lansbury, George Hearn. This film version of Stephen Sondheim's musical about a barber who gets revenge by slitting the throats of his customers is an example of how serious subjects can be the source for a sung-through musical.

The Taming of the Shrew (1966). Dir: Franco Zeffirelli. Cast: Richard Burton, Elizabeth Taylor. Shakespeare's play in which Petruchio marries a reluctant bride, Kate, and tames her temper is an example of the genre of farce.

——— (1976). Dir: William Ball. Cast: Marc Singer, Fredi Ostler. The stage production by San Francisco's American Conservatory Theatre was broadcast on television for PBS Great Performances. It is an example of Theatricalism.

——— (1982). Dir: John Allison. Cast: Franklyn Seales, Karen Austin. This made-for-television production demonstrates how a great play can transcend the work of lesser actors and directors.

——— (1980). Dir: Jonathan Miller. Cast: John Cleese, Sarah Bade. This BBC Television production demonstrates how a director can interpret a script in an unexpected way.

Terms of Endearment (1983). Dir: James L. Brooks. Cast: Shirley MacLaine, Debra Winger. Thirty years of a mother and daughter, their lives and loves, makes this domestic story an example of melodrama.

Till the Clouds Roll By (1946). Dir: Richard Whorf. Cast: Robert Walker, Van Heflin, Judy Garland. This bio-pic of the songwriter Jerome Kern provides examples of how book musicals came to be written and how songs and dances contribute to them.

Tom Jones (1963). Dir: Tony Richardson. Cast: Albert Finney, Susannah York. The characters break through the convention of the fourth wall and look directly into the camera and speak or wink directly at you. This example of presentational performance is a rollickingly funny film, the tale of a rascally youth's misadventures in eighteenth-century England.

Touched by an Angel (TV situation melodrama). This popular television series in which angels help people solve their problems in each sixty-minute episode demonstrates why melodrama is the most popular genre of play.

Treemonisha (1982). Dir: Frank Corsaro. Cast: Obba Babatude, Carmen Balthrop. Scott Joplin's ragtime musical brought to life on the screen is an example of the contribution of African-American culture to American musical theatre.

The Truman Show (1998). Dir: Peter Weir. Cast: Jim Carrey, Laura Linney. The plot of this film demonstrates the theory behind the style of Postmodernism, as the central character's life becomes a performance.

Victor/Victoria (1982). Dir: Blake Edwards. Cast: Julie Andrews, James Garner. In 1930s Paris, a penniless singer poses as a gay Polish count to earn a living. The success of the musical film inspired the Broadway musical, also done by Edwards and Andrews. The film and musical both demonstrate how a character's gender need not be the same as the actor's gender.

Waiting for Godot (1977). Dir: G. Arner and C. Dubin. Cast: Donald Moffat, Ralph Waite. This Los Angeles Actor's Theatre production of the twentieth-century's greatest tragicomedy was broadcast on television on PBS's Great Performances series. This is a Realistic production filmed on the Mojave desert.

———— (1988, B&W). Dir: Alan Schneider. Cast: Zero Mostel, Burgess Meredith. This production was directed by Beckett's leading English-language director, so it is a trustworthy example of the correct mood and tone of this tragicomedy.

———— (1990). Dir: Walter Asmus. Cast: Rick Cluchey, Alan Mandell. The San Quentin Drama Workshop production was done under playwright Beckett's tutelage, so the interpretation reflects the playwright's own, even though the actors are less accomplished than in the other recorded versions.

Wall Street (1987). Dir: Oliver Stone. Cast: Michael Douglas, Charlie Sheen. This film about wheeling and double-dealing in the world of the stock market provides fine examples of how costume tells us about the characters' economic status.

West Side Story (1961). Dir: Robert Wise, Jerome Robbins. Cast: Natalie Wood, Richard Beymer. The Romeo and Juliet story updated to the 1950s in New York City with rival white and Puerto Rican gangs. The film is an adaptation of the great American musical of the same title and demonstrates the importance of dance in the mature musical.

What's Love Got to Do with It? (1993). Dir: Brian Gibson. Cast: Angela Bassett, Laurence Fishburne. The story of Ike and Tina Turner illustrates that a movie actor such as Fishburne remains pretty much the same from one role to another, as opposed to a stage actor who tries to alter his or her appearance, speech, and manner.

Wuthering Heights (1939, B&W). Dir: William Wyler. Cast: Laurence Olivier, Merle Oberon. Laurence Olivier plays Heathcliff, a foundling Gypsy boy who loves the spoiled daughter of the wealthy family who takes him in. Olivier changed his appearance, voice, and posture in his portrayal of Heathcliff. The film is an example of Romanticism and of melodrama.

Zoot Suit (1981). Dir: Luis Valdez. Cast: Edward James Olmos, Charles Aidman. Adapted from the musical of the same title, this is a fictionalized version of the Sleepy Lagoon murder case that took place in 1942. It is an example of the contributions to American musical theatre that have been made by the Latino culture.

Glossary

501(c)3 A designation by the Internal Revenue Service for not-for-profit businesses that applies to hospitals, schools, and arts institutions that provide a public service; a 501(c)3 designation authorizes a business to accept charitable contributions, it relieves it of the obligation to pay certain taxes, and it prohibits it from distributing profits to investors.

aesthetic distance A description for the condition in which an audience is close enough to the stage to be emotionally involved in the play and yet far enough away to be physically separated from it; the proper "aesthetic distance" gives the audience the most rewarding experience of the performance.

arena theatre A theatre with seats completely surrounding a stage that is circular, oval, square, or rectangular; sometimes referred to as theatre-in-the-round.

black box theatre A theatre space that is an empty space, painted black, and that may be adapted to whatever play is performed in it; it is usually small and used for experimental theatre.

blocking The term describing the patterns of movement that the actors follow in a performance.

book musical A musical or musical comedy that has scenes of spoken dialogue between the songs; it is different from a sung-through musical that has no "book scenes."

Broadway 1. The wide avenue that runs diagonally through Manhattan from southeast to northwest. 2. The section of midtown Manhattan in which most commercial theatres are located. 3. The description of commercial theatre. 4. A description of high-quality theatre. 5. A description of popular theatre that does not challenge the values of society.

Classicism A theatrical style in which the artist strives to imitate an idealized reality based on the power of reason; Classicism is commonly associated with the ancient Greek notion of "the golden mean" in which excess is considered improper and in which balance and proportion are considered desirable.

codpiece A fabric pouch sewn to the front of a man's hose in medieval clothing to accommodate the genitals; it tied shut with laces.

collective A word used by sociologists and anthropologists to describe a group of people who do not share basic beliefs but who agree to join together for particular reasons, such as safety.

community   A word used by sociologists and anthropologists to describe a group of people who share common beliefs and for whom the welfare of the group is more important than the welfare of any single individual.

convention   A rule or procedure in the theatre that is understood by actors and audience alike, in the same way that the rules of a sport are understood; the "convention of the fourth wall" is a good example.

cue   1. The theatrical term for any change in lighting or sound effects. 2. The moment when any scenery moves. 3. The line of dialogue or physical activity that happens immediately before a character speaks.

dramaturg   The literary consultant to a theatre; the word is borrowed from German.

dress rehearsal   A rehearsal near the end of the rehearsal period when the actors first wear their costumes; dress rehearsal is normally scheduled after the technical rehearsals have been completed.

element (of design)   A basic component that a designer uses to create a design; the four elements of design are color, line, mass, and texture. Each is a basic component that a designer uses to make a design.

emotional recall   A tool of the Stanislavsky System of acting by which an actor remembers how he or she felt in real life and substitutes that feeling for the character's emotional state during the performance of a role.

end stage theatre   A theatre with the stage at one end of a large space, but without a proscenium arch formally separating the stage from the auditorium; end stage theatres are commonly built in rooms not originally intended for performance.

ensemble musical   A musical that does not have starring roles, such as *Rent* or *A Chorus Line.*

Expressionism   A theatrical style in which the artist strives to imitate subjective reality as it is experienced in nightmares, and in which the visual world is distorted and abstracted to demonstrate how the central character feels about it; as a literary genre, Expressionism presents the story through the central character's vision and voice.

flashback   A scene in a film or play that takes place in an earlier virtual time than its placement in the structure of the plot.

found space theatre   Name for a performance space that was not intended for that use: the steps of a government building, the courtyard in a mall, a railroad station, and so on.

genre   Categorization of dramas on the basis of their emotional impact on an audience; there are also literary characteristics of each genre. The six most common genres are tragedy, comedy, farce, melodrama, serious drama, and tragicomedy.

hubris   The Greek word for excessive pride, which was considered to be a flaw in the character of an otherwise ideal person; the common flaw in the tragic heroes of ancient Greek dramas.

League of Resident Theatres   An organization of not-for-profit theatres across America that forms a collective bargaining unit to negotiate with unions and that shares common information.

libretto   All the spoken and sung words in a play for the musical theatre; the term is used most often in describing operas, operettas, and sung-through musicals.

LORT   Acronym for League of Resident Theatres.

mansion stage   A platform stage used in medieval Europe that had a long stage with a number of separate houses attached to the back of it, each depicting a unique location.

mechana   A large crane that was used to "fly" actors into the air in ancient Greek theatres.

Naturalism   A theatrical style developed in the nineteenth century that is based on the philosophy of Determinism, and that strives to present on stage an exact imitation of everyday life; Naturalism and Realism are closely linked and sometimes the words are used interchangeably.

not-for-profit   A business that serves the best interests of the public and is not required to pay certain taxes but is prohibited by law from distributing its profits to its investors; a not-for-profit corporation must be awarded a 501(c)3 status by the Internal Revenue Service.

Off Broadway   1. The name for theatres and theatrical productions that are not presented in the Broadway district in midtown Manhattan. 2. A description of intellectually challenging plays. 3. A category of union contracts that permit lower salaries than for Broadway productions and that therefore encourage less expensive productions.

orchestra   1. The flat circle of earth at the center of an ancient Greek theatre where the chorus sang and danced; the word means "dancing place." 2. The main floor audience seating in a proscenium arch theatre. 3. The musicians who play during a musical theatre performance and who usually sit in front of and below the stage in a place called the "orchestra pit."

parados   1. The passage between the audience seating area and the skene in ancient Greek theatre that was used by the chorus for entrances and exits. 2. The descriptive name for the choral ode sung by the chorus when it entered at the beginning of an ancient Greek play.

playbill   The printed program distributed to the audience at a performance; it contains information about the play and the artists.

plot   The major action of the story that is told and that takes the audience on a journey from the status quo at the beginning to the changed circumstances at the end. Aristotle described plot as "the life and soul of the drama."

Postmodernism   A theatrical style that evolved from Surrealism in the late twentieth century and that combines an imitation of the subjective reality of Surrealism with the objective reality of Theatricalism; it is sometimes equated with imagistic theatre.

presentational   A style of performance in which the actors acknowledge the presence of the audience and sometimes speak directly to them; the actors "present" the characters.

preview   A final rehearsal for which tickets are sold at a reduced rate. Actors and directors learn how audiences will react to the performance and make adjustments before opening night.

principle (of design)   A basic tool for organizing the four elements of design into a coherent composition; the five principles of design are focus, balance, proportion, rhythm, and unity.

property   Anything that may be owned, like real estate; in the theatre, it refers to the intellectual property that may be protected by copyright, including the words and music written by a playwright, lyricist, or composer.

proscenium arch theatre   A theatre building that has a proscenium arch in it. The most common kind of theatre today, it was developed in the seventeenth century. Proscenium arch is the name for the architectural separation between the stage house and the auditorium. It is frequently decorated very ornately, and the audience looks through the arch at the performance on the stage the way one looks through a picture frame at a painting.

proskene   A platform attached to the front of the skene in ancient Greek theatres that actors stood on.

Realism   A style of theatrical production and dramatic writing that imitates selected traits of the language and appearance of everyday life. It evolved from Naturalism, and today the words "Realism" and "Naturalism" are used interchangeably.

representational   A style of performance in which the actors pretend the audience is not there and the audience pretends the actors do not know they are there; the actors "represent" the characters.

Romanticism   A theatrical style in which the artist strives to imitate an idealized reality based on the importance of emotion; Romanticism evolved in the early nineteenth century as a reaction to Classicism, and it values excess of emotion.

role   The entirety of a character's part in a play.

royalty   A percentage of the gross revenue that is distributed to the creators of a production: author, director, composer, and so on.

skene   A free-standing building that was a part of an ancient Greek theatre; it was behind the orchestra, and actors made entrances from it and changed costumes in it. The word "scenery" derives from skene.

Stanislavsky System   The organized method that actors use to analyze and create a character; invented by the Russian Constantine Stanislavsky.

style   1. A categorization of artistic works by their literary or theatrical characteristics. 2. A categorization of plays by *how* they imitate reality; there are six main theatrical styles: Realism, Theatricalism, Expressionism, Surrealism, Classicism, and Romanticism.

super objective   The main objective of a character in a play; the term is part of the Stanislavsky System.

Surrealism   A theatrical style in which the artist strives to imitate the subjective reality as it is experienced in whimsical dreams; surrealism uses associative logic instead of cause-and-effect logic to move from one incident to the next.

technical rehearsal   A rehearsal when the scenery, lighting, and sound are first added to the actors' performances; one or more technical rehearsals are scheduled toward the end of the rehearsal period, just before costumes are added for the dress rehearsal.

Theatricalism   A theatrical style in which the artist strives to imitate objective reality as it is traditionally presented in the theatre; theatricalism is based on the belief that we are all self-conscious creatures who "act" our lives.

theatron   The seating area in ancient Greek theatres; we get our word "theatre" from this word, which means "the seeing place."

thrust theatre   A theatre without a proscenium arch and in which the stage thrusts forward so that the audience is seated on three sides; an excellent example is the Guthrie Theatre in Minneapolis.

thymele   In ancient Greek theatres, the altar to Dionysus, the god of wine, fertility, ecstasy, and theatre; it was erected in the center of the orchestra.

upstage   The portion of the stage furthest from the audience. It got its name when stage floors were raked upward so that the audience seated on a flat floor could see all the actors.

willing suspension of disbelief   A phrase coined by the nineteenth-century English poet and critic Samuel Taylor Coleridge to explain the convention by which an audience can enjoy a theatrical performance.

Text Credits

Pp. 10, 12, "Putting It Together" by Stephen Sondheim. © 1984 Rilting Music, Inc. (ASCAP) All Rights Administered by WB Music Corp. (ASCAP) All Rights Reserved. Used by permission of Warner Bros. Publications U.S., Inc., Miami, FL 33014. **P. 11**, "Color and Light" by Stephen Sondheim. © 1984 Rilting Music, Inc. (ASCAP) All Rights Administered by WB Music Corp. (ASCAP) All Rights Reserved. Used by permission of Warner Bros. Publications U.S., Inc., Miami, FL 33014. **P. 145**, From "En Gggarrde" in *Modern French Theatre* by Michael Benedikt and George E. Well Warth, (New York: E. P. Dutton and Co., 1964). Translation copyright © 1964 by Michael Benedikt. Reprinted by permission of Georges Borchardt, Inc. for Michael Benedikt. **P. 159**, "That Terrific Rainbow" by Lorenz Hart and Richard Rogers. © 1951 (Renewed) Chappell & CO., (ASCAP). All Rights Reserved. Used by permission of Warner Bros. Publications U.S., Inc., Miami, FL 33014. **P. 187**, From "Waiting for Godot" by Samuel Beckett. With permission from Grove Press. **P. 256**, "dianoia" from *The Oxford English Dictionary, Second Edition*, 1989. By permission of Oxford University Press.

Photo Credits

Chapter 1 1.1–1.2, Courtesy of the authors **Chapter 2 2.1**, Courtesy Robert Clayton; **2.2**, Courtesy of the authors **Chapter 3 3.1**, Courtesy Comité Départemental du Tourisme de la Dordogne; **3.2**, Courtesy of the authors; **3.3**, Courtesy Robert Clayton **Chapter 4 4.1–4.2**, Courtesy of the authors; **4.3**, Martha Swope, © Time, Inc.; **4.4**, Courtesy Robert Cohen **Chapter 5 5.1–5.4**, Courtesy of the authors **Chapter 6 6.1–6.2**, Courtesy of the authors **Chapter 7 7.1**, © Colonial Williamsburg Foundation; **7.2**, Courtesy of the authors; **7.3**, Photo by Karl Hugh. © 1999 Utah Shakespeare Festival; **7.4**, Courtesy Eric Fielding **Chapter 8 8.1**, Photofest; **8.2**, © Michael Le Poer Trench/Performing Arts Library; **8.3**, Courtesy Robert Clayton; **8.4**, Courtesy Robert Clayton; **8.5**, Courtesy Children's Theatre Company; **8.6**, Martha Swope/© Time, Inc. **Chapter 9 9.1**, National Park Service/Ford's Theatre NHS. Photo by Edwin L. Kesler; **9.2–9.5**, Courtesy of the authors; **9.6**, Used by permission, Utah State Historical Society, all rights reserved.; **9.7–9.9**, Courtesy of the authors; **9.10**, Photo courtesy of Alley Theatre, Houston; **9.11**, Tyrone Gutherie's 1963 production of The Three Sisters at The Gutherie Theatre. Photo provided by The Gutherie Theatre; **9.12–9.13**, Courtesy of the authors; **9.14**, Photo by Peter Morenus/University of Connecticut; **9.15–9.17**, Courtesy of the authors; **9.18**, Courtesy Eric Fielding; **9.19**, Courtesy of the authors; **9.20**, © Ronald Sheridan/Ancient Art & Architecture Collection; **9.21–9.25**, Courtesy of the authors; **9.26**, Used by permission of The Great Passion Play in Eureka Springs, AR; **9.27–9.29**, Courtesy of the authors; **9.30**, © Alinari/Art Resource, NY; **9.31**, Courtesy of the authors; **9.32**, © Alinari/Art Resource, NY **Chapter 10 10.1–10.6**, Courtesy of the authors; **10.7**, Photo by Josef Svoboda, courtesy of J.M. Burian; **10.8–10.9**, Courtesy of the authors; **10.10**, Courtesy The Museum of Modern Art.; **10.11–10.12**, Courtesy of the authors; **10.13**, Virginia Museum Theatre, Virginia Museum of Fine Arts, Richmond. © Virginia Museum of Fine Arts; **10.14**, Courtesy of the authors; **10.15**, Photo by Joseph Varga; **10.16**, Courtesy of the authors; **10.17**, Courtesy Robert Clayton; **10.18–10.19**, Courtesy of the authors **Chapter 11 11.6, 11.10, 11.11, 11.17, 11.19, 11.20, 11.21, 11.23–11.27**, Courtesy of the authors; **p. 183**, University Productions, University of Michigan, David Smith Photography **Chapter 12 12.1**, University Productions, University of Michigan, David Smith Photography; **12.2–12.4**, Courtesy of the authors; **12.5**, Photo by Cornelia Lee/Playmakers Repertory Company; **12.6**, Courtesy Robert Clayton **Chapter 13 13.1–13.2**, Courtesy of the authors; **13.3**, Courtesy Kim Pereira; **13.4**, © Joan Marcus/Shakespeare Theatre, Washington, DC; **13.5**, Everett Collection; **13.6**, Courtesy of the authors **Chapter 14 14.1**, Courtesy of the authors; **14.2**, © Joan Marcus; **14.3–14.4**, Courtesy of the authors **Chapter 15 15.1**, Courtesy of the authors; **15.2**, Courtesy Robert Clayton **Chapter 16 16.1**, Courtesy of the authors; **16.2**, Courtesy of the authors; **16.3–16.4**, Courtesy of the authors **Color Section CP#1**, Photograph © Art Institute of Chicago. Helen Birch Bartlett Memorial Collection. All Rights Reserved; **CP#2**, Courtesy of the authors; **CP#3**, © Joan Marcus; **CP#4**, © Joan Marcus; **CP#5**, Martha Swope/© Time, Inc.; **CP#6**, © Joan Marcus; **CP#7**, © Clive Barda/Performing Arts Library; **CP#8**, Courtesy Luanne Brownd; **CP#9**, © John Tramper/Shakespeare's Globe; **CP#10**, Courtesy of the authors; **CP#11**, Courtesy of the authors; **CP#12**, The Metropolitan Museum of Art, Gift of Frederic H. Hatch, 1926. (26.97). Photograph © 1999 The Metropolitan Museum of Art; **CP#13**, Salvador Dali. *The Persistence of Memory (Persistance de la mémoire)*. 1931. Oil on canvas, 9 1/2 x 13" (24.1 x 33 cm). The Museum of Modern Art, New York. Given anonymously. Photograph © 2000 The Museum of Modern Art, New York. © 2000 Foundation Gala-Salvador Dali/VEGAP/Artists Rights Society (ARS), New York; **CP#14–CP#19**, Courtesy of the authors; **CP#20**, Courtesy Eric Fielding; **CP#21–CP#24**, Courtesy of the authors; **CP#25**, © Carol Rosegg; **CP#26**, Courtesy of the authors; **CP#27**, © Jennifer Lester; **CP#28**, © Joan Marcus

Index